Geering
Interviews

Geering
Interviews

Mike Grimshaw

POLEBRIDGE PRESS
Salem, Oregon

Copyright © 2018 by Mike Grimshaw

Polebridge Press is the publishing arm of the Westar Institute, a non-profit, public-benefit research and educational organization. To learn more, visit westarinstitute.org.

All rights reserved. Printed in the United States of America. No part of this book may be used or reproduced in any manner whatsoever without written permission except in the case of brief quotations embodied in critical articles and reviews. For information address Polebridge Press, PO Box 346, Farmington, Minnesota 55024.

Cover photo by Baxter Holly, Melbourne, Australia, 2010. Used by permission.

Cover and interior design by Robaire Ream

Library of Congress Cataloging-in-Publication Data
Names: Geering, Lloyd, 1918- interviewee. | Grimshaw, Mike, 1967- Interviewer.
Title: Interviews with Lloyd Geering / Mike Grimshaw.
Description: Salem, OR : Polebridge Press, 2018. | Includes bibliographical references.
Identifiers: LCCN 2017057846 | ISBN 9781598152142 (alk. paper)
Subjects: LCSH: Geering, Lloyd, 1918---Interviews. | Presbyterian Church--New Zealand--Clergy--Interviews.
Classification: LCC BX9225.G44 A5 2018 | DDC 230.092--dc23
LC record available at https://lccn.loc.gov/2017057846

10   9   8   7   6   5   4   3   2   1

Contents

Introduction 1

"Go into All the World" 41

   1. Early Life, University, and Entry into the Church 47

   2. Parish Life, Queensland, Then Return to the
      Theological Hall 59

   3. The Trial and Then Escape to Religious Studies 69

   4. From Religious Studies to Public Theologian 83

   5. Lloyd Geering's Notebook, 1965–1990 123

Appendix 1: Geering's Reading, 1965–1990 135

Appendix 2: Biographical Sketches 189

Notes 201

Bibliography 207

Preface

Why a biography of interviews?

A Note on Lloyd Geering and Me

The interviews that follow are drawn from an original set of seven interviews I conducted with Lloyd Geering between 2010 and 2016 in Christchurch and Wellington. The first interview arose out of questions that came to me as I re-read *Wrestling with God*. My copy became heavily annotated with comments and questions, and I decided that there was a need to, in effect, fill in the gaps identified in my reading. I had been thinking about an intellectual biography of Lloyd Geering for a number of years: I first began academic work on him back in 1988 looking at the Geering controversy and public opinion from 1966 to 1967.

Sir Lloyd Geering (1918–) was famously tried for "heresy" in 1967 by the Presbyterian Church of New Zealand. At the time, he was professor of Old Testament Studies and principal of Knox Theological Hall in Dunedin. However, his public statements on the historicity of the resurrection of Jesus in 1966 and the immortality of the soul in 1967 were what made him a figure of national debate and controversy. After a public trial at the General Assembly, the charges were dismissed with a decision that no doctrinal error had been established. In 1971 Geering was appointed foundational chair in Religious Studies at Victoria University of Canterbury. Here, as a teacher, prolific author, religious commentator, and a popular public speaker, he consolidated his position as a noted public intellectual, activities that continue in his retirement even as he turned 99 on February 26, 2017. His status and influence were recognized when he was awarded the New Zealand Order of Merit in 2001 and New Zealand's highest honour, membership of The Order of New Zealand in 2007.

I was born in the year of the trial, and Lloyd Geering has been a constant identity in my life. My father, Frank Grimshaw (1934–85), was taught by Lloyd (as he was always referred to in our house) when he underwent his studies at Knox Theological Hall, 1968–70. My mother, then a speech therapist, knew Lloyd's second wife Elaine, also a speech therapist. I grew up in manses where Lloyd's books (including some inscribed) were on the shelves, his ideas freely discussed. The trial was always referred to as a sad day for the church. My parents stressed that Lloyd's position was one that had offered both freedom and a future, especially as the conservative and evangelical forces began their steady takeover of the Presbyterian Church in New Zealand. This led me as fourth-year student at Otago University in Dunedin to consider the Geering controversy as a topic of inquiry. So I scoured all the newspapers and other print media for a sense of just what had gone on some twenty years prior.

A few years later, to my surprise, I found myself a student at Knox Theological Hall in Dunedin doing a Bachelor of Divinity and training, I thought, for the Presbyterian ministry. The Theological Hall was yet again embroiled in a time of great disruption and conflict between both staff and students. A number of theological battles were raging between a liberal-radical faction and a Barthian-Evangelical-Pentecostal faction. I entered the Theological Hall as a liberal-radical and quickly converted to a radical and secular theology. Already well versed in Geering's work, I discovered the 1960s death-of-God writings of Thomas Altizer and Gabriel Vahanian in a little-read dusty corner of the marvelous Hewitson Library. The librarian Beth Nichol, wife of theologian Frank Nichol, also pointed me to the work of Frank's friend William Hamilton, with whom he had studied at St Andrews. Theologian and clergyman Clive Pearson introduced me to the work of Don Cupitt, who also appeared in Geering's writings from time to time. All this reading combined with various forms of postmodernism that I had first picked up before turning to theology, from my reading of UK style, culture, and fashion magazines such as the marvelous and edgy *Blitz* (1980–91) and *The Face*. So it was of little surprise that I found myself quickly at odds with the Barthian line of the theology programme. I soon discovered it was counter-productive to mention Geering in classes, essays, and tutorials—let alone Altizer, Cupitt, and so on! Church history luckily offered a far more sympathetic home, even though I kept up my growing fascination and then obsession with radical and secular theology. I also joined the local Sea of Faith network, and I will always be extremely grateful to that wonderful eclectic mixture of clergy and laity who supported and encouraged me as I struggled through my studies within a church and theological hall that seemed to have little place for radical theological thought. All this culminated in my acknowledgement that I could not see a future for myself within the ministry of the church. I knew what had happened to Geering—and I also knew there were very few parishes where someone of my radical views could find a home.

I was able to win an Otago university scholarship to embark on a Ph.D. studying New Zealand church history. While up in Wellington in 1994 for a year of archival research, I was extremely fortunate to gain some work tutoring in the Religious Studies department at Victoria University of Wellington. In one of those life-changing coincidences, Paul Morris was visiting on a sabbatical from Lancaster University, and we forged a deep friendship. After two years back in Dunedin finishing my study, I then returned to Wellington at the start of 1997 to undertake research in the Alexander Turnbull library while I awaited the marking of my thesis. I was able to gain work tutoring and then teaching in Religious Studies at Victoria University because Paul Morris had returned, this time as chair of the department. Lloyd taught Paul in his early days at Victoria. Another colleague, Jim Veitch, was taught by Lloyd at Knox back in the 1960s and, later, became a notable supporter of Lloyd as a colleague. In this setting I remade myself from dissident theologian into religious studies scholar in an unconscious echo of Lloyd's move that I had not really considered until I wrote this piece. Also like Lloyd, I had not had a religious studies background and so, again in a very similar fashion, my reading speed trebled as I taught for two and half very happy years in the department. At the end of 1999 I relocated to Canterbury University to teach religious studies, now with my partner and young daughter. While in Wellington I renewed my acquaintance with Lloyd via various department functions and forums (including the department-hosted visits by Robert Funk and John Dominic Crossan), and I was fascinated at the way he continued to read and write prodigiously in his retirement.

In my new role at Canterbury I also came to give seminars and public lectures on Lloyd Geering and his thought, and reviewed his books for various publications. With Paul Morris, I co-edited *The Lloyd Geering Reader*. We had identified a need to gather together a companion volume of his talks and writings after the publication of his autobiography. The *Reader* in turn, out of further public lectures and discussions, gave rise to this book, as I was aware that there was far more to Geering's thought than had been captured in written records. I had been steadily gathering Geering material for a number of years, not only books but also copies of articles and papers I discovered. Initially the interviews were to provide the basis for a traditional intellectual/theological biography, for which Lloyd agreed at the end of July 2010 to my proposal for a series of interviews. However, at 4.35 AM on 4 September 2010, Christchurch was struck by a 7.1-magnitude earthquake. So began a year of constant earthquakes including the most devastating 22 February 2011 6.3-magnitude quake that destroyed the central city and many suburbs, killing 185 people. Thousands of sizable aftershocks, including a number over five on the Richter scale, continued into 2012, and years on some aftershocks still rattle the city, thankfully far less occasionally.

In the aftermath of that first quake, I began work on this book. The university was closed and I knew I needed a project, especially in the evenings. Little did I know what a period of earthquakes, devastation, and disruption was in store, and so this book has taken far longer than I thought it would amidst the ongoing effects, not only at a personal level but also at university and city levels, that the quakes created. My first interview with Lloyd in October 2010 was undertaken in a house now no longer here. It was situated on the hills of Mt. Pleasant overlooking a city that, at that time, believed that it had managed to come through a major earthquake with significant disruption but not too much destruction. Of course that soon, tragically changed.

All this disruption, and the ongoing changes in my university as we came through the quakes, including my relocation from a disestablished religious studies department into sociology at the start of 2011, meant that the Geering project (as it soon became named) struggled to find a space for concentrated engagement. The interviews were wonderful and full of rich material; it was, I knew, a privilege to be able to so frankly and repeatedly talk with Lloyd. Then when I undertook archival research, I gathered more background and supporting material that helped give a fuller context to what had happened to him in the 1960s. Yet over time I realized that a traditional biography would in many ways only repeat what he had so richly laid out in his autobiography. A different approach was called for and this evolved into the realization that what I needed was to construct a different sort of intellectual and theological biography composed of the interviews. For in conversation I was able to get Lloyd talking with a clarity and honesty that I deeply appreciated. Here was Lloyd communicating who he was and what he thought and why. Lloyd has always been a most excellent communicator of his thought—especially in his public talks. I wanted to be able to take what he provided in the interviews and enable him to speak for himself. As I noted down after that first interview:

> From the start I found a series of set questions not the best way; it was far more fruitful to develop questions as we talked, which will be the model for future interviews, for what I realized [in that first interview] is that too great a constraint on interview topics stifles the conversation and Geering is really a conversationalist.

Each interview drew on questions that arose as I transcribed the previous interview. Some also came from that aforementioned archival research undertaken in the Presbyterian archives at Knox College, Dunedin, and in the National Archives in Wellington. But the discussions always quickly took on their own form and direction as a question or answer sparked off a new focus. The engagement never stopped after each interview, for often there were supplementary emails between myself and Lloyd in which either I raised various queries and issues, or he commented on something he had been thinking about since the interview.

This process meant that each interview in itself covered a number of topics and, more importantly, different stages of Lloyd's life and thought. While I went into each interview with a series of framing questions, I constantly found that as we talked we would range far and wide through his life. Therefore, when transcribed, there was no particular chronology or focus to each interview as it developed; in short, they were true conversations. Meanwhile the traditional narrative planned for the biography had repeatedly stalled. As I came to realize that I didn't want to write a traditional "life and thought," I kept coming back to quotes I had taken down back in 2010 when I read Geoff Dyer's marvelous *Out of Sheer Rage*,[1] his account of not succeeding at writing a biography of D. H. Lawrence. The first spoke to my current predicament, whereby Dyer noted, "All over the world people are taking notes as a way of postponing, putting off and standing in for."[2] The second gave me hope and impetus: "… books, if they need to be written, will always find their moment. The important thing was to avoid paralyzing uncertainty and indecision."[3]

I decided that the interviews were in themselves central to the planned biography and in fact would come to comprise the central text. I was then faced with a quandary. Did I keep each interview as it was or, as I did in fact decide, did I draw on all the interviews and reassemble the questions and answers into a chronological narrative? I decided to do the latter because this enabled what is, in effect, an intellectual and theological biography to be developed via the interviews. In our conversations the biography occurs; in effect it is co-written (or perhaps co-narrated?) and then assembled by me. I transcribed all the interviews and printed off a copy of each one. Then, perhaps in what many would view as a very old-fashioned approach, I took over the dining table at home in the evenings and went through each interview with a pair of scissors, cutting it into sections that fit the chronology of Lloyd's life. These literal snippets were put into large envelopes and labelled with the headings that became the interview chapters. The segments were then assembled into a chronological interview that was arranged under the headings of each phase of Geering's life. This book is, therefore, composed of interviews that have been reassembled as a type of conversational biography, a process I discussed with Geering and had his agreement to so do.

To my delight and surprise, what is presented here is all of our conversations except for a mere nine lines comprising two questions and answers wherein we "got off topic" in our discussion. So what is presented is almost 100 percent of what we discussed, reassembled as a biography by conversation. It is supplemented by this Preface, an Introduction in which I situate Geering and his thought in both New Zealand and international currents and moments, a general chronology and an overview of the events leading up to and surrounding the heresy trial, an essay discussing his reading from 1966 to 1990 and the accompanying transcription of his reading notebooks, and a transcription of the relevant sections of his 1963 conference lecture that drew him to the attention of the conservative faction upon his return to New Zealand from Australia.

Working on this with Lloyd has been an honour and a deep privilege; it may sound clichéd, but he is a true "scholar and a gentleman" who has gone out of his way to support and encourage me in this project over too many years. In writing this piece I went back through my old notebooks I kept over these years. Right at the beginning I had jotted down the following quote from Christopher Hitchens' *Why Orwell Matters*: "… the sheer ill will and bad faith and intellectual confusion that appear to ignite spontaneously when Orwell's name is mentioned in some quarters. Or perhaps not so spontaneously; it can be seen at a glance that the various authors attribute immense potency to Orwell, that they make the common mistake of blaming him for his supposed 'effect.'"[4] As I then commented, this reaction holds very true also for Geering. His name creates such an outpouring of misunderstanding. Further the "Geering effect" is one that can be claimed to have been in existence for almost fifty years—to which it must be asked, why has no group or individual been able to "successfully" oppose or even refute him? This book could easily have been called "The Geering Effect" or "Why Geering Matters," for, especially in New Zealand, Geering has been misunderstood by those who oppose him and not fully understood by those who support or align themselves with him. Yet, especially for New Zealand society and indeed also for wider theological and religious thought over the past century, Geering does indeed matter—and his effect has been a positive one. Hopefully this book and these conversations can help us understand why.

—Mike Grimshaw
  9 February 2017

Acknowledgments

This book could not have been undertaken without the constant support, generosity, and encouragement of Lloyd Geering. I deeply appreciate his willingness to not only undertake such an honest series of interviews but also his lending me his notebook of reading and the selected correspondence and papers he had kept in his personal archives. I also want to thank Shirley Geering for her hospitality when I called on them at home at Herbert Gardens, and especially for the sustenance she provided us during our interviews.

A special thank you must be made to The Presbyterian Archives at Knox College, Dunedin, in particular to Jane Bloore who, when I, either in person or via email, raised a query, was able to hunt down and provide invaluable material. I also want to mention the magisterial Register of Presbyterian Ministers, first compiled by Rev. Ian Fraser, that is available via the archives web page. This resource made my footnoted commentary so much easier, providing the base material on which to build so many of the references.

The staff at the Macmillan Brown Library at University of Canterbury have also been very helpful and supportive as was the National Archives when I accessed the APL papers. I want to thank Jane Simpson for allowing me to access the Kemp and Blaiklock papers at the Alexander Turnbull Library, Wellington.

Paul Morris has been a constant friend and support throughout this process and I appreciate being able to talk with him over generous food and wine when I stayed (and many thanks here also to Mary Morris), and to be able to email him or phone him about points and queries that arose. I also want to note the importance of being able to give, in 2016, a seminar at Religious Studies at Victoria University with feedback from staff and students that served to centralize my thoughts and approach.

I appreciate the research funding made available to me by the College of Arts, University of Canterbury, that provided an initial research grant and then ongoing research support throughout the years of this project.

I also want to acknowledge my aunt and uncle, Jan and Ron Cormack, for being prepared to honestly share their memories of the 1962–63 Gore Conference where Lloyd made his controversial comments.

Deep thanks also to David Galston and Cassandra Farrin of Polebridge for their willingness to take on and support this project.

Finally, I want to thank and acknowledge my wife and family who have lived with various elements that made up "The Geering Project" as a constant presence for over a decade. I especially want to thank my wife for her unfailing encouragement, support, interest, and particularly her willingness to act as a sounding board, especially through those times of stalling and writer's block. Without her this book never would have been completed, it still would be a work in progress.

Introduction

A New Theological Century? Geering, God and Modernity

In a well-known delineation put forward by the British historian Eric Hobsbawm (1917–2012), the "short twentieth century" ran from 1914–91 and was bookended by World War I and the collapse of Soviet Communism and the Soviet Bloc.[1] It was preceded by the long nineteenth century that began with the French Revolution in 1789 and ran to the start of the World War.

It is interesting to think what a theological equivalent would be. The start of the short twentieth century would most probably be Karl Barth's *Der Römerbrief* of 1918/1919, for as Robert W. Jenson claims, Barth's commentary "theologically divides the twentieth century from the nineteenth."[2] However, when did the twentieth century end theologically? Could it be dated to April 8, 1966, with the infamous cover of *Time* magazine asking "Is God Dead?" in reference to the work of, in particular, Thomas Altizer and William Hamilton? Or was that merely the start of a long interregnum? It may be the case that, theologically speaking, we find ourselves not yet free of the twentieth century but also not yet into a new century. If I wished, a case could be made for the return to theology within Continental Philosophy, in particular the engagement with religion, god-language, and theology by, in no particular order, Derrida, Vattimo, Badiou, Agamben, Zizek, and many others. But is this engagement necessarily a theological turn, or is it a philosophical turn making increasing use of theology? The difference is important—and in particular, has this movement crossed over into the church itself? It would be a rare church or even seminary that made repeated and sustained use of the continental turn to religion. I am not saying such usage does not occur, but in general the church exhibits little uptake, or even sustained knowledge and engagement. Perhaps the rise of theological feminism and womanism, of liberation theology, of queer theology, of black and post-colonial theologies, of ecological issues could also make a stronger case for an epochal change. But again these movements have all been either accommodated in various and to varying degrees—or sidelined and often neutered.

So is theology actually still—in contrast to political and social history—in a long twentieth century that continues, splintered into a myriad of possibilities and articulations, not yet secular but not fully religious, as mixed in its approach to the revitalization of Islam as it was to the rise and fall of communism? Or did the twentieth century theologically end with the decline and marginalisation of broad-church, liberal Christianity? For, from within the twenty-first century, it is too easy to forget there was a time when, in Protestant churches in particular, the mainstream was a church and theology decidedly liberal in ethos, drawing on the theological legacy of Schleiermacher and the scholarship of the historical-critical method. This was a liberal and broad-church Christianity supporting a generic sense of a Christian culture and Christian values. It was based on the expounding of Christian experience and the relating of it to all other knowledge. This was not a pietistic theology of sermons as to how "Jesus died for our sins"; rather, as cultural and social theology it focused on how to live a Christian life within a broader Christian—or at least Christian-based—society. But such theology and church was in decline from the 1960s, under challenge not only from an increasingly secular society but also with the rise within Christianity of stridently anti-liberal and anti-secular opposition. So we can also ask, did the twenty-first century emerge early, with the rise of conservative, evangelical Christianity and also Pentecostalism as global and political movements? Here the attack on theological liberalism initiated by Karl Barth succeeds—but not in a way that Barth would have expected, or indeed wished. Barth sought to signify a clear difference between religion and revelation, with the latter being a biblical Christianity in opposition to all human undertakings. However, while Barth's aim was a revitalization of broad-church Christianity, in effect the replacement of liberalism with neo-orthodoxy, the dogmatic focus and ethos of Barthian-derived neo-orthodoxy proved unappealing to the vast majority of liberals and, indeed, also to many in the broad church who were in effect cultural Christians. Facing a call to become more dogmatic, more conservative, and more biblical in focus, the effect has actually been that both the mainstream broad church and the liberal church have tended to dissolve into secular society. This is especially so in the Protestant church—and particularly in the Protestant church in western societies. Even neo-orthodoxy itself, which sought to reclaim a broad-church Christianity, albeit versus liberalism, has retreated and increasingly is a minority theological and especially ecclesiastical position. What we see is instead an eclectic mix of theologically, politically, and socially conservative evangelical, charismatic, and Pentecostal Christianities that are extremely fluid in membership, ecclesiology, and theology. We also see a resurgent Roman Catholic Church that, however, continues to face significant issues in western societies in particular.

So perhaps we need to clarify that something seemed to happen theologically, and we now find ourselves in a new century theologically that we have yet to fully delineate. Perhaps it is a century that began somewhere between the end of the 1960s and the mid-1980s. I am aware that the sociological norm of the secularization thesis was publicly recanted by one of its most prominent supporters, Peter Berger, in 1999,[3] but, conversely, the secularization thesis seems to have held true for the Protestant mainstream broad church and the Protestant liberal church. In other words, educated populations in the West, especially those who are liberal in their social and cultural views, have from the 1960s increasingly stopped attending churches and also, perhaps more significantly, stopped seeing a value in the Christian narrative and history. In effect they seek to live what can be called not only a post-Christian but also a post-religious life. It is important to note that the "return of religion" is the return of theologically, socially, and culturally conservative forms that exist in opposition to not only the continuation of secularized society but also to any remnants of liberal or radical religion, especially Christian but also other traditions. The new century is therefore signalled by the movement of members of broad-church and liberal Protestantism in particular, but also Roman Catholicism, particularly in the West, into secular society. The churches therefore have become far more conservative institutions that operate in increasingly eclectic ways. The West in particular has become a secular society for many who in the past would have been practicing, but now are often, at most, nominal Christians. This is especially so for an older generation who were brought up in the church but, from the 1960s and 1970s onwards, struggled to find a place or reason to remain within increasingly conservative churches. This group often abandoned traditional parishes and gathered in the decreasing number of liberal or radical churches, left the church outright, or became affiliated with parachurch groups such as the Sea of Faith that began in the United Kingdom in 1984 in response to radical theologian Don Cupitt's book and television series of the same name. The Sea of Faith has now become an international organization with national networks in the United Kingdom, New Zealand, and Australia, and other members elsewhere. Geering has become a significant figure in the Sea of Faith, both in New Zealand and internationally. We also must not forget that others retained an interest in religion and theology but saw little point or need to remain affiliated, practicing Christians. Instead they turned to reading and discussion as the source of spiritual and theological interest, often undertaking a Christian-based new age eclecticism.

In such a time of change and decline of the broad, liberal, and radical churches, Christians and post-Christians still needed thinkers to help point ways through the unfolding process, to articulate possibilities, and to assist in steering clear of dead-ends. In New Zealand from the late 1960s, and then increasingly internationally, Lloyd Geering has been taken up as one such thinker. His popularity becomes understandable if we consider Geering in light of what might constitute the short twentieth century, both historically and, more importantly for our discussion, theologically. For Lloyd Geering, born in 1918 in the small town of Rangiora in the South Island of New Zealand, has lived his life from the start of Hobsbawm's twentieth century and continues to write and talk on what it might mean *theologically* to have lived through such a short century, endured the interregnums, and found himself in a new one.

In a stark and centrally important contrast to most who were or remain some shade of theological liberal or radical, Geering was a convert to Christianity in the late 1930s while a mathematics student at Otago University in Dunedin. His conversion was primarily to Christian community, initially to that of First Presbyterian Church and then, centrally and crucially, to that found in the Student Christian Movement (S.C.M.). Thus, he was converted to Protestant Christian liberalism, not the ascendant Barthianism seeking to gain hold in the S.C.M. at that time, and certainly not to the pietistic alternatives of the Evangelical Union nor in particular the Oxford movement, also known as the Buchmanites after the founder, American Protestant missionary Dr. Frank Buchman (1878–1961). Renamed Moral Rearmament (1938), it was an influential revivalist and non-denominationalist movement based in calls for a moral and spiritual awakening. Geering's conversion was one that also directed him very quickly toward seeking to train for the Presbyterian Ministry. Despite his ongoing marginalization (and indeed often demonization) by an increasingly conservative church, he has remained a minister of the Presbyterian Church of Aotearoa New Zealand since his ordination in 1943.

Geering's theology was framed through two crucial influences from the start. The first was that he possesses a most able scientific mind. Prior to his theological training, he was a top flight mathematics student. His approach is that of a scientific mind seeking proofs and clarity, with no time for what he sees as the abstract nature of much theological thought. From ordination right through to the late 1960s he remained what could be termed an old-fashioned liberal in his theology, primarily influenced far more by biblical scholarship than contemporary theological currents. As he has noted, it was not until 1963, twenty years after his ordination, that he actually undertook his "first real piece of theological research."[4] Tellingly, this project was an invitation to examine the influence of Charles Darwin upon theology. This research enabled him to discover a new way to think about theology, to see it as in conversation and debate with science, not necessarily in opposition or dismissal. It also enabled Geering to seriously think about the ways theology and science have engaged in discussions on not only what it means to be human but also what it means to be a modern person. His philosophical interests are likewise understandably directed far more toward questions of science and religion than they are toward theology itself or debates within continental thought. Here we can see the reason for his long-standing interest in the work of the Jesuit philosopher and scientist Pierre Teilhard de Chardin.

The second, long-standing influence is that the young Geering's non-theological outlook, in tandem with an existing interest in comparative religions, led him to concentrate on the Old Testament. Here the debates in the field regarding biblical history and biblical scholarship provided another entry to questions of how to reconcile faith to the twentieth century. The way the Jewish texts and beliefs developed over time and place enabled him to develop his comparative interests in religion. Consequently, Geering came to a very early understanding of religion as a human action and creation—even if at this time it was still in response to what would be a broad-church liberal conception of the reality of God. At this time, as discussed in the interviews, he also much preferred the teaching offered in church history by Helmut Rex (1913–67) to the liberal theology offered by John Dickie (1875–1942). Yet Dickie's influence remained strong for many years in forming a basic liberal theological approach that was not seriously revised until necessitated by the impact of the controversies in which Geering was embroiled during the 1960s.

Geering's conversion to Christian community meant that his central focus was on becoming a parish minister, a role he served in the Kurow (North Otago), Opoho (Dunedin) and St James (Wellington) parishes. He also acquitted himself as a most able churchman, serving on local and national church committees. He then made the move into theological education by securing the position of lecturer in Old Testament at Emmanuel College in Brisbane, Australia (1956–60). Here his theological knowledge was broadened by being able to participate in an academic community that took seriously the work of Rudolf Bultmann (1884–1976) and Paul Tillich (1886–1965). He also got a chance to teach comparative religion at the University of Queensland.

Geering then returned to New Zealand in 1960 to take up the role of Professor of Old Testament Studies at Knox Theological Hall in Dunedin, a position that from 1963 he combined with principal of the Theological Hall.

A report for the World Presbyterian Alliance[a] by Rev. Dr Albert Moore on the state of theology in New Zealand in 1964–65 makes two important points that now help us understand why there was such a response to Geering when the controversies occurred:

> The Presbyterian Church is reputed to be among the more theologically-minded, yet there is little response to theology in the lay membership: apparently theology offers little stimulus to thought or direction for living and its guidance is seldom sought in the life of the church, either at parish level or in the higher courts. The 'ordinary believer' still expresses a mixture of Biblicism and liberalism which the theologians, in their sophistication, have long discarded. A great gulf is in evidence.[5]

Moore, who would consider himself a theological modernist and, as will be noted, had described Geering at this time as "an old fashioned liberal," demonstrates just how much the conservative faction was underestimated:

---

a. Or to give it its full title, "The Alliance of Reformed Churches throughout the World Holding the Presbyterian System."

In seeking causes for this situation, one would have to ask: Who reads theology? Who participates in the 'theological circle'? By what channels can it effectively influence the members of the church and of society at large? In the church, there seems to be lacking an audience which is really interested theologically, so that ministers come to feel the irrelevance of their theological training for much of the church's life. This lack of interest can doubtless be traced to the colonial inheritance of 'practical mindedness' ... Religion in New Zealand has been summed up in Mathew Arnold's definition—'morality tinged with emotion.' As the New Zealand man of letters, M. H. Holcroft, points out, it rests more on social than on religious foundations; the bias is towards *doing* rather than believing or speculating. A widespread comfortable feeling of toleration and vague moralism of a humanist sort give encouragement to efforts of inter-church co-operation and good works but discourage sharp theological disputes or the systematic development of theological positions.[6]

Importantly, not only had this report been approved by Rev. Jim Bates, chair of the Presbyterian Church's Doctrine committee, but Geering, in his role as Theological Hall principal, had also read and approved the report, providing additional information.

Therefore, at least on the broad-church and liberal side of the Presbyterian Church, there was no expectation that there would be any such theological controversy as soon occurred. Yet the roots of what became known as the Geering controversy go back many years and involve a number of events that combined to make him the focus of conservative concern and opposition. The first event is one not previously considered. As discussed in the interviews, in 1941 Geering broke off his engagement to Joyce MacGregor, daughter of the conservative Presbyterian minister Rev. John MacGregor. As Geering recounts, an outraged John MacGregor "wrote to every vacant parish warning them against me as a person who couldn't be trusted." Consequently Geering was noted as "problematic," especially by those in the conservative faction of the church, over twenty years before the trial.

In 2011, a short while after Geering shared MacGregor's response, I undertook research in the National Archives into the papers of the anti-Geering faction, the Association of Presbyterian Laymen (APL). In the process I discovered how the APL got hold of a tape-recording made illegally of Geering's closed-venue talk on "Man's Ultimate Destiny" at Canterbury University on April 24, 1967. Geering only knew a copy of his talk had been made and somehow leaked to the APL,[7] whereupon at the heresy trial, one of his accusers, Robert Wardlaw of the APL, sought leave of the Assembly to have copies of it distributed. Geering, seeing it as being able to aid his defence, raised no objection.[8] In the National Archives I discovered the tape-recording was made available to Austen Ward of the Nelson APL, who then passed it on to Wardlaw. Excited by being able to solve this mystery, but knowing nothing of Austen Ward, I let Geering know about it, whereupon he was able to make a further connection of which I—and he up to that point—was unaware. As Geering wrote to me: "probably you did not know, Austen Ward had been married to Joyce MacGregor, whom you asked me about. But I do not think Joyce would have been behind it—indeed she may have disapproved of what Austen was doing. But a lot can happen in twenty-five years. I had not spoken to her since 1942 and that was to congratulate her on her engagement to Austen. That was a little over a year since we had broken up. But wheels within wheels eh?"[9]

Only now can it be documented how the tape of the Canterbury University talk came to be part of the charges laid against Geering in 1967. On August 4, 2011, I became the first researcher to read the Association of Presbyterian Laymen files of Geering's opponent, the educationalist, historian, and academic Rollo Arnold, held in the National Archives, Wellington. The narrative of events is a fascinating insight into what was involved. On May 10, 1967, Austen Ward of Nelson wrote to Rollo Arnold stating:

This is a copy of the tape I told you about. I doubt if L.G.G. knows of its existence for he apparently stated that he wanted no publicity for his lecture. The young man who loaned me the tape is concerned that he should not be identified and I respect his wish for he is only a youth and wonders if he has acted ethically in allowing me to copy it. ... My own view is that if Geering makes statements like these he must believe them and therefore welcome their dissemination. ... I regard the attitude that such speeches to University students are suitable for them but unsuitable for the general public as intellectual snobbery.[10]

Arnold obviously quickly informed the APL leadership of the existence of the recording, as on 12 May, 1967, Robert Wardlaw wrote to Arnold:

I am *most* anxious to receive a copy of the tape-recording made by the ex Bible Class member of your friend from Nelson. Would it be possible to write or wire urging haste, and informing your friend that we will be very happy to pay the costs of duplication of the tape—both for yourself and myself— as this is a legitimate charge against our funds here?[11]

The basis of Ward's concerns—and a fascinating insight into a growing culture split in the church—is outlined in a letter to Wardlaw, which was also passed on to the Assembly Secretary Stan Read:

To me, the really disturbing feature of the present situation is not merely the Professor's position in the church, although this must be resolved, but the most alarming feature is the amount of support he is receiving from ministers in the church. ... It would appear that many of our ministers have a standard of ethics inferior to that normally expected in the hard world of business.[12]

A second, more often noted event was the return to New Zealand in 1961 of the conservative Presbyterian Minister Rev. Arthur Gunn (1912–2000). The son of a Presbyterian minister,

Gunn studied at the conservative Auckland Bible Training Institute and established the lay evangelical body the Christian Men's Business Association in the 1930s, which became a forerunner of supporters for the APL's opposition to Geering in the 1960s. Gunn undertook missionary work with the China Inland Mission (1939–41), then became a Bomber pilot in World War II. A period of post-war theological study and parish work in Scotland was followed by his return to New Zealand and the South Auckland parish of Manurewa in 1961, where he stayed until retirement in 1978. A noted evangelical, Gunn was editor the *Evangelical Presbyterian*, the journal of the conservative Westminster Fellowship within the Presbyterian Church of New Zealand. As such, Gunn was a driving force in the opposition to Geering and liberal Presbyterianism, and South Auckland became a noted conservative hot-bed from the 1960s that was increasingly concerned as to what type of theological education was being undertaken down south in Dunedin.

A third, not previously noted contributing factor occurred in 1963 when Geering, in his role as principal of the Theological Hall, gave three evening addresses at the Presbyterian Summer Conference, Gore, 27 December 1962 through 3 January 1963: "Discipline through Disaster"; "Go into All the World"; and "God's People in the World Today." It was the second talk, "Go into All the World," that elicited a concerned response from the conservative and evangelical wing of the Presbyterian Church,[13] wherein Geering stated:

> Our mission is not to make committed Christians. That may surprise you! My reason … is that it is both unbiblical and inadequate. The Bible speaks of believers, of men of faith, of being in Christ; but not of being committed Christians. What does it mean? I don't know. It seems often to be used to describe a man who is wholly dedicated to God in Christ. Where does one find such a person? I know I am not. I would like to think I were. But I find that Christian faith and practice is a continual struggle within myself. I am continually being pulled up with a start as I

find areas in my life which are not committed to God. It would be hypocrisy for me to set out to make other people committed Christians with the assumption that I am.[14]

However, Geering's statement, coming as it did from the principal of the Theological Hall, was noted across the theological spectrum of the church, not just by the conservatives but also among those who considered themselves part of the modern wing, who had moved past liberalism. For example, it is interesting that Geering's colleague, Helmut Rex, the ill and soon-to-retire professor of church history (and onetime teacher of Geering in the 1940s), upon hearing of Geering's talk felt he did not know where Geering sat theologically and so wrote enquiring to Rev. Albert Moore, at this time minister in Tapanui in west Otago. Moore's response is telling:

> You ask about Lloyd Geering's theological position. As far as the Gore Conference is concerned, I was not able to be in Gore on the evenings when he was speaking; but apparently he proved the most—perhaps the only—provocative speaker of the Conference with his statement, "I don't know whether I'm a committed Christian myself"; he was having a crack against certain narrow pietistic labels in order to emphasize the content of the Gospel rather than the personal qualifications of the Christian bearer. This statement was apparently widely discussed and argued and was given subsequent explanation. But I hope it does not play into the hands of conservatives who might repeat up and down New Zealand, "That dreadful new Principal of the Theological Hall doesn't even know if he's a Christian!" My two years of association with him on the Faith & Order Commission in Dunedin give me the impression that he is an alert and questioning mind but that he has never applied it previously in a thoroughgoing way to the basic questions of Systematic Theology. This may be due to the theological era in which he studied, or perhaps to his concentration on Hebrew and Old Testament. But now that he has started discussion on the theme "What is our Gospel?" the

questions all come flooding in. One might say that he is discovering Systematic Theology a bit late in the day and lacks a formulated position as yet; hence his questioning gives the flavour of an old-fashioned Liberal, as you express it.[15]

My aunt, Jan Cormack (then Jan Clark), who at that time had undertaken a year of study at Knox "to check out my theology" before taking up a position in the Christian Education Department of the Presbyterian Church, was "Leader Singing" for the conference and remembered the controversy Geering's second lecture aroused. This was seconded by her husband, Ron Cormack (who also attended), when I mentioned the lecture to them in 2016. They give two differing perspectives on that talk. Jan said she was in agreement with Geering, having "had the experience that year of studying under Geering and delighting in it. I had never been 'saved' but rather joined the church because that was a community of people whose way of life I wanted to be part of—and the life of Jesus seemed to make sense as a goal for life. The language of the church has always been a mystery to me—mission, faith, good news, gospel, evangelism, being saved—it *is* the language of the church and not really about the life of Jesus, which is much more challenging."[16]

Her husband Ron said, "it's more correct to say I was challenged by it, and in due course moved on to a greater understanding. For me, at that time, I had had the experience of 'having been saved' and Geering's challenge moved me on to 'having been saved: being saved: will be saved'; a continuum of relationship with a living spirit. Geering's address certainly gave me a sense of freedom and spaciousness; a release from *shoulds* and *oughts*, and it was good to have affirmation of relief from the literal interpretation of the Bible. I liked the call to action, and the call to mission in the sense of sharing the good news (what I was glad about Christianity) that I could share. I lived life for many years with this sort of understanding."[17]

Like Geering, both Jan and Ron found the ever-increasing conservatism of the church problematic and, as Ron notes, "when the church struggled to be inclusive, negating the fundamental of the value of each person," they found they had to leave.

I mention these three events because they provide a background of the longer momentum that resulted in the controversy. It seems in particular that it was the Gore address that provided a real emphasis for a growing opposition to Geering and the Theological Hall more generally in conservative circles in the church. For Geering here was not only speaking to theological students but to a broad spectrum of young people from across the Presbyterian church—and speaking in his role as principal of the Theological Hall. Yet, as the comment by Moore to Rex demonstrates, there was also a wide gulf between "old fashioned liberalism," and those who considered themselves more modern in their theology. But many in the church were not even ready for, nor prepared to accept "old fashioned liberalism"; rather, they bided their time awaiting their opportunity.

As Geering had demonstrated in Gore, what he was able to do was clearly and succinctly state issues of liberal concern and thought to and for the wider church. His role as principal gave him the perfect platform for doing so, a fact that was identified by Peter Smith, the editor of the official church journal *The Outlook*, who began to call upon Geering to write articles for the paper. This in effect gave Geering a national pulpit and so a wider disquiet occurred in September 1965 when he wrote an article published in the Presbyterian journal *The Outlook* asking, "Is a New Reformation Possible?"[18] and covering very similar ground to John Robinson's *The New Reformation*. The accessibility of such a question was problematic, for here was controversial theological debate and discussion venturing outside the Theological Hall and expressed in a manner applicable and approachable for a non-theological and often non-intellectual audience. That the principal of the only Presbyterian seminary was making public statements of such a nature was seen by his opposition as a provocation they could not ignore. Liberals—and radicals—were of course making such statements across the western Christian churches at this time;

in raising them Geering was therefore part of a much wider set of questions. So it needs to be understood that the problem was not that Geering was a liberal (for they could be ignored) but rather that, as principal, his views were taken to be a direct, representative challenge to a section of the church that felt ready to challenge its marginalization. As Geering and others have noted, his colleague, the systematic theologian Frank Nichol, at that time a committed Bonhofferian, was far more radical, but he was very careful not to make public statements.

The APL certainly viewed Nichol as the real concern and in their archival papers a correspondent in 1967 notes that, having spent time in Dunedin, including discussion with relatives and some students at Knox:

> It is quite evident that Geering has very little real influence on their Spiritual Life and is regarded <u>by most</u> as simply a good lecturer. And from what I have learned I would consider Nichol is the more radical person and he is sized up adequately by those who have to suffer him and his efforts to be clever. An example from his examination papers shows the type of man: "Biblical hermeneutics demand a constant dialogue of the exegete and his texts; he who questions is as well aware that he himself is questioned. Analyse and assess."[19]

This concern with Nichol continued after the trial, as evidenced in a further letter dated 31 May 1971 on APL letterhead from Reg Gardner of Roslyn Church, Dunedin to Euan Campbell of Wellington. Gardner discusses issues of the appointment of a successor to Geering as principal, then has handwritten at the bottom: "If Frank Nichol is appointed to the position of principal I think our church will slide faster down-hill—he is more radical than L.G."[20]

Furthermore, as Geering reports, he had had a run-in with one of his accusers, Rev. Bob Blaikie, in the mid-1960s when Blaikie attacked Nichol. As Geering told me, "at the next Assembly in 1965 I took Blaikie aside and I said, 'You attack me and not my staff'. Now I didn't mean him to take it literally!"[21] Fiercely loyal to his staff, a gifted communicator and an increasingly public figure known throughout the church, Geering soon became a symbolic figure for both liberals and conservatives and the focus of the rising conservative opposition in the church.

What can be called "the Geering Controversy" began in 1966 with the publication in *The Outlook* of a short Easter message from Geering entitled "What does the Resurrection mean?" Quoting from Ronald Gregor Smith's *Secular Christianity*, the fateful passage for what followed was, "we may freely say that the bones of Jesus lie somewhere in Palestine."[22] Geering calls for a reading of the resurrection as a future hope that was expressed metaphorically by the disciples as the resurrection of the physical body. The editor of *The Outlook*, Peter Smith, was delighted with the uproar that resulted. It is worth quoting him at length from a letter he wrote to Geering on June 15, 1966:

> One thing your Resurrection article has done, and no one, surprisingly, appears to have cottoned-on, so to speak. You have taken this vast, complex subject into the streets: you have provided so-called secular man with a talking point, with food for thought. ... Letters have poured in here from all sorts of people 'outside' the church requesting copies of the original article. So much so that by [the] June 25 issue we hope to have reprinted it one thousand times for free distribution. ... I am hoping all this will not end with the General Assembly. It is my sincere hope that there will be a coming together of protagonists. ... As I say this dialogue has jerked many to their intellectual feet: it has brought the real issues of the Faith into places where one never thought it possible, and I personally know of agnostics and near-atheists who have gone to ministers for enlightenment. Students, even, of no faith at all have been debating your viewpoints: homes have been set aflame with healthy enquiry, and, as I ask in the Talking Point, is this a good or bad thing? There are some of course who are medieval paralytics. They refuse to read: it would

kill them to glance at Metzger's "New Testament: Its Corruption, Restoration and Transmission." One fundamentally-inclined churchman flung the Bible at me the other day and demanded: "Do you think God would allow this book to contain all these textual errors over such a long period?" While realising it is useless to dispute with such people, I meekly replied: "Evidently He is doing something about it now."[23]

Geering suddenly found himself in the midst of a wider public discussion and debate involving both clerical and lay factions, notably the creation of the influential Association of Presbyterian Laymen, which grew to over fifteen hundred members. Theology, piety, and folk-belief collided both within and outside the church, and the wider secular media became very interested in this news of strong dissent within the Presbyterian Church. The debates that had arisen in the church seemed to connect New Zealand to debates happening elsewhere: those of Bishop Robinson and *Honest to God* in the United Kingdom and those labelled the death-of-God theologians in the United States. New Zealand, it seemed, was actually becoming modern and part of the new theology: a place where the tacit acceptance of a normative Christian piety could now be critiqued—from inside the church! The discussion continued throughout the year and culminated in a seven-hour debate at the 1966 Presbyterian General Assembly. Finally, a compromise statement was issued by the church in such language that neither liberal nor conservative factions could disagree. While peace was not restored, at least a truce was declared.

Hopes that the controversy had died down proved false, and the second phase began when Geering accepted an invitation to preach at the annual inaugural service for Victoria University of Wellington in March 1967. Thinking of what would interest a primarily student audience, Geering chose to speak on the book of Ecclesiastes because he saw in it a similarity of attempting to make sense of unsettling times. Focusing on issues of conflict between the secular world and Christian doctrines, he made what proved a problematic statement that the human sciences had provided an understanding that "man is a psychosomatic creature whose psyche cannot live independently from his body. Man has no immortal soul."[24] In support of this statement Geering, drawing on his knowledge as both Old Testament scholar and student of comparative religion, noted that Jewish and early Christian thought alike also had a similar understanding of mortality. However, because Geering was already such a public and controversial figure, a religiously conservative journalist in the audience reduced the sermon to the statement "man has no immortal soul" and headlined it along with the reactions of church leaders he had telephoned for comment. The second stage of the controversy had begun.

It was the changing nature of the controversy that resulted in the trial later in 1967. For the reported statement in particular became the touchstone for a deepening and wide-ranging uproar that reached throughout New Zealand society. The resurrection was, in the end, an in-house theological issue, but the question of whether the soul is immortal or not created national debate at an unprecedented level amongst both religious communities and the wider population. Geering and his views became a public controversy filling articles and letters in newspapers and church and secular journals, and being debated and discussed on radio and television. In early May 1967, Geering's colleague Frank Nichol was sufficiently concerned to write privately to Stan Read, who that year was both Clerk and Moderator of the General Assembly. Nichol stated:

> I believe I should repeat to you my firm belief that the Presbyterian Church of N.Z is reaching a "moment of truth" as regards its relation to the Bible as the supreme standard, and the freedom of its ministers, not to speak of its Professors and teachers, to question current interpretations of the Bible and to suggest fresh and sometimes disturbing reinterpretations. It is really a question of whether the Bible is to be muzzled by confessionalism, or allowed to have free course in the church's life. This,

I think, is the question really at issue in the present controversy, and it takes shape in the debate about Principal Geering.

Nichol then effectively upped the stakes, warning:

If—as I fervently pray and believe shall not happen—he should be dismissed from his post either as Principal or as Professor of Old Testament, I should feel bound to tender my own resignation from my chair; and I do not think I would be alone on the staff in that matter.[25]

Nichol was correct to state this, as his colleague, the New Testament professor Evan Pollard had, in 1968, stated the same to a clerical colleague, observing that if the decision had gone against Geering, "I know of a number who had their resignations already written out just in case, and they would have been joined by many more, the whole of the staff of the Theological Hall included."[26]

Nichol also further warned Read that if Geering was dismissed, then Knox Theological Hall's standing would be diminished internationally "to such a degree that it would be impossible to attract here scholars or teachers of any repute or adequacy whatsoever." He concluded by stating: "In respect of our principal, I consider we are far more fortunate than almost any other theological college in the entire Presbyterian world—and yet we are allowing, and for far too long have allowed, our people to entertain entirely groundless doubts about him."

Stan Read replied on 9 May, that: "I see no possibility of a decision being given against Lloyd. On the other hand, I think there is a need for a more exact statement regarding the freedom of a theological teacher."[27] Yet Read was personally opposed to Geering's position and a few months later counselled Geering's opponent Rev. Bob Blaikie to stay in the church when Blaikie wrote and said he felt he should leave the ministry of the Presbyterian Church in New Zealand. Read's comments to Blaikie are telling, not only in comparison to what he had said to Nichol but also as to what happened after the trial and Assembly decision of 1967 when the conservatives, and indeed many of the now conservative-turning-broad-church clergy, increased their pressure on Geering. Read stated:

> I consider that you could do much more to the cause which is obviously so dear to your heart by remaining in the Church. There may be opportunities which we cannot discern at present by which your point of view could receive wider acceptance. I do not imagine that we shall reach finality at Assembly in November. The debate on the doctrinal issues will go on and it is right that it should do so.
>
> A surprising number of ministers feel that if Lloyd Geering continues along the present lines he will reach the stage where he will have to go. They are not prepared to align themselves with those clamouring for his dismissal now but they are keeping an open mind about the future. I do wish you could see the necessity of continuing your witness even if progress and support seem slow. To leave the Church would place you in the position where your influence would cease.[28]

The debate, both within the church and especially in the public realm, grew vociferously throughout the year and it was uncertain at times whether charges would be formally laid—and if so, what would be the outcome. The forces of the liberal church swung into action and a leading liberal churchman, Rev. Graham Ferguson, was in regular correspondence with both Geering and Nichol. In October 1967, a month before the General Assembly, Ferguson wrote to Nichol noting the possible effect of public opinion:

> With the papers getting hold of things a new element is present, namely that public reaction is likely to be hostile to any prosecution for heresy. The *Sunday Times* yesterday was less than polite on the subject in its editorial. Before the public reaction became a factor I thought that we should be going for a mediatory position. Now I wonder if we shouldn't aim at victory all the way down the line without attempting to mollify tender—and ignorant—consciences.[29]

Other liberals, especially in Auckland, were not so sure that victory would be so clear-cut, observing deep-seated splits within the church that neither a liberal victory nor, as it later proved, a compromise statement could heal. One such liberal minister in Auckland was Ross Miller, who wrote regularly to Ferguson and Nichol updating them on what was happening in the largest city in New Zealand. His observations give a different view as to what was developing, especially the concerted push by the Westminster Fellowship to plant conservative ministers into previously broad-church parishes:

> The only consistency to be detected in Auckland Presbytery's theological position at present is bloodymindedness. I would never have credited that a court could be so swayed by its liver. In fact, any trend here is to the conservative—a trend which will show itself even more clearly when Greyfriars, Orewa and Grey Lynn each get their W. F. [Westminster Fellowship] ministers.

Miller believes the cause is a breakdown between the laity and the clergy:

> The real trouble is not anyone's doctrinal views, but the state of mind into which many have been cajoled, by the propaganda of the W. F. and the Layman's Association, in which you live and breathe in mistrust of anything said by the minister (save a trusted few). The "peace of the church" (whatever that may be) is threatened precisely by the rank disloyalty and lack of faith of the ultra-protestants. It is this, in Auckland, which more than anything else is inhibiting the real work of the Gospel.[30]

Geering, in his interviews, agrees with this observation of a growing anti-intellectual sentiment amongst his opponents. This opinion actually fits in with the previously noted antipathy to new theological thought in New Zealand mentioned by Albert Moore in his report to the World Presbyterian Alliance. The sizable and growing body of conservative lay people—and indeed many of their clergy—desired theological conformation, not confrontation; they practiced a conservative common-sense piety and selective biblical literalism that confirmed existing suspicions and prejudices, especially in the midst of both a changing world and antipodean society.

Geering has observed that it was in fact only the rise of the A.P.L. that led to the trial, for in his opinion Bob Blaikie would not have acted alone. Yet it was actually Geering who, in effect, allowed the trial to proceed because charges had to be brought to the presbytery of the complainant and Wardlaw, in Auckland Presbytery, was in the wrong presbytery to be able to win a convincing vote to do so. Geering, however, because he held a national position in the church, decided to allow the charges to be brought to the general assembly and, in doing so, give up his Court of Appeal because, as he puts it, he was "fairly confident" that he would win.[31]

It is important to note that two different charges of doctrinal error were laid. One, more nuanced, by Reverend Bob Blaikie, concerned Geering "gravely disturbing the peace and unity of the church by making statements which appear to be contrary to the church's teaching."[32] The other, from the fundamentalist and intemperate Robert Wardlaw of the Association of Presbyterian Laymen (with the strong influence of the conservative Westminster Fellowship), was a charge of "grave impropriety of conduct" arising from denying the Christian doctrine of the Christian Creator God; "the Holy Scripture as the Revelation of God"; the deity and the supernatural power of Christ; that Christ has been raised from the dead; and "a life to come."[33] These denials, believed Wardlaw, were contrary to both the Bible and to the 1646 Westminster Confession of Faith, to which all clergy in the Presbyterian Church had to assent. As Ross Miller had earlier wryly observed to Nichol and Ferguson, "Wardlaw & Co. use 'heresy' synonymously with 'apostasy,' which is confusing."[34]

The discussion of the charges during the 1967 General Assembly, held in the city of Christchurch, attracted over a thousand people and was covered by television, radio, and print media. Following considerable debate by all involved, it was declared that "the Assembly judges no doctrinal error has been established, dismisses the charges and declares the case closed."[35] The declaration was, however, a statement aimed at church unity, for not only did the Moderator conclude by thanking Geering's accusers for bringing the charges but did not mention Geering, there also followed a Pastoral Letter for the church that, as well as stating confidence in Geering as a theological teacher and minister, expressed appreciation for the faith and devotion of his two main accusers.

The effects of the trial were widespread—and ongoing to this day. The church was split and no pastoral letter, especially such an innocuous one focussed on attempting to prop-up an already collapsing "church unity," was going to heal the breaches. The effects were also both immediate and longstanding, affecting the views in what was an expanding secular society. That in 1967 the second largest New Zealand church[a] could have what became, in the media and popular opinion, a heresy trial,[b] only served for

---

a. In the 1966 census the Presbyterian Church, with 582,976 members, was the second largest denomination after the Anglicans (901,701 members) in a national population of 2,386,331. Since that time the Catholic Church (third in 1966 with 425,280) has risen to become the largest denomination—but at just under 500,000 out of a total national population now approaching 4.5 million. The Anglicans (now around 450,000) and Presbyterians (now around 330,000) in particular have suffered a massive decline alongside an exponential growth in those identifying as either "no religion" (over 1.6 million) or "object to state" (at least 170,000). Interestingly, the decline this century in those "objecting to state" seems to be the result of a relocation into an ever-growing "no religion" category. The largest non-Christian grouping is now Hindus (around 90,000) followed by Buddhists (around 60,000) and then Muslims (around 46,000). All recent numbers are provisional given the last census was in 2013 and immigration and societal change created significant shifts in each prior census. Contemporary figures arise from my analysis of the 2013 national census; figures from the 1960s arise from Hoverd, "No Longer a Christian Country?," 41–65.

b. In fact, the Presbyterian Church itself issued a booklet containing "information about the doctrinal charges and related matters" brought before the General Assembly in 1967. Tellingly, although the official term for the charges brought is "doctrinal error," the booklet is headed, "A Trial for Heresy." See Presbyterian Church of New Zealand, *A Trial for Heresy*. The booklet contains an explanatory statement by many both to create and to support distrust of both churches and theology. For a heresy trial in 1967 seemed to signal a discordant medieval process and expectation that had no place in a modern society—or, for liberal Christians, a modern church. In many ways this was the beginning of the end of the very short theological—and indeed Christian—twentieth century in New Zealand.

What then of the future for theology—and of the future for Geering—following the theological uproar of 1966 and 1967? In a prescient article in 1970, Frank Nichol, Geering's colleague throughout the years of uproar, threw down a challenge to both theology and religious studies in New Zealand. Writing in the liberal Roman Catholic journal of culture and opinion, *Comment*, Nichol stated that the "principal feature of the present scene, as I see it, is *the collapse of orthodoxy*. ... The very concept of orthodoxy has, by the acids of modernity, been eroded to vanishing point; and the varieties of Christian belief have conspired to achieve a collapse from within." Of course, as he noted, the voluntary nature of belief in New Zealand, coupled with "pluralism, relativism, and scepticism" all help to contribute to such a situation. But Nichol's real concern was his assessment that there was still very little real theology being done in New Zealand. What occurred instead was the churchly captivity of theology; that is, theology sought merely to reaffirm the church, its authority, and its expectations. Such captive theology was concerned with church maintenance and thus lost both its prophetic and intellectual task. For theology held captive does not seek to act as challenge to the church but rather becomes an in-house activity of self-affirmation and self-belief. In 1970 Nichol conversely saw religious studies as a place to let into

---

the moderator and clerk of the General Assembly; the charges brought by Mr R. J. Wardlaw and Rev. J Blaikie; a copy of the address "Man's Ultimate Destiny" that Geering delivered at University of Canterbury on April 14, 1967—and was subsequently leaked to Geering's opponents (as discussed in the interviews); the Addresses and Final Replies to the Assembly of Geering's accusers and Geering; and, in conclusion, The Pastoral Letter to the Church from the General Assembly.

the church a "few bracing, if also chilling, breezes,"[36] because, free of churchly captivity, religious studies could be the place where the radical, critical questions about humanity and beliefs could and should be asked. In his own way, Lloyd Geering has continued to blow his version of a "few bracing, if also chilling, breezes," first from within religious studies and then as a public intellectual over the subsequent years. The problem is that the church, by and large, has opted to keep all breezes at bay. Interestingly, in the American context Van A. Harvey, who at that time had recently returned to the University of Pennsylvania from Perkins School of Theology at Southern Methodist University, was arguing a similar role at the same time. Reflecting on not only his own "zig-zag career—from department of religion (four years) to seminary (ten years) back to department of religion,"[37] Harvey raises the issue of "the possibility and even the relevance of traditional systematic theology in our pluralistic and secular culture."[38] In such a culture, traditional theology strikes "a crisis of credibility" and yet, like Nichol, Harvey sees a new home and possibility for theology in religious studies. In particular, for Harvey this includes the possibility of "a new and probably non-Christian theology of some sort" being developed that is "more strictly philosophical and does not at all understand itself as a servant of a church or a tradition."[39] Referencing Victor Preller of Princeton, Harvey terms this a "meta-theology"[40] or "a genuinely secular theology"[41] that is to be thought, critiqued, and argued in departments of religion.

That Lloyd Geering, for over half a century, continues to make us think, engage with, and challenge him as he works out his local and now global articulation of "a genuinely secular theology" is the central importance of his work. For he forces us continually to respond, to rethink, and, importantly, to reinterpret Christian origins, institutions, and beliefs. In regard to issues of religion and identity in the modern world, Geering continues to demand that we situate and resituate ourselves and our position from a position of informed knowledge that includes a central ongoing engagement of science and religion and scholarship. Therefore, the chilling, bracing winds of Geering's thought that blow from the collapse of orthodoxy are derived from the fifty-year engagement of Geering's wrestling with modernity, the end of the short theological twentieth century, and his hope for a new, secular theological future.

Lloyd Geering's freedom from churchly captivity meant he became New Zealand's public theologian in an age when religion seemed to be losing its relevance in public life; but how do we come to grips with Geering's move from heretic to knight, from being tried for heresy to being considered a foremost public intellectual? Why did New Zealand decide to embrace and endorse such a religious thinker?

If we begin by considering the public and archival papers of the New Zealand Presbyterian Church, it becomes clear that Geering's treatment is only a touchstone of a wider anti-authoritarian move in the 1960s. For any attempt to state and extend statements of authority and singular meaning within the institution, within the collective known as a church or denomination, had been lost in the sense that unity itself was recognized as something that even a church's doctrine committee could not agree upon or enforce. Further, as the requested need at the time for a "simple" Statement of Faith exposed, what eventuated in the church was a communal language of piety and not theology. The tensions that were exposed and exploded with Geering's trial were actually a matter of *when* and not *if*. These tensions also existed within the students at the Theological Hall at the time, as the "Hall Report" in the Knox College magazine for 1966 makes clear. Written by John McKinlay, who was soon to embark for mission work in Hong Kong and was later a co-convenor of the conservative "Presbyterian Affirm" body, it helps explain why there was soon a substantial conservative shift in the Presbyterian Church:

> Let's probe a little deeper, because I think that an analysis of the Hall student body reflects the thinking and attitudes of the Presbyterian Church of New Zealand at large. That might not sound very significant but for once it is, because this year the

Presbyterian Church of New Zealand has hit the headlines from one end of the country to the other. Professor Geering set the ecclesiastical world alight with his theological articles in the official church paper. The fantastic response to his writings has staggered everyone and demonstrated clearly that lots of people still consider Christian faith a vital issue, at least for discussion.

What about the response within the Hall? There has been little open debate. That much is understandable where the views of a staff member are involved. Hall men have at least refused to share in public attacks which sadly have often been directed at the principal himself. However undercurrents of opinion and discussion have not ceased to flow since the articles appeared.

For what it's worth, most Hall students disagree with the views which have attracted so much attention to the Hall. But what staggers this student is the bewildering variety of opinion. Fundamentalist, conservative, neo-evangelical, Thomist, neo-Orthodox, post-Barthian liberal and Pentecostal—you name it, we've got it. The confusion of tongues at Babel pales by comparison. All this illustrates the confusion of a church which does not know which way to turn. At least the cards are on the table. Today's churchly catch-cry is "unity"! It is certainly appropriate.[a]

But was Geering at the time of the trial actually a radical? Helmut Rex's critique, endorsed by Albert Moore, of Geering as "an old-fashioned liberal" also helps to signal the rationale behind the response to him. Those opposed to Geering thought he was contemporary and radical; yet he was not, even at that time—as Rex

---

[a]. John McKinlay, "Hall Notes," 71. The *Collegian* is the annual magazine of the Presbyterian Church's University residential college next to the Theological Hall. At this time a male-only college, it housed theological students, amidst a majority of Otago university students. When he became a theological student, Geering moved into Knox College, having been in private accommodation while completing his study at Otago university. I want to thank Jane Bloore of the Presbyterian Archives, Dunedin, for drawing this report to my attention.
Chapter 1: Early Life

and Nichol suggest—up to date with Bonhoeffer or more recent theology. Moreover, Geering himself admits that he was a liberal and not a radical at this time. His radical turn came later as a result of his move into religious studies and was a self-radicalization that occurred primarily by prodigious reading. At the time of the controversies in 1966–67, Geering primarily represented the perspective of an Old Testament scholar who was unversed in both contemporary New Testament scholarship and systematic theology but very much engaged in late nineteenth-century and early twentieth-century liberal Christian biblical exegesis. Here we must remember that Geering was never a theologian, nor was he ever really interested in theology, as he honestly admits, because he found it too abstract.

So how do we explain Geering's move from the mid-1970s to a type of atheistic theology that was not informed by the death-of-God theologians and only partly by Nietzsche? Central to Geering's success is his formidable ability to take control of a wide range of ideas and debates (as evidenced by his reading) and express them in an accessible manner for the contemporary world. We could use the word *populist* to describe his work, if it was not likely to be pejoratively misunderstood. In fact, we could say that his clarity and honesty was his undoing during the 1960s. Geering's work is the accessible exposition of a scientifically-inclined mind who, via engagement with biblical scholarship, sought to express a logical version of Jesus the good man as exemplar par excellence. But quite quickly, due to his experience and especially his reading, while keeping an emphasis on the importance of Jesus the good man of faith, Geering's god becomes both a noun for value and meaning and a verb for responsive action; a noun arising from within the Jewish and then Christian traditions that also underpins Western civilization and the rise of modern society and a verb that humanity uses to create institutions, beliefs and also, importantly, cultural and social change. Because of his interest in comparative religions and then his career in religious studies, he was able to then expand the noun as expressing a formative human search for value and meaning that takes different forms in different ages, peoples, cultures, and faiths.

This change in thinking about God is the key to Geering's success with the liberal wing of the Christian churches and his acceptance amongst the wider body of a secular, liberal New Zealand. Geering's acceptance occurred in two ways. Firstly, because of Geering's trial, many people moved out of the church but still held on to a type of liberal good works ethos and lived a good life of piety underwritten by an acceptance of modern science and secular society. They made up a substantial number of the audiences for his very popular nationwide continuing education courses and public lectures. They also read his newspaper and magazine columns. Some migrated to the Sea of Faith movement. Alternatively, we must not forget that Geering chose to remain in the Presbyterian Church as a minister. As a convert to Christianity, Geering then had to make the decision to remain a convert. He was not like so many in the liberal church who had been born into the church and had moved towards a liberal position, whereby the decision was now to leave. Geering was that very rare creature of the short theological twentieth century, a non-Christian who became an adult convert to liberal Christianity. His decision was for liberal Presbyterianism—and for liberal Presbyterian community. He remains a Christian, or perhaps even more so a radical Presbyterian, far more accepted—and at home—outside his church than in it.

To return to the 1960s, Geering was not like the death-of-God theologians who we might think of as his contemporaries. Unlike Hamilton, Altizer, or Vahanian, Geering did not come to his position through a deep reading of and wrestling with Barth, Bonhoeffer, or even Tillich amidst the rise of modern secular society. He also lacked the engagement with art and literature that so underscored their work. If theirs could be expressed as an intellectual critique undertaken by applying theology and philosophy to both high and popular culture in American secular society, Geering's religious piety arises as a response to being a rational, "scientific" everyman unencumbered by abstract thought. His central quest was for clarity and logic; it was how to make a common-sense, rational Christian faith for the modern world. While this may seem overly critical, it is actually what made him so accessible and so successful. New Zealand society in the 1960s was certainly not like America at that time: Geering, the churches and general society were not influenced by study in Europe nor did they have access to either that great diaspora of European thinkers who fled to America from the 1930s or the post-war wave of scholars who moved into American seminaries and universities.

Another key to understanding Geering and his thought is to be found in the title of his autobiography: *Wrestling with God*. The Genesis 32:22–31 narrative of Jacob wrestling with God is a favourite of Protestants, in part for its reaffirmation that a strong work ethic will gain both spiritual and temporal rewards. Its other attraction, especially for Presbyterians, is its re-reading whereby physical wrestling becomes re-imagined as intellectual wrestling. The scholastic tradition of Presbyterianism runs deep; not so long ago, theological and intellectual competency were seen as a hallmark of Presbyterian clergy and laity.

The *Wrestling with God* analogy often overlooks the fact that while Jacob's wrestling gains him a new name (Israel) and the blessing of God, he is also wounded. God dislocates Jacob's hip-socket so Jacob will continue to carry the permanent legacy of the cost of his struggle. To read Lloyd Geering's autobiography is to be reminded time and time again of the cost involved in his wrestling. And yet I want to add a caveat: his wrestling was not actually with "God," for he has never been centrally concerned with theology. Rather his wrestling was always secular: on the one hand with the search for and demands of community and on the other with modernity itself. To properly understand Lloyd Geering is to think of him as a modernist, wrestling with modernity. As Paul Morris and I named him in the subtitle of *The Lloyd Geering Reader*, Lloyd Geering is first and foremost a "Prophet of Modernity." But how can we understand this claim? What does it mean to be modern? To understand Lloyd Geering and his engagement with modernity, and to further make sense of my claim that he is not wrestling with God but rather with modernity itself, we need to venture back one hundred years ago to Vienna.

In 1908 the Austrian architect and critic Adolf Loos first presented a lecture that was to impact radically upon the modern world's self-conception. Loos's topic was "Ornament and Crime."[42] He asked the question, within the cultural framework of the day, who in the modern world besides the child and "the civilised Papuan" unnecessarily decorates themselves and their environment? Loos as promoter of modernist, middleclass, bourgeois values offers two replies: either the degenerate aristocrat or those with criminal tendencies. The modern person, by comparison, will live a life *without* unnecessary ornamentation—and for us, crucially, he includes God as an example of such unnecessary ornamentation.

Loos's manifesto was taken up in the early 1920s by the French Purist movement in their journal *L'Espirit Nouveau* and mistranslated as "Ornament Is Crime." Out of this arose the square white box of Bauhaus-inflected architecture and the modern cityscape of the square-topped glass tower most notably influenced by the great German architect Mies van der Rohe.

Why should we venture to Austria and modernist architecture when ostensibly the topic under discussion is Lloyd Geering's "God"—or dismissal thereof? Surely Geering and his erosion of God have little if anything to do with Loos, the Bauhaus, or Mies— let alone the rise of modernist architecture. And yet if we find ourselves asking such a question, we have, paradoxically, given our own answer. For if we ignore the bigger picture of the influence of Loos and the banishment of unnecessary ornamentation as one of the dominant narratives of twentieth-century modernity then we can never really understand Lloyd Geering's gradual banishment of the unnecessary ornamentation of God in his writings.

Loos did not arise out of a vacuum. He was a product of the history of cultural and intellectual debates that flowed out of the Enlightenment and the counter-rise of Romanticism into that cultural meeting point of *fin de siècle* Vienna. Here, Jewish and

Christian culture swirled in a melee influenced by those forces that came to dominate the twentieth century: nationalism, incipient fascism, and communism. Loos's claim that modern secular progress was the history of the banishment of unnecessary ornamentation was also a statement of humanist hope. The past was crucial for shaping how we had gotten to now, but the future—and most crucially the present—must not remain in thrall to those past elements that sought to continue the past into the present. To do so would be to deny the modern world, and to deny the realisation of the modern person.

It is into this world that Lloyd Geering was born. As has been discussed, the year of Lloyd's birth, 1918, was perhaps the real beginning of the twentieth century and Lloyd is perhaps the antipodean example of the modern man *par excellence*.

Too often the response against Lloyd Geering has been framed primarily within a sectarian viewing of the Christian faith where, in anti-Loosian terms, God and indeed Christianity are viewed as "fundamentally necessary ornamentation." In such a schema, admittedly broad-brushed here, the post-Enlightenment modern world has been viewed as "a fall from a state of grace." Christianity and modernity are therefore viewed as inherently oppositional, and transcendence is a reality that, if not exactly still a three-tiered universe, is at least some form of sub-gnostic (but self-evident within faith) two-tiered reality of this world and a good after life that those possessing "knowledge" are aware of. To understand Lloyd Geering's God we need to move outside of a sectarian view of the Christian faith and of Lloyd himself. He needs to be placed within a general history of the intellectual's debate with modernity as it has developed, especially from the Enlightenment.

Geering's god-talk was and remains also that of a convert. His conversion was twofold. He first moved from a non-Christian, scientific identity into Presbyterian Christianity. This move led to a focus on the centrality of the sermon and value of the academically and theologically educated teaching elder. Moreover, his conversion was, as noted, to liberal broad-church Presbyterianism. At this time (1937) in New Zealand, this was a counter-cultural choice. Conversions to communism, socialism, or the evangelical Oxford movement were far more common amongst university students at that time. Nor was he ever tempted by Barthianism, as a number of fellow bright young Presbyterians of the time were.

His second conversion was forced upon him by circumstance. The trial of 1967 and the related ongoing difficulties he faced meant that a decision to move into religious studies was much easier than it might otherwise have been. This decision set up a second conversion into what can be termed radical Christianity. Had Geering remained an Old Testament professor in a Theological Hall and, most likely, continued on as principal of that Theological Hall, certain institutional, disciplinary, and ecclesiastical limitations would most likely have kept him in the situation of being an increasingly problematic theological liberal. In such a context, even the exponential growth of his reading habit after the trial might not have been enough to push him into radical theology. Of course, he might have faced yet another charge of doctrinal error. One signal of this likelihood can be seen in the response to his comments during a television interview in Brisbane in 1970: answering rapid-fire questions, he rejected the virginity of Mary, stated "Son of God" was a metaphorical but not literal term for Jesus, and defined a Christian as one who chooses to live in response to the heritage arising from Jesus. But these statements were really still part of a liberal Christian faith for Geering. However, in moving to establish religious studies in a new university, he encountered an intellectual and academic freedom that he could never have experienced if he had chosen, or indeed managed, to stay on at Knox.

In many ways, harking back to Frank Nichol's call, the first "cold winds blowing from religious studies" blew into the theology of Lloyd Geering himself. Yet his conversion to radical Christianity was not a dramatic damascene moment. Rather, it was a slow move that arose out of his teaching and culminates in his book *Faith's New Age* (1980). Here is Geering at the age of 62 really emerging as a radical thinker, charting the rise of modern secularity and seeking to outline the basis of a radical faith. Yet in many ways the demands of establishing and running a new discipline and department meant that his radicalism was kept in check. So for the decade preceding the book, Geering was a liberal in transition to radicalism; but this was a very important transition because much of it occurred in front of his students, in front of his nationwide continuing education classes, in public lectures, and in his columns in the media. Therefore it was not an abrupt, confrontational transition but rather one that, most probably unwittingly, also liberalized and radicalized a fair number of his audiences. In that decade Geering, as academic and public intellectual, became a figurehead for New Zealand's transition into a secular, liberal, urban society that increasingly sought connection to the wider world.

Even so, during the 1960s and 1970s in particular, Geering was working and thinking in an almost defiantly provincial country. Lacking academic and intellectual resources and populations, constrained by distance and cost, New Zealand was not part of the major byways of academic or theological movements. This insularity meant, especially in those pre-Internet days, that Lloyd was forced to make do in the best "Kiwi No. 8 Wire" mentality; that is, constructing what he could by using the limited materials and resources at hand. He could not rely on others to do his thinking for him, nor could he ride on the back of a constant flow of visitors, trends, and information. Yet this is not to knock the provincial dilemma. Rather, the provinces tend to force two reactions—either a retreat into safety and the aping of a second-hand orthodoxy (for fear of being thought provincial) or a defiant attempt to make do, to attempt to overcome such limitations, to make up one's own mind and to take risks.

Charles Brasch noted a similar issue in his inaugural editorial of the seminal New Zealand journal *Landfall* in 1947:

> In every good artist in every European society that main tradition is reincarnated. Working in his own place and time he is drawing on a tradition which has been formed in so many places

and times that it now belongs to none exclusively but to all. In one sense he is working on the periphery, wherever he may be, even in London or Paris or Vienna, because at the same time the tradition belongs to and is being reincarnated in a dozen other places as well; but inasmuch as the tradition is alive for him it has become localized and he is working *from a centre*. There is no single centre; the Yugoslavia of Mestrovich, the Finland of Sibelius, the Ireland of Yeats, are as much centres in respect of the work of these artists as the Italy of Dante or the France of Cezanne.

If this is so, there is no reason why a New Zealand artist too, ours being a European society, should not absorb the tradition and work within it and add new forms to it in New Zealand. But the first condition of good work here is that for the artist the tradition must be localized, in himself or in a group to which he has access, so that he may feel himself, just as an artist working in Europe would, to be working from a centre, and can see his subject matter, which will be local at least in the sense that he belongs to this particular time and place, quite naturally in terms of the tradition. He must at the same time reincarnate the tradition in a local form, and embody his local and personal material in terms recognizably of the tradition, however modified.

It is true that New Zealand is a long way from Europe. But it is true also that the European tradition can take root here and grow, if we wish it to do so. To think of this country as a *mere* province, a poverty-stricken outpost where nothing original can be expected to arise, is false and stultifying and the best way to ensure that in fact nothing will arise. Every province has something to contribute to the centre—provided it continues to welcome what the centre can give it; every province can be a centre in its own right—provided it does not imagine that it can be self-sufficient.[43]

What I want to argue is that Lloyd Geering can only really be understood if we frame him in the legacy of Brasch's comments. Today's society is of course not the "European society" as articulated by Brasch. Yet Geering's work up to the 1990s and his turn to ecological issues could be read as existing in the province's dialogues with a series of theological centres variously European and North American. So I want to emphasize the degree to which his theological approach is framed by Brach's *Landfall* ethos. *Landfall* played a significant role as the in-house journal for New Zealand intelligentsia up to the late 1960s. Brasch's stated interest in religion[44] made *Landfall* a sympathetic frame for liberal Christians to interact with culture.[45] The fact that the later Geering has been taken up by radical religious groups in Britain and North America as a prophet of global humanism, selling out book and lecture tours, is something we here in New Zealand need to appreciate more fully. There is a degree of the infamous tall poppy syndrome at work—whatever our theological perspective.

Geering is indeed "reworking the tradition in a particular time and place," and so perhaps his most important contribution locally is that he has added to New Zealand's long history of secularisation an awareness of the religious implications of modernity. We now not only have such a history but, for many, a new way of understanding how and why this has come to be. This is Geering acting as public intellectual for New Zealand and his success in doing so has resulted in his deserved public honours of a CBE in 1988, followed in 2001 and 2007 with gradations within the Order of New Zealand. These all occurred under centre-Left Labour-led governments, for Geering's supporters have always tended to be far more on the Left than on the Right politically, and Geering himself has always been a man of the Left. It could be said that Geering represented what the liberal Left in New Zealand saw as the ideal type of churchman: one prepared to seriously engage with and support a secular society and challenge conservative Christian beliefs and institutions. Then in 2009 a change in the honours system under the centre-Right National-led government saw the redesignation of one of the Orders of Merit into a Knighthood. That a "heretic" could become a Knight within a forty-year period signals not only that New Zealand society secularized while the churches were marginalised, but also that Geering's transition into a public intellectual of increasingly radical theology became normal in New Zealand society. Central to this is, as noted, his admirable ability to clearly communicate a way to think through and respond to the challenges and changes of modernity. He enabled a conservative, provincial society to engage with theological and intellectual currents and ideas that enabled a sense that we, too, here could become modern. Yet he did so in a manner, due to his location in religious studies, that enabled many questioning liberals to retain a spirituality and form of faith that probably slowed down the decline of the churches in the 1970s and 1980s.

Importantly, during these decades, Geering expounded a turn toward an emerging global humanism in which many on the centre-Left, even if no longer part of the church, could participate. His politically centre-Left humanism, which spoke directly to such issues as human meaning, technology, evil, ethics, ecology, and global society, also served to make him an acceptable public intellectual for the growing post-Christian society, especially those who had come to adulthood in the late 1960s and 1970s.

Out of this time of transition, drawing on his teaching, Geering comes to write *Faith's New Age*. He signals his radical turn, explicitly distancing himself from "Christianity in its orthodox or classical forms."[46] God and Christ are reaffirmed as symbols that must be reworked afresh in each age as a means to help humanity work out their own salvation in the new era, a salvation in which "the sincere and concerned atheist is more religious than the half-hearted theist or nominal Christian."[47] We can see, in this statement in particular, the influence of a concentrated period in the mid-1970s of reading on and about Dietrich Bonhoeffer. *Faith's New Age* is in many ways an eclectic book into which Geering deposits all his reading and thinking arising from his lectures, including his longstanding interest in issues of religion and science. Secularization is presented as an inevitable movement of the modern world and of modern thinking. The question was articulated elsewhere at least two decades previously in the northern hemisphere: what does it mean to—and how can I—have a secular faith? Yet this is no criticism because this was a most honest and thoughtful book, and New Zealand and New Zealand Christians were, in the main, by no means ready, willing, or able to engage with such questions in the 1950s and early 1960s—as Geering's own trial exposed. *Faith's New Age* is the book that in many ways can be read as a type of theological confessional in which Geering emerges as a fully radical and secular theologian. Importantly, it was a book that spoke to audiences both inside and outside the church, a guidebook on how we came to be modern.

Central to the book and to Geering's thinking at this time is Nietzsche's challenge, to himself and us, of who we are and how we make our way in a new secular age. But Geering expresses this as a task for each individual to complete, drawing upon one's own resources, for "we can no longer appeal to a God up there, or to former authorities—not even to Nietzsche himself."[48] Instead, as outlined in the book, we must seek out the prophets of change and development,[49] who no longer focus on theological issues but rather on socio-anthropological ones. The new age of faith is without a transcendent, objective, singular god. Rather, in an unwitting echo of Geering's own original conversion, the focus turns to issues of personhood and community. That turn would draw heavily upon Martin Buber who, in his next major text, is taken to exemplify possibilities for a relational "god" in "the post-theistic age."[50]

We can understand this post-theistic emphasis as the culmination of the Loosian basis of modernity. The unnecessary ornament of the theistic God is banished; religion has now become explicitly understood to be a human activity involving a human search for meaning that is *neither* atheist or theistic. Influenced here also by the work of Don Cupitt, "god" is now a symbol for humanity's relational encounters with others and with the world. Geering's "god" is thus also an iconoclastic challenge to traditional, orthodox Christianity (and is in a direct lineage from Bonhoeffer and "religionless Christianity"). From here on, the use of the symbol "god" to facilitate human interrelation with others and the environment becomes his focus. Geering's work becomes more explicitly theological. Now he expresses a radical, relational theology as a basis for a series of engagements with the environment, technology, science, and urbanisation that Geering undertook as he entered his retirement from religious studies.

By the mid-1980s an additional influence, the work of Carl Jung, comes to play an important part in his theology. In Geering's newly radical theology-driven critiques of what being human might entail, god is now a human idea created by a collective human consciousness.[51] In good modernist fashion, the call is for a new religious form for a new global future because "the old religious forms will not do and a new one has not emerged."[52]

Geering seeks to answer his own call with *Tomorrow's God* (1994), in which the new religious form is now that of an emergent global culture. God is understood as a functional word in that the way we use it affirms "something about ourselves,"[53] precisely because it is a word that "has no external referent that is open to public confirmation."[54] In an echo of the title of his book on the resurrection, to use the term "Tomorrow's God" is a prophetic statement of hope that we *can* affirm a future. In Geering's case, it must be tied inherently to the ecological future of the planet. Such a reimagining of god, he later argues, stands in the lineage of the Judeo-Christian tradition. For in its first five centuries, Christianity rethought and created "an entirely new way of talking about God … [by] … simply relating the Jewish heritage to their current experience. So must we."[55] Here is the basis of all his later radical writing and theology: how to relate the heritage we inherit to the world in which we find ourselves. This period sees Geering writing what is essentially a companion volume to *Faith's New Age* for a twenty-first century radical Christianity in *Christianity without God* (2002). Perhaps his most explicitly Christian work since the late 1960s, here Geering secularizes the death of God into a rethought radical Christian humanism focussed on the figure of the non-incarnational Jesus. His argument is more fully articulated in what I consider to be his second autobiography, *Such Is Life: A Close Encounter with Ecclesiastes* (2010). A combination of biblical scholarship (and notably a return to the Old

Testament) and spiritual autobiography, *Such Is Life* exhibits a new personal freedom. While tracing a continuity from within a dissident biblical tradition to today's new sceptics of Dawkins, Hitchens, and Sam Harris, Geering emphasizes that scepticism plays a central part in the biblical tradition. Most telling is his repositioning of *Ecclesiastes* as a sage and the text as part of a sage tradition that includes Jesus and, on through the centuries, Geering himself. It is here that, against all who have sought to label him a heretic and a dissident, Geering reclaims a place for himself within the Jewish and Christian traditions. He finds the freedom to finally, clearly, state what he believes and why.

His central premise is that the wisdom stream of the biblical tradition, as best exemplified in Ecclesiastes, now finds its counterpart in the modern secular age's rejection of the supernatural and in the rise of "this-wordly" society. He calls for a rediscovery and rearticulation of the secular wisdom tradition from deep within the roots of Western culture. Like the sage of Ecclesiastes, Geering turns to the wisdom of the world around him to confront the big questions of meaning and how to make good decisions. God is here rewritten and reargued as Nature—as the force of life itself that we exist within and amongst, as individuals first and foremost. Now, in "wrestling with life," questions of finitude come to the fore wherein Geering finds hope and possibility, expressed as how to both rethink and live out life as a series of hopeful possibilities, even amongst times of despair.

For over fifty years Geering has been engaged in a most public—and publicly accessible—exploration of what it means to be modern. Throughout he has argued, clearly, coherently, rationally, and intelligently for the central role of a rethought religious and theological expression and engagement as part of this exploration. His own particular approach, now in the twenty-first century, is for a radical theology based in a secular, post-Christian Jewish-derived wisdom approach to life. Here is perhaps the starting point for a new theological century.

"Go into All the World"

A selection from the Address by Rev. Professor Lloyd Geering, MA, BD, to Presbyterian Summer Conference, Gore 1962–1963, evening meeting, Tuesday, 1 January 1963. This selection was transcribed by Mike Grimshaw (April 2016) from original handwritten notes and checked by Lloyd Geering (April–May 2016). Page numbers in { } relate to original lecture notes. Where necessary, missing words have been inserted in [ ].

This is the address that caused debate and discussion as to Geering's theology amongst not only the conservative faction of the Presbyterian church but also (as evidenced by the correspondence between Helmut Rex and Albert Moore) amongst those who considered themselves modern but not 'liberal' members of the church. The address came up in conversations between Grimshaw and Geering and resulted in Geering hunting in his own archives to see if he could locate a copy. Luckily, he found the original conference folder that still contained the handwritten notes of all the addresses he gave at the Conference. The transcription below begins thirteen pages into Geering's address. Up to this point Geering had undertaken a non-controversial, liberal discussion about mission. Then, having set the context biblically, Geering made the statements below that, as principal of the Theological Hall, formed the basis of the concerns of the conservatives in the church.

But what does this mean for us? What is *our* mission? Now it is a very heartening and encouraging thing to observe that just in [the] last twenty years there has been an amazing rediscovery of the sense of mission in the church. Until twenty years ago the word "mission" mainly meant something that went on in heathen countries overseas, or a revival meeting at home by a special evangelist. But there has been a growing concern lately with *our* task of mission and with the practice of evangelism. But though heartening, [this new concern] does not mean we have not got a long way to go and a lot to learn.

Let me start off by saying what I think *our* mission does not mean!

(a) It does not mean going around badgering people.

I have a feeling some of our early attempts at personal evangelism smack of this. It is not our mission to be a pest to people by asking them questions intended to niggle at their consciences …

(b) It does not mean proselytizing.

There are various forms of this—it sometimes even happens within our own denomination. It has been known for a minister quietly to encourage a Presbyterian from another congregation to come and join his congregation and swell its numbers. What has been achieved? Nothing! That is proselytizing.

We go a little further.

And if we encourage a Methodist to become a Presbyterian, have we in some way been successful in our mission? No! It is not our {14} role to persuade members of other Christian denominations to come and swell our numbers. That also is proselytizing?

But if it is a Roman Catholic who becomes a Presbyterian, I imagine that most of us would be really secretly pleased about it. But should we? Have we performed our mission by turning Roman Catholics into good Presbyterians? Some may wish to think so! I don't. I call that proselytizing also.

But what if he is an agnostic or a Hindu? Surely that's different! Surely we have a clear mission to make that person a Presbyterian. You may be surprised when I say no! The deliberate attempt to change anybody into a Presbyterian or even into a Christian is proselytizing. Our mission is *not* to persuade people to join our church?

Now don't throw me out just yet!

Do you remember what our Lord said about the Pharisees?

"Woe to you, scribes and Pharisees, hypocrites! For you traverse sea and land to make a single proselyte, and when he becomes a proselyte, you make him twice as much a son of hell as yourselves."

What were they doing wrong in going to such trouble to make proselytes? They were converting non-Jews to the Jewish faith? Wasn't this a good thing? Jesus was a Jew—a devout Jew. But he condemned proselytising. Proselytising is the attempt to persuade another person to conform to your own faith and practice. Are we so wonderful, you and I, that we think everybody else should join our church and become like us?

(c) {15} Our mission is not even to make committed Christians.

That may surprise you! My reason for saying this, especially to those individuals who use this phrase and who think of our mission is just in these terms, is that the term is both unbiblical and inadequate. The Bible speaks of believers, of men of faith, of living in Christ, of being in Christ, of being Christian; it does not speak of being committed Christians.

What does it mean? I don't know. It seems often to be used to describe a man who is wholly dedicated to God in Christ. Where does one find such a person? I know I am not. Perhaps I would like to think I am. But I find that Christian faith and practice involves a continual struggle within oneself. I am continually being pulled up with a start as I find areas in my life which are not at all committed to God. It would be hypocritical for me to set out to make other people committed Christians with the assumption that I am. This phrase suffers from over simplicity, for it is just not possible for us to make a division between those who are committed to Christ and those who are not. If it is simply a matter of varying degrees of commitment, then we must accept the fact that one comes across elements of genuine faith and even genuine commitment in the most unlikely places—even outside the activities of church life altogether. So encouraging people to become committed Christians is not an adequate way of describing our mission.

{16} What then is our mission? How are we to describe it? I noticed yesterday in a workshop that four different attempts were made to define evangelism—all said something true but not one used the word Gospel! When we remember that *evangel* is the Greek word for gospel and literally means Good News, it is hard to see how we can define evangelism adequately without using this term. We have a mission because of the very nature of the Gospel. The Apostles went out because they had some Good News for their fellow Jews. From the day of Pentecost they were bubbling over with it. They could not keep it to themselves. None of us tell good news out of a sense of duty—we just can't help sharing it. Yet I cannot help feeling that so often when we think about personal evangelism, we think of it as a duty laid upon us, one which we take up rather unwillingly. If this is so, then we must ask ourselves, "Have we a Gospel to preach? Have we nothing concerning Christianity in our own time to be glad about—nothing that we want to share with others?"

The sense of mission comes alive in us all when we discern within our own hearts what the Gospel is! What it was through the ages! What it has done for other people and what it has done for us! …

Let me illustrate it this way, for you might have been holding your sports meeting this afternoon instead of sightseeing. Supposing you dreamt that you were running in the relay race only to be woken up when the baton hit your hand and you found that you really were. {17} It's like that with the Gospel. So often we stand on the side-line as spectators and some stay like that all their lives. It is of no use trying to talk to spectator Christians about mission. It is not till the moment when we wake up to find we are involved in the race ourselves that, becomes the moment when God speaks the Gospel directly to us. That's when we receive something good from God. That is the moment our sense of mission begins. God does not speak to us for our sake only,

> He speaks to us that we may speak to others.
> He leads us that we may lead
> He teaches us that we may teach

And so ran the story of the people of God, whenever the Word of God spoke with power—to Moses, to Isaiah, to Jesus. They began to speak of being *sent*—they discovered they had a mission. It is to the extent that we have heard the Word of the Gospel in our own lives that we have a mission.

> And our mission is twofold—
> it is to tell the Gospel
> and to live the Gospel
> …

Let me conclude with a word about the first part of our mission. It is to tell the Gospel, that is, to tell *our* Gospel, to tell what God has done in the past, to tell what God is {18} doing now—to tell what God is doing for us.

It may well be that this will cause some people to want to join your church, to want to commit themselves to Christ—but if it does, God through the Holy Spirit will see to this. That is the Holy Spirit's task, not ours. This is why our mission is not to be defined in terms of getting people to join the church. It is not our task to go to people and say, "You miserable sinners, why don't you come to Church every Sunday like us. You miserable Catholics, why don't you surrender yourselves to God the way we have."

But we are all Catholics. We have been sent to tell our Gospel—to tell it because we are glad to. Everyone who has received the Gospel can do this. And because there is such great variety in our responses, in the forms in which we have received the Gospel, there will be great variety in the way in which we tell it. This need not surprise us. The Gospel is not tied down to any one form of words, to any one pattern. The Gospel is within us who have received the Good News of what God has done and who know firsthand what God is doing in us.

I said earlier that I find it misleading to describe myself as a committed Christian. So what then, you may ask, do I mean by being a Christian?

Whether I am a Christian or not does not really concern me—this was not a title coined by the first believers but by their enemies.

Whether I am among the elect I do not know. I make no claim to be a better person than the so-called non-Christian.

I cannot even claim to be a good church-member.

{19} But this I do know. In the past God encountered men like Moses, Amos, Jeremiah—and took hold of them and used them. God sent his Son—in him we see grace and faith such as we see nowhere else.

And this I know—that without any choice or decision on my part, indeed against my will, I have been caught up in this living tradition of faith that we call the fellowship of the church—and I am glad I have been caught up in it because I never would have chosen it of my own free-will.

I am not a Christian theologian because now I know all the answers. My study of theology has taught me how much I do not know—how many of my questions are still unanswered.

But this I know—that in the worship of the Church I encounter the meaning of life and death in a more real way than anywhere else.

That in the fellowship of Christ, such as we experience in conferences like this, I find a quality of life that I have not found elsewhere in the world.

That in the service of a worker in the Kingdom of God I find the deepest satisfaction. All this came to me from God unsought. This God has done for me! This I gladly bear witness to as I tell you. I tell all who would listen.

What has God done for you? Do you not rejoice about it?

Then go into the world and tell the world.

This is your mission!

1

Early Life, University and Entry into the Church

MG: I want to begin by asking, what was involved in the "sudden flash of illumination"[1] you experienced when a boy of fourteen in Dunedin?

LG: Jung had a similar experience at the age of eleven. It was a sudden realization of self-hood, of being a self. I was just walking, but it left its mark. I often used to go back to it; it was a time of adolescent reaction. I was a very insignificant creature but academically motivated. I had a lonely life in some respects.

MG: You mention in your autobiography that on your initial visits as an undergraduate to First Church[a] you were struck by the preaching.[2] I wonder if you could expand on why it made such an impact?

LG: I had spent a whole year boarding in a Roman Catholic home. My time there had aroused my interest in things religious in a general sort of way and this flowed over as I encountered the Presbyterian context. In Presbyterianism I discovered that the sermon was central, all the rest was padding. Alan Stevely* was the minister of First Church and he was quite a dramatic sort

---

*For short bios of people marked with an asterisk, see Appendix 2.
  a. First Church of Otago, Moray Place, Dunedin. A magnificent gothic style stone church, often labeled New Zealand's finest nineteenth-century structure, it is a Heritage New Zealand Historic Place, category one.

of preacher who preached extempore. It was this initial interest in the sermon that led to my soon becoming a member of First Church.

MG: You also seem to have been a convert to the SCM;[a] I was wondering, were you never tempted by the other great student movement at that time of Moral Rearmament?[b]

LG: No, I was always SCM. Of course I knew about Moral Rearmament from Harold Turner* and Ian Dixon*, but I kept myself aloof from Moral Rearmament because it seemed too intense and too concentrated on confession.

MG: It seems like you had a very sudden conversion, a very quick conversion both to the SCM and to First Church. It seems almost like Paul's Damascus moment!

LG: It was very like a Damascus moment, but remember I was very anti-evangelical and would have run a mile from "conversion." My background didn't fit with fundamentalism and emotionally I didn't fit because after all I was primarily a mathematician and so moving more toward rationalism.

---

a. Student Christian Movement. The New Zealand SCM was founded in 1896 under the umbrella organization of the World Student Christian Federation, founded in 1895. In contrast to the Oxford Group (see below), the SCM was a more liberal and progressive group and saw itself as more academic and political. The SCM in New Zealand published its own influential journal under various names. See Berry, *The New Zealand Student Christian Movement*.

b. The Oxford Group was a pietistic Protestant movement founded in 1921 by the American evangelist F.N.D. Buchman (1878–1961). It gathered a strong level of support at Oxford University, hence its name, but it was also known dismissively by its opponents as Buchmanites. The focus was on personal prayer, sin, conversion, and evangelism involving a call to a total surrendering of life to God. In the New Zealand SCM in the 1930s there was a battle for influence between those identifying as "Oxford Groupers" and those following a Barthian neo-orthodox line. In 1938 the name of the group was changed to Moral Rearmament as a result of a call for such action by Buchman, and in 2001 it was again renamed, as Initiatives of Change.

MG: I get the feeling, too, from what you have written and said, that it was also a conversion to a particular type of community?

LG: Yes, I was attracted to the SCM by the fellowship—before that I was a loner.

Ellis Dick[a] introduced me to the SCM and from this involvement I continued into the church and became a member of the church in about eight weeks. During the year—about August—the SCM ran a mission to the university and one of the brief speakers was Hubert Ryburn.* The mission was not that successful but I was really struck by what Hubert Ryburn said. We had a lot in common—he was a mathematician too and a man of some experience—he had fought in World War I and had been a Rhodes Scholar. What he said niggled in my mind and so I thought that if I was going to be a Christian I should go in boots and all. I wrestled with this idea for a few months.

MG: Given this quick conversion, why did you decide to put yourself forward as an ordinand for parish ministry?

LG: Because I felt I ought to. Parish ministry was the only model that I knew.

MG: So was Alan Stevely a role model?

LG: No, Stevely wasn't a role model—but I didn't know enough about Parish ministry. Ministry seemed to be taking Christianity seriously—you go the whole hog.

MG: What did your family think of this sudden conversion and change of plans?

LG: When I told my brother he said, "Oh you're wasting your time. The churches will all be closed in thirty years!" While my father, referring to Nordmeyer* and his time in Kurow said, "it could lead you into Politics".

---

a. Ellis Dick, a high school friend of Geering who was a medical student and became a surgeon.

MG: Given that you didn't have a strong religious background and you found yourself in a Roman Catholic boarding house of which you write and speak so warmly, were you never attracted to Roman Catholicism?

LG: No—not one little bit. I suppose it was my anti-Catholic background. Protestants were more anti Catholic than they were Protestants in those days.

MG: So how did you come to be in a Roman Catholic boarding house?

LG: One of my friends when I was at High School—a fellow train boy[a]—from Mosgiel[b], Ossie Pringle, went to school at Christian Brothers. He went to Otago University a year ahead of me and so when I went, I arranged to board with him. But Ossie failed his medical exams and so had to leave the boarding house, so I ended up the only one in that Roman Catholic Boarding house.

MG: How did the Roman Catholics handle your embrace of Protestantism?

LG: They accepted me very warmly and never tried to convert me. It was a very Catholic environment; one of the daughters had become a Carmelite nun and another of the boarders was the driver for the Catholic Bishop of Dunedin.[c]

MG: Was it Helmut Rex* who, in a way, made you who and what you are theologically? Was it Rex who enabled you to take the paths you did—in the sense you are always continuing and extending the influence of Rex?

LG: Rex's first lecture—on the Philosophy of History—changed the way I thought. I now saw history as changing and on the move.

---

   a. High school and university students who caught the train from Mosgiel into Dunedin.
   b. A town 15 kilometres southwest of Dunedin, at this time home to the Mosgiel Woollen Mill and now a satellite and commuter town.
   c. James Whyte (1868–1957), Third Bishop of Dunedin (1920–57).

In my first parish[a] I decided to study all the subjects in turn, starting with the Old Testament, then the New Testament, then church history and then theology, but I got stuck on the Old Testament. However I did quite a bit of reading in church history. I was becoming radical and now was a radical in the sense of going to the root of the matter—not being reactionary.

MG: How do you define radical?

LG: I see radical as clear, logical thinking—not necessarily as radical philosophy or theology. All this time I was trying to see what is true in past traditions. All of life is a type of search for clear, logical truth.

MG: You seem to exist at this time outside the wider political and cultural debates of the time.

LG: I don't think politics was important to me at this time. I had a passing interest and would always favour Labour. I took up an interest as my small world expanded, widening into the active Christian tradition and movement. The SCM was the life.

MG: Why did you enroll in a mathematics degree?

LG: I loved it. It was so orderly, so logical; it was teaching you logic. I just loved solving problems. I still do the cryptic crossword.

MG: Why didn't you do analytic philosophy?

LG: I didn't know much about philosophy.

MG: At that time, what career did you envisage?

LG: I assumed I would go teaching—secondary or later on, tertiary. I was against abstract thought and this position led me into biblical studies out of maths and it was logical compared to theology. Maths is a very good training ground for thinking clearly.

---

a. Kurow Presbyterian Church, North Otago. Geering was minister here, 1943–45.

The Professor of Mathematics, Bobby Bell,* was a Congregational Scot attending Moray place.[a] He was very encouraging of me for the Rhodes, and later when I went for the Christian Ministry.

MG: What career options had you considered?

LG: If not the ministry, then it would have been maths as I mentioned. Within the church it was as a parish minister. Not a missionary. I had no idea of teaching in the church. My sense was that if one was to be a Christian then one should live a Christian life and so I could be active as a parish minister.

Before that, when I left school, I had the opportunity, and was advised by my teachers, to do medicine. But I was too timid to take on anything new, so I decided to carry on in what I was best at in school, so there was no decision. I have often thought back to that time, for there was another train boy doing medicine and he said, "It's fascinating stuff."

MG: So is that a sense of regret?

LG: I have a central maxim from my teenage day: "One should be brutally honest." And so I had strong convictions. I was noted as "pretty frank" by my psychology lecturer, and this goes back to my frank statements. At the end of the year I had to give the thanks for the psychology course and I mentioned the student dissatisfaction with the course. The lecturer mentioned it to his colleagues.

MG: What was the impact of the SCM?

LG: The SCM was a community, but my connection to the church had begun a month or so earlier. It was through Ellis Dick that I had connection to both the SCM and the church. That year of being nineteen was a year of tremendous intellectual and spiritual growth—a turning point. My life took on a purpose.

---

a. First Church.

Early Life, University, and Church

For me, Christianity was embodied in the SCM, it was making friends. I had no close friends before the SCM. I had a sense of being almost an only child and at school I was a "train boy."

The year boarding in the Catholic house had a great influence on me. I had a close friend there—not in a romantic sense—a boarder, who became a nun.

MG: So are you really a convert to the SCM and to SCM theology and community?

LG: The SCM was a chance to engage. I saw SCM as within the church and not versus the church. I never really played a role in the wider Bible class movement. The SCM was much more active, more theologically alive, certainly, than the Bible class and the SCM was the seedbed of the ecumenical movement.

MG: Given that this was obviously a time of transition, I am wondering what framed your worldview at this time?

LG: The SCM formed my worldview and Christianity was read via the SCM. I didn't read much; some novels, detective stories. Any theology I read was not of any great significance; I didn't read much theology until the 1960s and then had to read fast!

Helmut Rex put me onto certain church history books, such as Hans Lietzmann.* I found church history much more interesting than theology.

In the sudden immersion into the Christian tradition I was spending time each morning reading the Bible and learning to pray. But the SCM mission to the university fell flat and this had an effect on me. I always had a call to activism and it continued with this new identity and new community. I felt that if I took Christianity seriously then I really should be doing something about it—but I had little idea of the Christian ministry.

There was no voice in the call,[a] rather the application to train for the Christian ministry gave a purpose and sense of going

---

a The "call" is the name given to the impetus behind the decision to apply for training for the Christian ministry. It arises from the biblical narratives of the call of God originating from the call of Abraham.

somewhere. Finding a purpose in life cemented me into the SCM first of all and, career-wise, carried me on. The funny thing is I never lost that at all; teaching was an extension; I was frustrated as a parish minister because I was not making any headway. I enjoyed teaching more than preaching.

MG: You stated in your paper "The Faith to Doubt"[3] that "faith is caught rather than taught. We catch it from others. ..." I am interested in what is that which is caught?

LG: What do we catch? An attitude, I think; an attitude of trust. If you live any length of time in a community there is a spirit in the community that catches you up and carries you along. I think sociology has not yet seen its real role: Sociology should be the study of what makes community work—this is what is meant by the Holy Spirit. We need to remember that community and the Holy Spirit are one and the same.

MG: So what was the community that you caught faith in? I keep getting the feeling it was not so much the church itself?

LG: I caught faith in the SCM more so than in the church. As I said, up to that year I was going through life without much sense of direction. I caught a sense of direction from the SCM because of the friendship and the example of a good number of theological students who were in it. So I caught faith from the SCM and it was this faith that led to my turn to the ministry.

MG: Who in particular was influential in you catching faith via the SCM?

LG: George Falloon.* He was president of the SCM. There was a group of theological students who couldn't afford to be at Knox[a]

---

a. Knox College, a student residential college situated next to the Theological Hall. Many theology students stayed in Knox for both their undergraduate degrees and/or for their theological training (which was post-graduate study).

[College] and had what was called "The Bach,"ᵃ and George Falloon was one of these.

MG: So if you can catch faith, can you also catch its opposite?

LG: Oh yes, you can also catch a loss of faith too. But faith is essentially an attitude of trust: trust of one's fellows, trust of the future.

MG: You often talk and write of the influence of Schleiermacher. Where did the influence arise from for you?

LG: My interest in Schleiermacher is due to John Dickie.* He helped us see the strengths and weaknesses of Schleiermacher. John Dickie also warned us against Barth, who he saw as leaving human reason behind.

MG: Wasn't there a strong Barthian group in the SCM in Dunedin at this time? It seems so from my reading of *The Student*.ᵇ

LG: Some were, but most of us in the SCM were not Barthians. John Dickie would call himself a Ritschlian. Ritschl moved away from Schleiermacher and thought of faith as a historical phenomenon—that faith moved and changed. So due to Dickie, the SCM was more Ritschlian, but probably didn't know the term. I would instead say that the SCM really absorbed the results of modern biblical scholarship.

---

a. George Fallon established "The Bach" (a house for bachelors, but also a New Zealand name for a small, simple weekend and holiday cottage) with a group of fellow students "studying divinity, medicine, education, and veterinary science." There were two Baches: the second, established in 1938, and the one Geering refers to, was at 208 Union Street. See Falloon, *The Day Thou Gavest, Lord*, 32–35 (photo of The Bach on Union Street, 32). Fallon was also a supporter of Geering in the heresy trial and is recorded as having constant run-ins with what he termed "pious fundamentalism" and stating, after such run-ins, "I'm sick of bloody religion" (107).

b. *The Student* was the Journal of the New Zealand Student Christian Movement, 1936–62; it replaced *Open Windows*.

MG: Given you are now one of the very few contemporaries of its tenure, I want to ask what are your memories of the *Journal of New Zealand Theology*?ᵃ

LG: Jim Steele* was a very good Calvinist scholar and I picked up bits and pieces from him. I was influenced by Jim ecclesiastically, and he led me away from a dead end future on the West Coast because I could have gone to Granityᵇ but Jim Steele told me to go to Opoho.ᶜ

MG: Bates* and Steel were strongly influenced by Calvin. Did Calvin influence you too? There seems to have been a strong Calvin influence in New Zealand theology in the 1930s.

LG: I actually did my mini-thesis on Calvin and read Calvin's *Institutes* from beginning to end and at one stage I had all his writings. But I never really took to Calvin; I read him out of a sense of tradition because Calvin was so important in the Presbyterian tradition and I thought we needed to do what Calvin did in his own context. That's another thing I have come to understand about Church history—I have come to see people in the context they were living. My resultant delving into evolution helps us understand thus: everything is in a process of change.

MG: Is this evolving a positive process of evolving?

LG: I don't think anything guarantees evolving towards anything—so it is a pushing forward rather than a directed push. Even Teilhard de Chardin emphasized this concept; there was no guarantee we would reach Omega. What I feel about evolution—about the essence of the evolution of the universe—is something I

---

a. *The Journal of New Zealand Theology*. A quarterly publication, Nov 1931–Aug 1935, with the aim "to encourage and give expression to original theological work in New Zealand."

b. A small, isolated coal mining town on the West Coast of New Zealand.

c. Opoho Presbyterian Church, where Geering was minister, 1945–50.

can't explain. Evolution has a capacity to produce more and more complex entities and any hope I have is about that and not about what we are doing [to our environment as a result of industrialization and population growth] which is disastrous.

MG: Is the real divide that comes to a head in the 1960s a legacy of the SCM versus Evangelical Union and Moral Rearmament?

LG: Yes, this divide is correct. If it hadn't been me it would have been someone else.

At this time in the Hall, while the liberals left conservatives alone, the conservatives couldn't leave the liberals alone. The *Evangelical Presbyterian* Editor[a] turned South Auckland Presbytery so it was ready to challenge. He was the turning point.

MG: I was wondering if you could tell me who is Joyce M[b] in your book and why is she not named?

LG: She is Joyce MacGregor and her father[c] was a fairly conservative minister. Joyce was in the SCM, but she was very traditional—she wouldn't go dancing. I loved dancing and took dancing lessons my first year at university because I felt out of step compared to others because I hadn't done dancing at high school.

The very first Sunday in the New Year at Church I met Joyce MacGregor. I recognized her from the French One class and talked to her.

She boarded nearby to where I did and we walked to church together.

---

a. Originally *The Evangelical Weekly*, the *Evangelical Presbyterian* was the journal of the conservative Westminster Fellowship within the Presbyterian Church of New Zealand. The editor at the time was Rev. Arthur Gunn (1912–2000).

b. See *Wrestling with God*, 41. In 1937 Geering met Joyce on his first Sunday evening service at First Church, recognizing her from his French class the year before. She became his girlfriend and they became engaged at the end of 1939 (*Wrestling with God*, 61).

c. Rev. John MacGregor (1877–1953), at this time Minister at Centre Bush parish, Southland.

However everyone thought it would be a disaster. Harold Turner[a] encouraged me to break it off. Harold was a close friend and I couldn't have broken it off without his support.

Her father wrote to every vacant parish warning them against me as a person who couldn't be trusted.

---

a. At this time (1941), Turner was Otago University Chaplain. Chapter 2: Parish Life

2

Parish Life, Queensland, Then Return to the Theological Hall

MG: I note that you were a pacifist in the war, but in 1941, while a third-year theology student, you filled in for Jack Sommerville* at Tapanui[a] so he could become an Army Chaplain. Why was this?

LG: While my own view was pacifist, I was never critical of those who had other views and I continued to hold this position for the rest of my life. Diversity is the aim; people must be free to think their own ideas. We are all different to each other. Diversity is as important in the thinking field as in the biological—it results in creativity, insight, and growth. I am always keen to find common ground.

MG: Looking back, do you think you could have survived as a parish minister?

LG: It is very hard to know; since I have been teaching I have evolved a lot. I liked teaching and even when I was a parish minister I did a variety of teaching. I instituted Wednesday night Home Groups, and when in Opoho I changed the prayer meeting to a sort of lecture meeting.

MG: Why did you do that?

LG: I found people needed to have an education widened on Christianity and Christian history—and the sermon was not the

---

a. Tapanui Presbyterian Church, a rural parish in West Otago.

appropriate place as the sermon is meant to inspire—so it was supplemented with the course. At St James[a] I instituted a parish forum in which I divided the Christian year into six lots of two months and every two months at the Parish Forum we discussed things of interest, such as, do we go back to the common cup [for communion]?

MG: I know that at St. James you got involved politically with the 1951 Waterfront dispute[b] and this raised a question for me. Many people who lived through the twentieth century as you have were attracted to Marxism. Was it ever attractive to you?

LG: Yes, I was attracted to Marxism as a sharing of life, but I was never attracted to Leninism—but then I believe you can't understand Marx via Soviet Russia.

MG: Did this attraction happen in the 1930s and '40s, as it did for many students?

LG: No, it didn't. My interest in Marxism occurred during my St. James days in the early 1950s. There was a woman who used to stand for the Communist Party in Wellington East and I used to have her come and talk to St James's. I had a Marxist friend and I used to talk with him, and I went to the Soviet Embassy on one or two occasions. I was interested in socialism, you see, and I was very critical of capitalism—and I still am in a way.

MG: Why were you so critical of capitalism back then?

LG: Capitalism is a form of economics, which always has the capacity to make the rich richer and the poor poorer, and I

---

a. St. James Presbyterian Church, Wellington. Geering was minister here, 1950–56.

b. The 1951 Waterfront Strike or Lockout lasted 151 days from February to July; it involved up to twenty-two thousand unionists at a time when the New Zealand population was only two million and more than one million working days were lost. The politics of the dispute, which were caught up in cold war rhetoric, caused a long-lasting split in the union movement. For Geering's involvement, see *Wrestling with God*, 101–2.

think—like George Soros[a]—that capitalism is doomed in the end. I was brought up in the days of New Zealand socialism and I was a Labour Party man, but I left it when it was being dismantled by Rogernomics[b] and joined the Green Party. I never joined the Values Party[c] because I could never see how it could grow, but once MMP (Mixed Member Proportional Parliamentary system) came in, the Values Party is the Green Party under another name.

MG: When do you think you became a theologian?

LG: I don't think I really turned to theology until I began teaching Old Testament and began reading Tillich and Bultmann. What interested me was the Bible. So it wouldn't have been until the 1950s. Tillich was my entry into the New Testament. I could see that Bultmann did to the New Testament what had been done already to the Old Testament.

MG: So we could say that your entry into theology was framed by Tillich?

LG: Yes, I think so. In Queensland[d] those of us teaching in the theological colleges met regularly for discussion. The Methodist

---

a. George Soros (1930–), Hungarian-American billionaire investor, businessman, philanthropist, author, and activist.

b. Rogernomics is the name given to the radical economic and social reforms (a version of neoliberalism) instituted by Roger Douglas (1937–), Finance Minister of the Fourth Labour Government elected in 1984. New Zealand governments, whether of the Left or Right, have continued with variations of a neo-liberal welfare state ever since.

c. The Values Party, launched in 1972, was the world's first environmental party to contest national elections. It always existed in tension between its socialist/radical factions and its environmental factions, resulting in its collapse in 1981. It was supplanted by the Green Party in 1990 which, under New Zealand's MMP (Mixed Member Proportional) parliamentary system, has gained a number of seats in Parliament.

d. Geering was Professor of Old Testament Studies, Presbyterian Church Hall, Brisbane, Queensland, Australia, 1956–60.

man[a] (who had studied under Paul Tillich in New York) introduced me to Tillich. As a result I began thinking theologically. I hadn't done so as a student because I found systematic theology dull. That said, I absorbed more from John Dickie than I realised. Although John Dickie seems old fashioned today, he really tried to get us thinking theologically.

MG: I get a strong sense that Queensland was a very important turning point for you in that it was here that you began to work on comparative religion.

LG: Yes, it very much was a turning point, and it enabled me to grow too. After Nancy[b] died, for a year or two I lost all interest in academic work and just threw myself into parish work. I was reading Tillich in Queensland, and Bultmann at that stage too, which was a turning point—and I had to do a lot of reading in Brisbane for my comparative religion lectures. What's also important is that I was sick in Brisbane and had to rest for several weeks. During this time I read the Hebrew Dictionary and picked out every word that was used more than ten times, and made my own list and tried to remember it. This study helped my Hebrew.

MG: One of the important influences in comparative religion occurs by Kierkegaard in *Fear & Trembling*, where he has the famous discussion about Abraham. Did that have any influence on you?

LG: I have read *Fear and Trembling* but I wouldn't say it had a great deal of impact. Helmut Rex, when he arrived and I was a student, used to talk about Kierkegaard, but I didn't take to him.

MG: Given all that you have so far said of your move into Christianity, I want to ask when, if ever, did you become a theist? Is your "God" a deist or a theist one?

---

  a. Rev. Gordon James, who also taught in the department of Philosophy of University of Queensland.
  b. Geering's first wife, Nancy Geering, née MacKenzie (1921–49), married 1943.

LG: God was a sort of unknown—a key to everything. I was never a believer in miracles or supernatural things. I was never a theist really. In saying the Creed I implied it, but I never thought of God in personal terms. I was never particularly happy about prayer. I participated because it was the thing to do, but I never practiced personal prayer. Corporate prayer, intercessions, these had some meaning, but I never expected God to do anything. So God was always deist; then moved into more pantheism thereafter.

MG: When was this move into pantheism?

LG: The move was after reading Teilhard de Chardin, in the early 1950s. Teilhard had a great influence on me. For me God is just a language, the language of the whole evolutionary process.

MG: So could we describe you as a Protestant Teilhard?

LG: Yes, in many ways you could. But Teilhard was over-optimistic about the future and I'm rather pessimistic about the future.

MG: Why is that?

LG: I think we are in the last human century—but then we may be in the birth pangs of something new. My fear is that we're rather like the condition in which Christianity came to birth, but on a global scale. George Soros believes capitalism is going to collapse because it depends on growth. The increasing competition for sources of power and food means the future is not very bright.

MG: I want to change tack to ask you about Arthur Prior,* as you not only knew each other but could be seen as pursuing parallel paths.

LG: I was not really influenced much by Arthur. Nancy[a] and Mary* were close friends, through school. Apparently Mary got me to introduce her to Arthur and I am the God-father of Martin

---

a. Nancy Geering.

Prior,[a] their son. While Mary and Arthur came and stayed at Opoho—I now suspect Mary got TB [tuberculosis] from Nancy—Arthur and I never really talked a lot. I would have felt out of his philosophical league at the time. I once stayed with the Priors in Christchurch and found Arthur reading Barth at the kitchen table at breakfast. I thought later he was reading the dogmatics but it was Barth on the Word of God. I ragged him on that. In those days I was not into systematic theology at all, I found it very dull.

MG: What were you into?

LG: I was into biblical studies. I felt theology was airy and wordy and with not much meaning. In comparison biblical studies was more solid because you were working with language, with meaning, and words and history.

MG: I saw this in the articles you were writing when you were in Queensland.

LG: In Queensland I never saw myself as a writer. It was Hodder & Stoughton who invited me to write what became *God in the New World*. I had to learn how to write it. My earlier books were all typed out three times by myself, I had no secretary. *Tomorrow's God* was the first one I did on a computer. The computer enabled me to continue writing.

MG: I note that on your return to Knox to teach Old Testament you state your only regret was no longer teaching comparative religion.[1] Was this what set you on your present course, that there was no wider context for you to debate and discuss—and further—for you to express your thinking?

LG: I had enjoyed teaching comparative religion in Queensland and did miss it when I returned. I had become interested in Bultmann in Queensland and so was reading Bultmann and Tillich before the resurrection controversy. I was fascinated by

---

a. Martin Prior (1944–), a linguist in the UK.

what I read, for at least theology was beginning to make sense. It seemed to have a reality about it and be relative to life, compared to Dickie, Brunner, and especially Barth. I couldn't stand Barth; he was a dogmatist and I didn't find it very real what Barth was saying. But I do use Dickie's definition that systematic theology should be reaching to the world outside.

MG: I now want to turn to the run-up to the 1967 heresy trial. From what I have discovered in the archives, your talk at the 1962–63 Presbyterian Summer Conference in Gore increasingly seems crucial in the events that followed. Albie Moore* wrote to Cappie Rex that he was worried that your statement, "I don't know whether I'm a committed Christian myself," might cause trouble with the conservatives and because of the fact that you were principal of the Theological Hall.

LG: I was aware as I wrote the lectures for that 1963 Bible class conference that I was challenging one aspect of orthodoxy: that Christianity proclaimed the absolute truth and so had to be missionary and going out. I questioned that.

MG: Why did you question it?

LG: I think the seeds really went back to Queensland and the group of theology teachers we had there studying Bultmann. You see, Bultmann's theology—his theological thinking—was very radical and that was beginning to have an influence on me, and Bultmann's classic essay on demythologizing[2] and the necessity to give fresh expression to Kerygma [proclamation of the Gospel] was stirring in me.

MG: What about Tillich at this time—was he also an influence?

LG: The influence of Tillich was just beginning and that, of course, was more on a personal note outside of the Old Testament. I was a little apprehensive in 1963 as I was aware that the Bible class had always been more traditional than the SCM. To my surprise it went down very well, and there are a number of people who have told me so since. I was still speaking about God in a reasonably traditional way

MG: Rex, in writing to Albie Moore in 1963, described you as an old-fashioned liberal.

LG: I suppose I was.

MG: In reading the papers in the archives it seems Breward* and John Allan* wished to put limits on what was taught by the Theological Hall.[a]

LG: John Allan and I were very good friends right up until he finished [retired December 1962] but there was a coolness there after the 1966–67 Assemblies. What stuck in my mind was a comment made to a student in my presence concerning a question on our eternal destiny and John Allan said something to the effect

---

a. While supportive of intellectual and theological freedom, Breward and Allan, who were more conservative in their theology, wished to ensure that Geering—or any other individual—were not taken as expressing representative views. Their concern was that Geering's position as principal could mean his public statements were regarded as official statements or expressions of the Theological Hall and its views. See Presbyterian Archives: 3/72 Nichol, Frank W.F. (Dr), Correspondence—Geering Controversy 1967 396/27/1 DC 3/2, Frank Nichol to Graeme Ferguson 6 Oct 67. Also, Ferguson to Nichol 9 Oct 67:

> Jack Bates wants the Book of Order amended to remove all suggestion that the WCF [Westminster Confession of Faith] can be used as an instrument of discipline, clarifying its role as a *confession* & *guide* to interpretation of Scripture. I know Ian Breward is concerned lest we give the impression that we are a Church in which a minister or Professor can teach anything whatever. Both points are important: I myself think it paramount to forswear publicly all fundamentalism & confessionalism.

Ferguson notes that also Prof. Allan is with Breward regarding the concern that it is a church in which one can "teach what they like," but Ferguson states that church as Catholic means "there is no question that one man's interpretation puts in question that fullness." Ferguson believes "that it is over this question of interpretation that the real trouble is."

that if there is no destiny after our death, we might as well give it all up.

MG: In 1967 Graeme Ferguson* wrote to Frank Nichol* that he believes that with the newspapers getting into the debate the public reaction is going to be against a prosecution for heresy. Was that how you read the situation at the time?

LG: Graeme Ferguson was a very loyal supporter of mine—as was his father-in-law, Ian Fraser.* I was very much aware that it was becoming a public debate rather than just one of the church and I felt I was speaking to those of a secular background.

MG: Also in the archives, I found that Ross Miller* states that in his view the issue is not doctrinal but that of the Westminster Fellowship and the Layman's Association, and resulted from and led to anti-clericalism.

LG: I believe it was not so much anti-clerical as anti-academic. Arthur Gunn's supporters were not anti-clerical but they were anti-modern scholarship and in many ways anti- the whole world of modern thought. Yet, for example, Gregor Smith's book *Secular Christianity* caused no stir in Scotland and also none in the Hall. It was Frank Nichol who drew my attention to it.

MG: Why do you think Frank did that?

LG: Frank was testing boundaries all the way. Whether he felt I should fire the bullets, I don't know. Frank was always cautious yet in himself he was really moving.[a]

---

a. 3/72 Rev. Prof. Frank W.R. Nichol Lectures 1959–72 396/38/30 DC 9/7 Biblical Interpretation & The Theologian. Australian C.E. Staff training Conference 21 November 1968 (Presbyterian Archives, Dunedin). Nichol calls for a constructive theology—which involves:

… working out what it means to worship, to pray, to serve and to engage creatively with what is happening in the contemporary scene.
… As it undertakes this task, theology will be faced not only with problems of interpreting Scripture or relating itself to the world of Biblical scholars; it will also be faced with the questions thrown up

MG: So would you say you were more secular in your thinking than others in the Hall?

LG: I think so. I was the only one who was a convert to Christianity, the only one who had had to make a decision for Christianity. My secular background meant that I understood the secular world whereas those brought up in the church are unconsciously programmed in the way others aren't. But I wasn't aware between 1967 and 1970 that I was actually raising issues about the reality of God. I know Blaikie* accused me of that and in a personal discussion we had I rejected that I had any personal relationship or support for Altizer.*

---

by the world and what is happening in it, by what people who live in that world believe about themselves, by the unseen and largely unacknowledged pressures which, thanks to psychology, sociology, economics and so on, we know humans to be determined and shaped. A constructive theology will have to take account, so far as it is able, of all these factors. ... Its primary aim will be a positive, constructive one—to sketch out, and perhaps fill in detail, a total vision of what Christianity means in the present. (11)

Christian faith is always in need of such construction—where it is wanting it is clear that the community of faith has lost its nerve. This seems to me to be abundantly clear in the New Zealand controversy—there is no lively Christian vision, and the Church has descended, with distressing speed, to cautious anxiety and acrimonious mutual accusation which saps the Church's energies to no good purpose. (11)

3

The Trial and Then Escape to Religious Studies

MG: Why do you think the APL [Association of Presbyterian Laymen][a] may have thought Frank Nichol was more radical than you?

LG: Is that so? In many ways Frank, without knowing it, helped me quite a bit in those days. He was like a breath of fresh air after Henderson.* Frank was in his prime then. His odd remarks made in the Common Room helped me orientate things. I remember before the resurrection controversy came about that Frank was the first ever to say "the empty tomb story." I had previously only seen it as part of the whole Christian story and that one remark changed my thinking. Frank was not Barthian then, he was more influenced by Bonhoeffer at this stage.

I can understand why they may have thought Frank a danger; at a refresher school that I wasn't at, Frank was up against Bob Blaikie and was challenged by Bob but Frank refused. Frank was a bit cautious but my feeling is that he was at this stage moving towards what I came to say.

---

a. Association of Presbyterian Laymen, which brought one set of charges against Geering. It was established in 1966 in the midst of the debate about the resurrection. See *Wrestling with God*, 151–52. Robert Wardlaw, an Auckland advertising executive with a Church of Christ background, was national chair. Following the Heresy trial he resigned from the Presbyterian Church and established his own, short-lived church.

So at the 1965 Assembly I took Bob Blaikie to task for tackling Frank and told him to leave the Hall staff alone and this probably resulted in him tackling me.[1]

Frank provided very full support throughout the controversy. Ian Breward was the least supportive; face to face he was very supportive but behind the scenes he was far less so.

MG: And Evan Pollard?* Was he supportive, especially when your statements ventured into the New Testament?

LG: He was supportive[a] throughout but overstretched in places.

---

a. Pollard makes his support for Geering clear in the following correspondence (3/164 Pollard, T.E. [Prof] Correspondence: Geering Controversy 1966–70. 394/58/1 DC2/4 Pollard to Bob Blaikie 30 April 1967):

> On the issue of 'the immortality of the soul' Lloyd and I are basically in agreement.
>
> I feel, Bob, that I must protest to you as strongly as I possibly can about what appears to me to be your thoroughly unchristian attitude toward Lloyd. ... Furthermore I find it impossible to understand how a minister with your theological training and your professed Christianity can allow yourself to be a party to the slanderous accusations levelled against all the staff at the Theological Hall in the Layman's Broadsheet. Controversial theological discussion must always have a part in the life of the Church if theology is to be a living thing and not merely dead dogma.

See also Pollard to Bow (H.O. Bowman—Balmoral church, Auckland) 2 Jan 1968:

> If Wardlaw or Blaikie had got their way, the Church would have become a police-state, with a security service keeping check on everything that every minister said; theological thinking and teaching would be impossible under those circumstances—honest thinking and teaching that is.
>
> I also object to conservatives claiming that they alone are evangelical. I am neither a conservative nor a liberal, but whatever I am I hope I am evangelical. Over a period of seven or eight years the Evangelical Presbyterian has been injecting poison into the minds of many within the Church.
>
> The situation created in the Church by the WF has resulted in a lack of openness to one another and an unwillingness for ministers and elders and members to listen to one another. This has become especially clear in the Doctrine Committee itself where some of the

MG: I am interested why, suddenly, in 1966 you were asked to write for the *Outlook*.[a]

LG: I don't know the reason why I was asked to write for the *Outlook*, as I hadn't written anything for it before. When it came to the Easter one, Peter Smith[b] got very agitated and when he died, his widow blamed me for his early death.

MG: This question of the principal of the Theological Hall being attacked for what he is taken to represent regarding theological education and the views of "progressive" clergy is, I have come to think, core to the issue. And it seems also to have arisen first in the talk you gave at the Gore Conference in 1963.

LG: If you take it further back to the Gore Conference, I was invited because I was to be principal, but I was not principal before December. Of course people like Les Gosling* were not happy that I was appointed to the chair in the first place. Yet Les Gosling was not a typical conservative either, he was more able and liberal than most.[c] Prior to the trial, at least by 1963

"conservatives"—not all of them, thank God!—simply refuse to listen to the rest.

One of the biggest challenges we have in our teaching is to establish communication with students who come out of a fundamentalist background. It is not that we want to make them think as we do; we simply want to be able to converse with them and make them aware there are other points of view.

a. *The Outlook*, the Presbyterian weekly journal that ran from 1899–1986.

b. Peter Smith (1910–67), Scottish journalist who came to New Zealand in 1957 to edit *The Outlook*.

c. In a letter to Geering, 15 June 1966, Gosling states: "You have certainly been selling Peter Smith's *Outlook* for him for the last issue or two. The position you take concerning the resurrection just raises more intellectual difficulties for me than it solves. I hope, however, that people who are really concerned for the truth will hear you out a little further before they come to drastic conclusions.

It has always been a personal regret that I have held a different point of view to you, especially as I remember with appreciation past associations. Every good wish …" (Lloyd Geering private correspondence, 1966. Permission granted to reproduce.)

or '64, we were becoming concerned about the tactics in the South Auckland Presbytery, which we learned of via a minister in Papatoetoe. He reported to us that he was concerned that Arthur Gunn was arranging behind the scenes of every parish that was vacant, calling only a conservative minister, as the evangelical Presbyterians were having an increasing influence.[a]

MG: All of this—Gore, the South Auckland moves, the writing for *The Outlook*—all created the heresy trial?

LG: Sometimes I think history reaches a point where factors unseen, and perhaps unknown, come together—similar to the Berlin Wall—when things never realized suddenly explode.

MG: What were these unseen factors and perhaps unknown outcomes? Are they collective, or do they perhaps involve individuals?

LG: You see, from 1940 onwards, Helmut Rex would have been the most radical theological teacher in the Hall. In the light of the 1960s, looking back, it seems so strange that Helmut went on so successfully without opposition—perhaps it was the way he did it, not mentioning traditional doctrines or dogmas. Alan Richardson* came out to New Zealand—about 1960 or 1961—and gave us the lectures eventually published as *The Bible in the Age of Science*[b]—

---

a. The same thing was also happening in the Auckland Presbytery. Rev. F.W. Winton of Onehunga Presbyterian Church wrote to Geering, 20 May 1966 and observed: "As you know, the Westminster fellowship is very active in our area, and is subtly infiltrating in many ways. They are doing their best not only in S. Auckland but in Auckland itself to seal off as many congregations as possible from other views than their own. For example, Maurice Yule is convener of our Life & Work Committee, and recently organized a Presbytery wide pulpit exchange. I noticed that invariably the Westminster fellows exchanged with one another. It may have been a coincidence, but I do not think so. They of course are regarded as the really keen and evangelical people" (Lloyd Geering private correspondence, 1966. Permission granted to reproduce).

b. Richardson, *The Bible in the Age of Science*; originally the Cadbury Lectures, University of Birmingham, 1960.

and was very critical of Bultmann, much to Helmut's annoyance, for in his own lectures Helmut really presented the modernist stance.

MG: In my impression it seems that it was the writing in *The Outlook* that really did it for you.

LG: I think even Bob Blaikie would have felt that if I had written what I wrote somewhere else and I was principal it wouldn't have mattered.

MG: Yes, that is my view of it; that it was you as principal in the official organ of the church that caused the eruption as it did.

LG: Yes, you see the principal was viewed as the theological voice of the church at that time and the Presbyterian Church was more hierarchical back then. In those days there were certain unspoken restrictions on what the Moderator would do or say between Assemblies—he would chair the General Assembly and have a pastoral role between assemblies, and was not to speak for the church. He could only do so if the particular committee had given approval.

MG: And did this hold in some way for you too—it would have been the Doctrine Committee?

LG: Yes, the problem for many is that I spoke out publicly without the support or approval of the Doctrine Committee—for example in the previous decade the church had published Bates's *Manual of Doctrine*, which had a certain authority because the Doctrine Committee had gone through it with him.

MG: Why was there such a lack of understanding?

LG: At congregational level not much thinking had happened. Theology in the late nineteenth century was moving very fast, but not taking the church with it. Protestant liberalism had no particular problem with the idea of evolution, for example. They were talking of the evolution of religion by 1900 and saw no conflict between that and divine revelation. But this acceptance didn't cross over to the pews, for such ideas needed a teaching medium, and preaching was not suitable. Preaching is to inspire, uplift, comfort. Some Protestants, such as Rutherford Waddell,* had a kind of prophetic voice for social justice, but when it came to theology, new ideas just didn't come through to the pew.

By the time I was a theological student I found students had a real fear if they spoke too much of what they learned in the Theological Hall. They felt they would upset people, so they didn't pass on their learning in the parishes. The result was that liberal theology collapsed and conservatism returned. If it had not been me in the controversy of the 1960s then it would have been someone else, for the liberals were receding and the conservative challenge was growing.

In my day in the theological hall, fundamentalists were laughed out of court by their liberal teachers. All the fundamentalists asked for was to be left alone. Yet in the 1960s they were strong enough to voice their opposition. An important element was the *Evangelical Presbyterian* and its editor.[a] He began the resistance to Church Union, was a voice for conservative theology, and was a real fundamentalist, which was a reaction to where theology was going. There had also been an earlier attack on John Dickie.

MG: Was there a type of sociological angle to it, different responses in different parts of the country?

LG: I felt it was more dominant in Auckland than in Dunedin. You would normally think the South conservative, yet there was greater resistance in Auckland. In already growing metropolitan Auckland churches felt under pressure and I suspect that this put them in defensive mode.

MG: In talking with you I get the strong sense that by the trial you were not really a modernist in theology.

---

a. Les Gosling, see Appendix 2: Biographical Sketches, p. 193.

LG: Looking back personally, I can understand why, when editing *What is our Gospel?* in 1961, I was dissatisfied with what Albie Moore and Hubert Ryburn had written, because they were expressions of modernism which I found unsatisfactory. So I can see I became postmodernist in the 1960s—and the whole heresy trial pushed me into it.

MG: A question that keeps returning to me is, What would have happened if Lloyd Geering had been found guilty of doctrinal error?

LG: That is a difficult one and illustrates (like chaos theory) how one event can change the lives of a whole number of people. First, the Assembly clerk, Stan Read,* explained to a reporter at the time that the possible outcomes of the "trial" were:

> I would be acquitted,
> I would be reprimanded
> I would be dismissed from my teaching post
> I would be expelled from the ministry

My hunch is that if either of the latter two had eventuated, a number of my friends and supporters would not only have protested vigorously but would have also resigned from the ministry. Three years later, when I put in my application for the chair at Victoria, three, possibly four, of my colleagues had also applied for positions elsewhere. (I did not find this out until later.)

Even though I was, in effect, acquitted, it left the church somewhat divided. Some left to go to more conservative churches and some left, or quietly faded out of the church because the church had shown by the trial that it was still living in the past. The Assembly was more anxious to preserve peace and unity than to face up to the theological issues involved.

MG: I find it a fascinating question [of what would have happened if found guilty] because on the one hand I need to unpick (as it were) all that you have achieved since 1967—and in fact unpick in many ways all that has occurred in religious studies and the Presbyterian church in New Zealand since then.

LG: I do not know what I would have done and did not even think about that possibility at the time. I must have felt reasonably confident about the outcome. After all, I knew most of the ministers and had a fair idea of what they thought about the matter.

MG: Of course the position at Victoria University of Wellington may still have been available, but I feel Rollo Arnold's* opposition may have been more successful. You may, of course, have decided to not pursue such a career. Would you have considered a move to Australia perhaps?

LG: When I did apply, Jack Bates tried to persuade me not to. But for me, the attraction of the chair was not primarily to get myself out of an uncomfortable position at Knox but to have the opportunity to take up again the study of comparative religion (as we still called it), which I had done in Queensland and which I reluctantly had to drop. I did not expect to get the chair and was quite happy continuing on at Knox.

MG: I also feel that if you had been "convicted" then Frank Nichol would have been the next on trial?

LG: Very likely, as one or two had already been gunning for him.

MG: There is also the possibility that the evangelical take-over of the Presbyterian Church would have occurred thirty years earlier, but in doing so perhaps the greatest losses would have been the non-ordination of women, the continued marginalization of the Pacific Church and the Maori Church, as all three were topics of the liberal/broad church. However, the Presbyterian Church would have also rapidly become marginalized in New Zealand society even more quickly than it has.

LG: Yes. The present trends would have accelerated earlier.

MG: Why do you think you were treated so badly?

LG: I have wondered that myself. I owe a lot to the church, so to reject it is like rejecting your mother, but I always felt you could be critical of the church.

I felt that the church had left me, not that I left the church. Once I came to Wellington I never went back to presbytery; I would have gone to presbytery here in Wellington except the Moderator of Wellington Presbytery[a] had written a critical letter saying he had no confidence in me, so I never went back.

MG: What about invitations to speak or to preach?

LG: The church never invites me to speak—outside of St Andrews on the Terrace and a couple of other parishes, but I am never invited to preach.

MG: I take it that this saddens you?

LG: Yes, I would have been glad to have been used by my church; instead now I preach to those outside of the church.

MG: So given all that happened to you during and after the trial—and that you had had that time in Brisbane—can I ask why you stayed in New Zealand?

LG: I stayed primarily because of family and family connection. I have never been attracted to apply to go anywhere else.

MG: So is this something to do with how you see yourself and your role here in New Zealand?

LG: Yes, I have always seen myself as a New Zealander. New Zealand has a rather unique position in the world because it is so isolated and this isolation has forced us to think about the rest of the world. Therefore, we are not so insulated as elsewhere and as a result we are world thinkers because we are so small.

---

a. Reverend R.D. Elley (1925–2012), studied at Knox Theological Hall, 1950–52; also undertook a ThM at Princeton, 1954–55. At this time, Minister at Khandallah Parish in Wellington, then lecturer at Bible College in Auckland, followed by missionary work in Malaysia.

MG: So would that be a way to describe yourself?

LG: Yes I think it would be—I am a world thinker from New Zealand.

MG: So given this self-description, how would you describe what being a New Zealander means to you?

LG: I don't really know how to answer that really—for me you are what you are. I was born here so I had to identify as that, but now I see myself as more of a world citizen.

MG: How did you find coming to Wellington after Dunedin?

LG: I had a new lease of life. I found the years 1965–70 in the Hall quite a strain so I felt a tremendous freedom coming to Wellington. For it wasn't much better after the trial as there were critics waiting at every point to pounce on me, and the Assembly in 1970 rejected me and my views.[a] So I was on the alert all the time. But I was already widening out my area of study and my interest. I rather enjoyed doing the comparative religion lectures because one of the things about the Old Testament is that it brings you into the study of the ancient world. It's quite notable the number of Old Testament scholars who moved into the study of world religions.

---

a. See *Wrestling with God*, 192–98. The rejection of Geering and his views at the 1970 General Assembly arose from Geering undertaking an invitation to Brisbane in 1970 that expanded from the original parish visit into a series of public engagements and media events. The visit culminated in his participation on the television programme *Meet the Press* where he was quizzed in a quick-fire manner on a number of topics of belief. A transcript of the show was made available to his opponents in New Zealand whereupon several presbyteries disassociated themselves from his statements. Following ongoing public discussion, the General Assembly in 1970 publicly disassociated itself from the statements Geering made in Brisbane. However, a notable number of Geering's supporters recorded their dissent.
Chapter 4: Public Theologian

MG: So given this preference, I must ask why you weren't writing on comparative religions at that time in the 1960s when you seemed to be instead moving into questions of the New Testament and theology?

LG: It was because I was more concerned to understand the present situation and in particular that of the Christian West.

MG: Given your longstanding interest in Buddhism and its influence on parts of your thought, did you ever consider a shift into Buddhism via comparative religion, as a number of scholars did at that time in the 1960s?

LG: No, I never considered becoming a Buddhist—as it evolved and diversified it did the same as Christianity and got bogged down in its past and it still hasn't moved specifically.

MG: What was the response from the rest of the country to the establishment of the chair in Religious Studies at Victoria University? How did your soon-to-be colleagues in religious studies react?

LG: I felt a little bit guilty about having the first chair but everyone was very supportive. Even Victoria University was a bit surprised that none of the others had applied for it. Victoria got Albert Moore to apply for it and Frank Nichol had applied for it too but when Frank learned that I had applied for it he withdrew. Albert was interviewed for the position but he didn't get it.

As soon as I was appointed I knew the religious studies people had developed the practice of meeting together once a year and we then decided to have the first year curriculum the same in all three universities and this provided a unity as to how religious studies developed. It was a new field internationally. What we did in Wellington had quite a rationale because we were trying to avoid religious studies becoming a place where we studied only one religious tradition. So there was no course in which we discussed only one religious tradition; rather, we had a curriculum in which ideas within religious traditions were studied. So there was no separate course on Buddhism or Christianity.

MG: What types of courses were developed?

LG: There were courses on philosophy of religion, phenomenology of religion, religion and change; these were courses on religious thought but not in one tradition.

MG: At Victoria University, when you established religious studies, what was your relationship with George Hughes* and Peter Munz* like?

LG: George was more in philosophy but at the interview Peter Munz said he would have taken me into history! But they both supported the chair in Religious Studies.

MG: What about Rollo Arnold who had been so opposed to you during the controversy?

LG: Rollo never spoke to me once I came to Victoria.

MG: What did you attempt to do in religious studies?

LG: I attempted to link religious studies with theology departments but this association never occurred. In my mind I was developing religious studies as a type of development of theology. Jim Thornton,* who was a very close friend, was critical of my attempt to do so.

I saw the time as past that of theology, which was to be replaced in universities by religious studies. I came to this opinion via Tillich and his understanding of religion as a dimension of culture. So what was once theology was now religious studies.

MG: Yet we have actually seen the decline of religious studies and the continuation—and often the growth—of theology. How would you explain this?

LG: It's partly because what religious studies tried to do has failed because there has been a strong resurgence of traditional thought, and religious studies was the secular discipline.

Also, the word "religious" is a problem, but we couldn't find a word that worked. Jim Veitch* wanted "world religions" or perhaps "religion studies."

MG: Yet also we had the decline of theological study and debate, especially of liberal, let alone radical theology. Why did theology collapse so badly in New Zealand?

LG: I think the collapse had already come earlier—what there was, was a revival of theology but it was pushed down.

In the Presbyterian Church more theology was done in the days of John Dickie, but that past ended when Dickie was in his dotage. When I was a young minister, I was shocked that ministers never talked theology; when ministers got together they only told funny stories and wouldn't go on refresher courses. When Henderson took over he didn't promote any new thinking at all because he saw theology as expounding Christian doctrine—what he termed "the Christian structure"—which climaxed at the Council of Nicaea.

4

From Religious Studies to Public Theologian

MG: Looking back over your life, would you do anything different?

LG: Sometimes I think to myself, what would have happened if I had not gone into the SCM because the SCM led me into the church and the church into the ministry. So why didn't I do medicine or science like I was advised to do? Instead I did arts—my maths degree was in arts.[a] I was a very immature person and so I just wanted to continue to do what I did well, and so I did maths and languages.

MG: Do you think you could have done medicine?

LG: I think I was put off medicine by the fear of responsibility for other lives —so it was a lack of decision—and once I got into the ministry I became a parish minister.

MG: And if you hadn't gone to Brisbane?

LG: I would have continued to be a parish minister—and to be pretty liberal.

MG: So in many ways the fear of theological education that the conservatives have is true—for further study radicalized you?

---

a. Geering did his maths degree as part of a Bachelor of Arts (BA). As maths is traditionally in both the Faculty of Arts and the Faculty of Science, Geering could have done the more usual choice of doing his maths degree as part of a Bachelor of Science (BSc).

LG: Yes, you see Gregor Smith's *Secular Christianity* had that verse regarding the bones of Jesus lying somewhere in Palestine[a] and that made me think and led me onto my view on the resurrection. So that was a type of turning point. For in doing parish ministry my view was that the resurrection was a historical fact—I was very traditional regarding that.

MG: That is interesting given the description of Albie Moore to Rex regarding you in 1963 as an old fashioned Liberal—and yet that changed very quickly. It seems something happened between 1963 and 1966.[b]

LG: Well, Gregor Smith—that helps explain the resurrection; and I had study leave in 1964 and went to Heidelberg—but I can't think of anything in particular that changed me.

MG: Do you think you could have stayed on at the Theological Hall after the trial?

LG: At the time I did but I knew there was a group in the church ready to pounce—and they did about my Brisbane television interview and caused trouble in 1970.

MG: And if there had not been the job in Wellington?

LG: I suppose it would have gotten worse. I would have stayed in the church, but what I would have done, it's very hard to know. It certainly would have been the finish of me as a theological teacher. Things worked out fortunately the way they did.

MG: Reading what you have written and stated about God and your preaching in those early days of your ministry, would it be

---

a. "We may freely say that the bones of Jesus lie somewhere in Palestine" (Smith, *Secular Christianity*, 103).

b. Also, in 1963 Geering began to undertake his "first piece of real theological research" to participate in the University of Otago public lecture series for the centenary of Darwin's *On the Origin of Species*. Given that Geering was ordained in 1942, he in effect had a twenty-year hiatus from theology. It is important to note that his return to theology was via the question of science and theology.

fair to describe you at this time as a liberal preacher of the ethical life arising out of the Christian tradition?

LG: Yes, it would be fair to say that. More of my sermons were about how to get the best out of life drawing on the biblical heritage—as much out of the Old Testament as the New Testament. You see, the Old Testament is more down to earth; it doesn't depend on the supernatural as much as the New Testament.

MG: And so how would you describe your preaching today?

LG: I see the New Testament as the way in which Christianity is really Paulism—which lead the way to the otherworldliness of Christianity; whereas the teaching of Jesus is much more this-worldly. The Jesus Seminar[a] has helped me with this since the late 1990s.

MG: I have been wondering, as we've undertaken these interviews, as to when you first began to engage in what could be called creative thinking theologically? My sense that has developed over our discussions is that the first expression of this thinking, at least publicly, is that address we discussed that you gave to the Gore Conference in 1963. It seems to me it was what brought you to the attention of the wider conservative block in the church.

LG: I suspect you are right in pointing to the address or addresses at the Gore Conference. That is why I am glad to find that they still exist and I look forward to reading them again.[b]

---

a. Founded by biblical scholar Robert W. Funk (see n. xx below), the Jesus Seminar (1985–98) was established to renew the quest for the historical Jesus with the aim of reporting its findings to the general public. Comprising over 150 critical scholars and laity, it produced new translations of New Testament works and also held many seminars and lectures. The Westar Institute continues its work and hosts a number of other seminars concerned with the critical study of biblical texts and theology. See westarinstitute.org/projects/the-jesus-seminar/

b. During our discussions, and after an email enquiry from me as to whether he still retained the Gore Conference papers, Geering found the Conference Handbook and lectures in his archives and loaned it to me, 2014–15.

Before that I wrote only sermons and lectures. The latter were simply summaries of what I read in books and I was digesting them for students. Some of the sermons may have contained a kernel of creativity as I tried to tease out the meaning of the text. (All of my sermons started with a biblical text.) I thought of them as learning how to expound the Bible for life in the modern world.

Now your queries on when did I first begin thinking in such ways have now made me historically interested in the third sermon I wrote. I no longer have it, as some years ago I began to cull my early sermons, being no longer happy with them. But I retained the title, "What is God like?" Looking back, I can see this was an attempt to find the answer for my own sake. I chose as the text John 14:8: "Philip said to Jesus, 'Lord show us the Father and we shall be satisfied.'" Having at that stage been in the church for only two years,[a] for I was not yet in the Hall, I was genuinely puzzled by what people meant when they talked so much about God and I was trying to get a clearer picture in my own mind. Goodness knows what the conservative Southland farmers made of it, and evidently I later did not think much of it myself. But I suspect it may have been an attempt to be creative.

But back to Gore. After that, the next attempts of mine at original or creative thought are the four documents (sermons and articles) which were published by *The Fourth R* [magazine] nearly fifty years later.[1] These proved to be the prelude to my first book, *God in the New World*. Though I do not think highly of it now, I can remember how I struggled to produce a chapter every fortnight, working on it each evening, and when I had completed it, reading it over to Elaine for her criticism. There was a deadline to have it in London before the impending heresy trial. It was original in the sense that I was attempting to work out just what I

---

a. This was in 1939 when Geering fulfilled a full day's supply (three services) in the small rural parish of Waikaka Valley in Southland. See *Wrestling with God*, 51.

thought. (The irony is that it is the only bestseller I have written, selling about fourteen thousand copies.)

My next book, *Resurrection—A Symbol of Hope*, was written after I had read everything I could find on the resurrection, including one source in German. This book had some originality in it, for after showing in Part I how the traditional understanding of the resurrection had now collapsed, I then traced the idea of resurrection historically to show that, far from the affirmation of the resurrection arising from a miraculous new event, it arose out of the context of an evolving cultural tradition. I later submitted this book to the Melbourne College of Divinity for a DD but it was rejected on the grounds that I had not quoted original sources but only translations of them.

From then onwards it was by writing books that my thinking gradually changed and, I hope, matured. (I am reminded of the man who said he did not know what he thought until he heard what he said, [or] in my case, until I read what I wrote.) So it was in writing on a topic, often not knowing how it would end, that my thinking developed. I found that writing a book had the effect of changing me, especially with *From the Big Bang to God*. Although I had long been influenced by Teilhard, I found that after writing the book, experiencing each phase as it were, I began to understand the human condition in a different way. The evolution of language—which includes the creation of such terms as gods, God, and so on—enabled us as a species to create our cultural world of thought through which we understand the physical universe and try to live meaningful lives.

MG: I am interested in how the term prophet has been applied to you—I think quite realistically—but I noticed in *Such Is Life* you sort of relocating as a sage, within the Sage Tradition.

LG: Well, that may be because I see Jesus as within that tradition, more than as a prophet. You see, for most of the twentieth century, until the Jesus Seminar, he was an apocalyptic prophet, but once you take that apocalypticism out as something actually added to Jesus at the end, which I think is more likely, then he's a sage and I see a lot in common with *Ecclesiastes.*

I always had a feeling for Ecclesiastes. My 1967 Wellington sermon,[a] the one that created the furore, expounded on Ecclesiastes.

MG: Therefore, given what appears the strength of your self-identification in *Such Is Life*, would you locate yourself in the Sage Tradition?

LG: Yes, I would, which is why I wrote that book—and I see Jesus also as part of that Sage Tradition.

MG: When did you come to see Jesus as a sage; I take it this is part of a change in your perception of Jesus?

LG: Yes, I came to see him as a sage mainly in the last twenty years. I never saw him as divine; of course, I implied I did in my ordination vows, but for me Jesus was a man. This view came in early in my thinking. Emil Brunner, one of our great heroes as students, said the doctrine of the virgin birth had to be reworked because it stopped Jesus being human.

MG: So in the ordination vows, did the term "the Christ" mean anything?

LG: No—"the Christ" is simply a title—as is its associated term, "the Messiah." At first, I accepted that Jesus may have seen himself as a Messiah, but I moved away from that, too.

MG: So as a minister and a preacher, how did you handle the "Christ" language? Was there a tension?

---

a. This was the sermon Geering preached at the annual inaugural university service for Victoria University of Wellington in which he stated, "Man has no immortal soul."

LG: I never talked about the Christ figure as such; I don't remember preaching that this was a unique figure—so I preached more about Jesus.

One of the tragedies of the story of the Christian tradition is that so early on they moved their focus from his teaching to him; so much of my focus has become to get back to what Jesus taught, away from the Church's focus on him—and this focus is also why the Jesus Seminar does so well.

MG: In writing on John Robinson you conclude that: "The theistic image of God had to go."[2] I was wondering if in turning from the theistic God you had turned instead to what could be called a deistic image or alternatively, given your ecological concerns, a pantheistic image of God?

LG: It is neither a pantheist or deist-derived image; I wouldn't use those terms myself. I now see ourselves as the creators of language and I tried to bring it out in *From the Big Bang to God*. We live in two worlds. There is a physical world but we see it and interpret it through our thought world. So Kant is right: we are one step removed from reality at all times. And the word God—in the Western tradition—has played a really important role as a centre-point. God is a symbolic word, the centre-point of which is values to live by. This understanding links up to much in the Bible: God is love; God is truth.

MG: So what might this idea mean for contemporary Christianity?

LG: I'm not sure how long Christianity in its traditional form will last. In many ways I deplore the ways moderns don't study our cultural past. The result is that our society is lacking in self-understanding, which means we lose our humanity. Remember that animals are only presentist. Without remembering and studying our past we become a directionless society. So it is very important to understand how we got to this point if we are to have that important global society. What we do have in common is our humanity. And we need to remember that of all the cultures that make up our global society it is the Christian culture that has contributed the most—and will contribute the most for some time.[a]

MG: So to go back to my earlier question, I am reminded that there was a famous series in *The Christian Century* in the 1960s, at the time of all that theological ferment, entitled "How my mind has changed." In it, theological figures would discuss precisely that idea. I wonder how you would answer such a question as, how has your mind has changed?

LG: My mind has changed mainly by becoming enlarged. I was rather narrow—not rigid like a fundamentalist—but going along the grooves held me in. In my Christian ministry years and in the Theological Hall I was still committed to defending certain basic affirmations—but not now, I am free in my thinking. So you could describe it as moving from a reasonably traditional theistic tradition to a post-theistic tradition and it has been a move of freedom. I never wanted to reject the past; I saw it as part of the process.

MG: So how did this change occur? What drove it and influenced it?

LG: It was undertaken by reading.[b] Rarely have I … I haven't had the advantage of regular contacts along my lines to work it out. The nearest was Frank Nichol. We got along pretty well, but never in regular periods.[c]

---

a. Here Geering is referring to his focus that what he terms "global society" is an emergent secular, scientific, modern society that arises primarily out of Western culture and civilization drawing on, in particular, Christian culture and faith.

b. See Appendix for the transcription of Geering's reading 1965–90.

c. In 1995 Nichol wrote to Albert Moore expressing how Geering had moved in his theology: "I have not had the nerve to bare my 'believer's breast' to Lloyd directly, fearful of his scorn, perhaps again. But he does know that he has gone another way than mine, I think. We

MG: What about prior to your time in the 1960s in Dunedin?

LG: Yes, I did have the meeting of a group when I was teaching in Queensland, and they introduced me to Bultmann.

MG: And now?

LG: The person I delight [in] talking with now is Jim Thornton.

MG: Why is that?

LG: Jim has a very acute philosophical mind which I value—he has rejected the whole ecclesiastical organization in a way I haven't.

But I have really had to do it all myself, even when teaching religious studies at Victoria.

MG: How do you see religious studies compared to theology?

LG: That's an interesting question and a point that Jim Thornton and I differed on at an early stage. He criticized me for turning religious studies into theology but I argued religious studies is the next stage in theological enquiry. Namely that theology is a discipline in which, from a Christian base, one is exploring how it relates to all other knowledge—and in the global world, when traditions move more into contact, religious studies is the discipline in which theology takes its next stage. So that is why I felt religious studies should be concerned with what is religiously true—whereas it has more come to explain what others think. So this is why I structured my undergraduate courses the way I did. At 100-level we covered all religious traditions; at 200-level we covered methods of looking at religious traditions and at 300-level

---

have been associated for a long time, but Lloyd does not make things easy for his friends. Why should he?" (Letter from Frank Nichol to Albert Moore 11 Feb 1995). It is also interesting to note that Nichol states that the days of Bonhoeffer, "those days of real theology were now gone" (Presbyterian Archives: NZ 640 A.C. Moore Lloyd Geering: Notes 1977–2003 2007/120/79 DC 16/3).

we focused on specific religious thinkers. But in any one course I ensured it was never tied to one religious tradition.

MG: And I get the sense you found the move into religious studies exciting.

LG: Yes, indeed it was! For it was the chance to see cutting-edge thought, and in a sense we were doing theology.

MG: And it enabled religion to become a public conversation in New Zealand?

LG: Yes, it did.

MG: If the controversy hadn't happened, what course do you think your life and thinking would have taken?

LG: It just would have gone on as it had. I had every intention of staying in the church, even after the trial, and I would have stayed in Old Testament. I don't think my theological thinking would have gone in the direction it did; I would have carried on in the liberal tradition.

Because of the controversy my reading speed trebled.[a]

MG: One of the things I noticed in reading your autobiography was that your discussion of the period of teaching religious studies was actually quite short within the book. Was there any particular reason for this?

LG: No, I wasn't aware of that. Perhaps I thought that there wasn't sufficient interest in prospective readers for what I was doing there. I couldn't give an adequate answer to that, for my thinking developed much more during that particular time.

MG: That is what interested me. For on the one hand because you were such a modern thinker you almost had to leave the theological institution behind …

---

[a]. As evidenced by the yearly list of Geering's reading, taken from his notebook, in Appendix.

LG: Yes.

MG: ... And you came into religious studies where you don't leave theology because you are still doing a type of theology within the limitations of the university as an institution. But I also think in some ways religious studies is almost a romanticist discipline, for in many ways people are looking for essences and there is only so long if you are a modern that you can stay within religious studies itself. So I was wondering, did you ever feel constrained within religious studies?

LG: No, not at all. Well, compared with where I had been, I felt completely free. The university does not attempt to control what is taught within any discipline in the same way as the church has some control over the teaching in its seminaries. The one constraint that should be evident in the university, in all of its disciplines, is the search for what is true. It is in that sense that I did not leave theology behind but, as you say, took it over into religious studies. On arrival at Victoria I was asked what my research interest was. I replied that it was to find out what is happening to religion in the modern world.

In the course of my research I was beginning to find that, on the narrow definition of religion (for example, belief in the supernatural), religion of the past was fast becoming superstition and hence obsolete. But on a wider definition of religion, as that which had to do with humankind's ultimate concern (and there are shades here of Tillich) religion was undergoing a radical change. In any case, a wide definition of religion has become necessary even to do justice to the diversity of religion in the past.

So I feel that the key to what I did is in *Faith's New Age*. I think that's my most important book. Well, more research went into that book than any other. This book came out of a second level course I developed, titled "Religion and Change." Here I set out that two-axial period division of religion and culture. Not only does it help to explain why the so-called world religions all originated at much the same time but it throws a lot of light on the present diversity, confusion, and radical change. And I was a bit surprised that others didn't take it up more in religious studies; as far as I can see it's just ignored, but you see people like Karen Armstrong have taken it up.

MG: I noticed that. When did you first come across the axial period, and Jaspers' work on the axial age?

LG: Well, first of all in Robert Bellah's classic essay—you know the one?[3] He has five periods and, as I said, *Faith's New Age* really came out of a course I developed on "Religion and Change" and it was in preparing for that course and delivering lectures that it developed, and I came more and more to the feeling that the first axial period from Jaspers and so on was important. I didn't actually use the term second axial period until the revision of *Faith's New Age*—you know the revision they brought out in America and called it *Christianity at the Crossroads*.[4] I called this the transition to modernity or something like that and I felt it made an awful amount of sense to everything else. After all, the study of religion and culture is tremendously complex when you look at it as a mass and trying to simplify it by this way at least put some order in it. It seemed to me to make a lot of sense.

MG: And did your students respond?

LG: Oh, they responded very well, no problem about that at all. As a matter of fact, that was a very popular course. They loved it, and when I started the course I had the intention of going on to deal with all religious traditions as they encountered modernity. Of course in the end that was impossible, but it also helped me to see that the modern world came out of the West. This is an actual fact, a cultural fact. It can't be denied.

MG: I agree, I always try to get my students to understand just how modernity itself is a form of secular Christianity.

LG: Oh yes, exactly—well, I'm using that term more and more now and I see it as a continuity and not a break. You see, the modern secular world carries through into a non-supernatural world all the values and so on. And something more than that—in a sense, you see, I view this as the flourishing of the doctrine of the incarnation. I mean there is no need for God up in heaven any more, God is *in* the universe. That is, if you are going to continue to use the word God, then God not only permeates the universe, but God is in us.

MG: In the early 1970s you gave a series of lectures on secular Christianity and various themes. I want to ask you what you meant by the term and does it still hold today?

LG: By secular I meant not Christian in the sense of holding particular beliefs. Christianity as a series of cultural streams expresses itself in a wide variety of ways held together by the Bible and the influence of Jesus of Nazareth. The secular world is a continuation of the Christian tradition. In the post-axial age, religion became de-secularized and focussed on what was taken to be the other world. Today, in what can be called the second axial age, it has become secularized again.

MG: I note that around 1970, for you God is becoming a symbolic word. For example, you use the phrase "spiritual values associated with the sense of mystery."[5] Can you elaborate on what you meant by "spiritual"?

LG: This is a bit of a difficult question to answer, and I now tend to move away from the use of "spirituality" as the values often taken to go with it don't fit in the class of moral values.[a] I see it as part of the human spirit—like art and music are part of it—and Nature fits in more and more.

I look with awe at Nature and at the universe generally. Evolution I find staggering and awe-inspiring, especially the

---

a. Here Geering is referring to the use of "spiritual" or "spirituality" amongst the New Age and referring to an eclectic, personal mixing of traditions, beliefs, claims, and values.

capacity of the universe, through our internal natural processes, to create.

MG: So this understanding of "spiritual" has resulted in a change in your theology?

LG: Yes, for me wisdom literature and ecology fit together, but I did not think this is in my earlier days. When I was young, ministers were very sniffy towards statements such as "I find God in my garden," because traditional theology—and of course the ancient prophets—were opposed to the gods of nature.

Now, for me, "God is nature," and I am much closer to Catholic and Celtic spirituality.

MG: Are there also connections here to Maori spirituality?

LG: I have been fairly ignorant about Maori culture but I have great sympathy to the Maori attachment to the earth. I feel we have lost what they have and so I have great sympathy. In the framework of the axial periods in the post-axial age we need to recover something from the pre-axial understanding to regain the feeling of a sanctity of the natural world. We are of the earth ourselves, we are earth creatures and this is the marvellous insight of the second and earliest creation narrative [in Genesis 2:4–25]. I can see it as early science, and the modern conflict between science and religion is a conflict between primitive science and modern science.

The opening chapter of Genesis confirmed the unity of everything and laid the foundation of the unity of the universe. From there, twelfth century CE, modern scientists built on this idea. So I can say "God is the unity of the universe."

MG: Living in New Zealand, we have seen the rise in Maori spirituality; its move into the mainstream has been a big change over the course of your life. How do you understand this shift?

LG: I can appreciate it more and understand how Maori culture has wanted to preserve its spiritual view of reality.

MG: Traditional modernists often say spirituality is something we have moved past. What do you think about this theory?

LG: In the modern secular world we have tended to lose the value and impact of spirituality a lot, because formerly spirituality was tied up with things that have become obsolete. But I think we have recovered spirituality in valuing human relationships—in things like personal counselling, helping people through their grief. All these quite secular forms of assisting and helping people understand how they depend on each other. In a funny way Facebook and the Internet are drawing people together—it's a curious form of spirituality—developing relationships.

MG: So is spirituality for you now about human relationships? And in this perception are we back to the Incarnation?

LG: Yes, that's right—of course it is not confined to the human race—so it is a feeling for all forms of life really.

MG: So a type of creation spirituality?

LG: Yes, that's right.

MG: Is your focus on the environment therefore something you come to via the Old Testament rather the New Testament?

LG: The Old Testament really keeps you in this world—it is permanent—we are from dust and return to dust. There is no doctrine of life after death in the Old Testament and this is a real step forward compared to the other religions of the time. The Old Testament gave it away, that belief in life after death.

MG: Are you more temperamentally Old Testament than New Testament?

LG: I suppose so, yes.

MG: I want to ask you about the similarities between yourself and Colin McCahon* in what you both seemed to be attempting to do. Do you think you were asking similar or different questions? I ask because of his gifting *Storm Warning*[a] to Victoria University of Wellington, in large part it seems because of you.

LG: Yes, there are similarities, but we came to it by different methods. I have always felt more in tune with McCahon, who I didn't know, than say James K. Baxter,* who I did know.

MG: Why was that?

LG: With McCahon it was the types of questions he raised. Whereas with Baxter it was not just the questions raised but more the way he did it I didn't take to.[b] This was especially true in his later years when he took on this persona and then the Jerusalem community[c] whereby he took up the role of being a critic of society without ever producing any positive solutions—whereas Colin McCahon was offering something positive.

MG: In what way did he do this for you?

---

a. In 1981 Colin McCahon gifted his painting *Storm Warning* to Victoria University of Wellington, in part because of what Geering had achieved in the Religious Studies department there and also via the university's continuing education programme. Gregory O'Brien (via a conversation with the curator Alexa Johnston) noted that "Geering's beliefs and non-conformist religious stance had greatly impressed McCahon over many years" (p. 252). The debate and issues of the university's decision to sell *Storm Warning* in 1999 are covered in O'Brien's essay, "Somebody Say Something." The painting was sold for between NZ$1.2–1.5 million and includes text from 2 Timothy 3:1–2. See mccahon.co.nz/cm001187.

b. Baxter and Geering also took on each other in verse published in the Otago University student newspaper *Critic* in 1966. Baxter, a Catholic since 1958, and at that time Robert Burns Fellow at the university, opposed Geering's stance on the resurrection and his poem "Thoughts on Ecumenism" was published in *Critic*, 8 July 1966. Geering's anonymous reply, "Celestial Greetings," was published in *Critic*, 4 Aug 1966. The poems can be read in Morris, Ricketts, and Grimshaw, *Spirit in a Strange Land*, 107–9.

c. A commune Baxter established in the small isolated Maori settlement of Jerusalem on the Whanganui River in 1969. See Newton, *The Double Rainbow*.

LG: Well, inspiration, I suppose, and, in his work on the New Zealand landscape, that there was something to rejoice about. But I never got that feeling from Baxter. I felt from him that he never had anything to rejoice about at all.

MG: So you are quite distinct therefore in how you saw them. How do you think they saw each other given that for many they were seen to be working in the same broad spiritual field?

LG: Did you know Baxter fell out with McCahon? McCahon got quite a lot of money for a painting, and Baxter wanted him to share it with him and McCahon was put out.[a]

MG: No, I didn't know that. Given the impact and religious focus of you, McCahon, and Baxter, do you think that can be explained by you all coming from the south and with a Calvinist heritage?

LG: No, I don't think so; it is just coincidence.

MG: I have always been fascinated by the fact that you and Colin McCahon are almost exact contemporaries and could be considered to be dealing with the same questions in different ways.

LG: Well, we actually never met, but we did attend the same school.[b]

MG: So when did you become aware of the interest in your work by McCahon?

LG: It took quite a while, as I am not an arty person; I was dragged into it by others. There was a special weekend in Wellington on McCahon.[6] I was invited to give a paper on the

---

   a. This would seem to be referring to an incident in 1969 when McCahon, by this time having become what Peter Simpson terms "a semi-Franciscan mendicant" ("Candles in a Dark Room," 178), and Baxter fell out over Baxter's request for money. For a superb overview of the relationship of McCahon and Baxter that engages with their work and beliefs, see Simpson, "Candles in a Dark Room."

   b. Otago Boys' High School in Dunedin.

religious component of McCahon's art. I was pretty reluctant, for it took me outside my comfort zone. Yet the organizers were delighted with it and published it. Then, on the basis of this endorsement, I was invited to give the first McCahon Memorial Lecture[7] in Auckland. I got access to McCahon's work in slide form, and the lecture was based on that and there was wide interest in the public.

MG: Why do you not have the despair of McCahon, especially in your approach to Ecclesiastes?[8] Why do you have hope compared to McCahon?

LG: It was alcohol that did it for McCahon. McCahon's passion for what he was doing was so great that he felt very disappointed that people didn't see what he was on about. There was little recognition of him by his peers, and so McCahon felt he had failed.

I actually didn't know at the time that McCahon was interested in my work. I learned of his interest from his son.[a]

MG: What about Baxter, who like McCahon also dealt with questions of faith in the modern world?

LG: I was fairly critical of Baxter, partly because he treated his wife badly. My wife[b] and Jacqui [Sturm]* had been in St Margaret's[c] together. We had Baxter to the Theological Hall a couple of times, but I felt Baxter to be a bit of a showman, to be quite honest.

MG: What about Baxter as a poet?

---

a. William McCahon, 1943–.

b. Elaine Geering (1927–2001), born in Dunedin. In 1945 she enrolled at Dunedin Teacher's College and then specialized in Speech Therapy. Geering's first wife Nancy, ill for eighteen months from tuberculosis, died suddenly during an accident in her medical treatment at the start of 1950, leaving Geering a widower with two children under four years old. Elaine had moved into a flat in Geering's Opoho parish, north Dunedin, and as recounted in his memoir of Elaine, a romance developed. They married in 1951. See Geering, *Every Moment Must Be Lived*.

c. University Hall of residence in Dunedin.

LG: Poetry is not in my field either. While of course Baxter was a poet of distinction, my interest was more in Baxter's father because of his pacifism,* as I too was a pacifist in World War II. You could say I had a love-hate relationship at a distance with Baxter.

MG: What did you think of Baxter's move to the Catholic Church?

LG: I often felt Baxter's Catholicism was not terribly sincere. If other Catholics had said some of the things that Baxter said, they would have been criticised or even pushed out, yet, because he was a poet and a public figure, the Catholic Church embraced him, rather uncritically I thought.

MG: What about Baxter's shift toward Maoridom?

LG: I didn't know enough at the time to be able to understand it. Of course, I have come to understand more over the years, but that was very early days in the Maori resurgence, compared with today.

My first contact with Maori was when I used to go to Whakatane once a year to give lectures at the Theological College for Maori.[a]

I also remember as a young minister in 1943[b] receiving the Moderator of the General Assembly John Laughton,* who couldn't bring his Maori wife[c] as she wouldn't be accepted. She had been refused entry to a hairdresser's in Wellington, which would be unthinkable today.

I do think Baxter helped to pioneer interest in Maori culture.

---

a. Te Wananga-a-Rangi, the theological college of the Maori Synod of the Presbyterian Church. Established in 1954, in 1972 it was relocated to Dunedin and incorporated within Knox Theological Hall.

b. This was when Geering was minister at Kurow in North Otago.

c. Horiana Te Kauru Laughton (1899–1986) of Nuhaka, graduate of Turakina Girls' School and a noted school teacher.

MG: I am interested in your turn to becoming what could be called a public intellectual.[a]

LG: Such a turn wasn't a conscious decision. I felt, after the heresy trial, pretty much an odd person in the church, so when I went to Victoria I felt now, as it were, to be working outside the church.

At Victoria I worked even beyond the university via seminars around New Zealand.[b] I did twelve a year. But I was never invited to speak inside a church. At the seminars I was always surprised that very few clergy turned up. Now, I was speaking outside the church environment, but on the main issues I felt the church should be talking about.

MG: So who did come to your seminars?

LG: People who were dissatisfied with the church. It was clear to me, at least, there was a group of people within the community interested in following things up. I did three seminars a year in Auckland for twenty years. The numbers began to fall off, partly because they put the price up, but in the early days there were two hundred at each seminar. I also did outreaches around the country every year at places like Tauranga, Te Kauwhata, and Masterton.

MG: Why was there such interest?

LG: In Auckland, in the third seminar of each year, we asked for suggestions. Otherwise we simply took up something being internally done in the university courses—Bultmann, Tillich, Martin Buber. The most popular was Jung; we did Jung five years running.

MG: Why was Jung so popular?

---

a. Geering's status as a public intellectual is demonstrable in the various awards and honours received as well as his multitude of public speaking engagements, and also by his inclusion in Simmons, *Speaking Truth to Power*, 128–40.

b. As well as teaching Religious Studies, Geering was reportedly the most popular lecturer there has been in Victoria University's Centre for Continuing Education.

LG: We called it "Jung, the Unconscious and God," or something like that. I found Jung's model of psyche[a] very helpful in self-understanding. I would explain the model and how it resulted in Jung's particular religious interest. I think Jung's idea of individuation (which comes to a stage of fulfilment in mid-life) suggests the human psyche is programmed to reach some understanding in which one's experiences are related to one's reality—the self. This notion means the archetypes of God and self are the same. There is a link here with Feuerbach, where God is a projection and it becomes clear via Bultmann that the question of God and self are the same. I always explained that we mustn't take Jung uncritically; rather we must use Jung as a model.

MG: So it sounds like these are the thinkers who have influenced you?

LG: Yes, Jung, Bultmann, Feuerbach for a start; I learned a lot from Feuerbach; he has been undervalued.

MG: What about Tillich?

LG: I was quite a Tillich fan. In the late 1950s or early 1960s I first read the three volumes of his *Systematic Theology*. Tillich understood what the problem of theology was, in a way few people seemed to do. In the early 1960s at a meeting at Seacliff [Lunatic Asylum],[b] I found doctors reading Tillich. Though I did have problems with Tillich, being not quite sure what "being itself"

---

a. A complex view of all psychic processes, both the conscious and the unconscious, involving the self, complexes, archetypes, the ego, persona, anima and animus, and the shadow. The search for wholeness is termed individuation.

b. Seacliff Lunatic Asylum located near Palmerston, north of Dunedin. When built in 1884 it was the largest building in New Zealand and noted for its extravagant gothic architecture. It closed in 1973. The noted New Zealand writer Janet Frame was held there in the 1940s as part of a misdiagnosis for schizophrenia and records the horrors of her time there in her autobiographical writing. Geering was invited to talk to a group of the doctors there.

really meant. There was also a limitation for me in Tillich because I felt Tillich was still carrying through his earlier Lutheranism, but I wouldn't rubbish Tillich even today.

MG: How about more recent influences?

LG: An important influence is Gordon Kaufman* and his little book on theology.[a] I used to use Kaufmann but I felt he overwrites a bit and needs to be simplified. Instead of trying to define God, Kaufman says let's see the role the word God has played in our thinking. My example that I used often is this: when our pioneers came to a new country, took over and surveyed it, the surveyor had to go to the top of the best hill and put in a trig station. The hill was humanly chosen but, having chosen it, we relate all land to that point. God as a word is like that, in our attempt to relate all of our experience to a central point ...

I feel I have a lot in common with Kaufmann. He got hold of my *Coming Back to Earth*, and he sent a marvellous email saying he hoped it would be widely read.[b] We had been previously in touch when I wrote *Tomorrow's God*, in which I quoted him.[c]

MG: Has there been an American shift in your thinking?

LG: I do feel an affinity with some American thinkers; another is John Cobb,* who I enjoyed particularly because of his great feeling for Buddhist culture.[9]

MG: What is your interest in Buddhism?

LG: Christianity has more in common with Buddhism than Hinduism or Confucianism. My interest in Buddhism is from an early stage in my career when I taught myself comparative religion

---

a. Kaufman, *God the Problem*. Geering read this in 1974, one of eighty-eight books he records as having read that year. See Appendix on his reading.

b. Kaufmann's comment is included on the back cover.

c. In *Tomorrow's God* Geering references four of Kaufmann's books: *God the Problem*; *An Essay on Theological Method*; *The Theological Imagination*; *Theology for a Nuclear Age*.

for my Melbourne BD. So I was interested from the 1940s and, as a result, I later taught comparative religion in Queensland. I had an interest in comparative religion from the beginning—almost from the last year of school—due to the SCM, which provided something to do in the lunch-hour. The Rector, Percy Kidson,[a] supported the SCM. He saw it as open-ended.

Also, an OT scholar whom I studied often wrote books in comparative religion.[b] So when I did my BD I was disappointed there was no comparative religion in theology, so I did it myself. Comparative religion was always viewed as a Cinderella. There was a certain fear in academic theological figures at that time that the study of comparative religion made one comparatively religious.

MG: Yes, you quote from Ronald Knox that "the study of comparative religion makes one comparatively religious"[10] in reference to your taking of that course on comparative religion from the Melbourne College of Divinity. Then of course you were invited to teach the first course on comparative religion at the University of Queensland. Would you say you are still "comparatively religious"?

LG: I'm a very religious person. I am passionate about what I see as religion and that is, a set of values to live by. For me these values come out of Christianity and while they do share things with other traditions, they are more pronounced in Christianity than in any other tradition. Consequently, the modern world came out of the Christian West because its values of justice and peace have their roots in the Christian tradition.

MG: What did you like about Buddhism?

LG: I felt affinity from the 1940s for the humanism in Buddhism and found certain parallels between what was then theistic Christianity and non-theistic Buddhism. It was the humanism in

---

a. Percy Kidson was Rector of Otago Boys' High School, 1934–47.
b. Here Geering is referring in particular to Robinson, *A Short Comparative History of Religions*, a book he used to own.

each of them. I never took to their doctrine of reincarnation. I personally feel that reincarnation is not necessary for Buddhism, but only Stephen Batchelor[11] agrees with me on that.

MG: So, associated with this subject, do you have what could be termed a personal myth?

LG: I have never been a person who has had a goal, an ambition to get to. I did at university and that was to be a Rhodes scholar, and in my second year I got close,[a] but when I came into the church I lost all sense of goals, as I was here to be used. Hereafter I became more Buddhist: I simply respond to the situation, I do what comes to me and accept it. This is more a Buddhist attitude of the Middle Way, the acceptance of what comes. This approach began from my days of studying Buddhism as a student, where I saw the significance of the Buddhist no-soul doctrine.

MG: So does that mean you may use Buddhism to help describe and define yourself?

LG: Yes, I think of myself as a secular Christian Buddhist.

MG: So could you also describe yourself as a Western Buddhist like Don Cupitt?*

LG: I am happy to describe myself as being in tune with Western humanist Buddhism. I am very much at one with nearly everything Cupitt says. The difference between us is this: his approach is from philosophy and mine is from culture.

MG: So that is how would you describe your position today?

---

a. See *Wrestling with God*, 47–49. In 1939 Geering, having been in 1938 Senior Scholar for New Zealand in Pure Mathematics, as well as SCM president and playing hockey for the Varsity A team, gained one of the two Rhodes Scholarship nominations for Otago University. This meant he was "one of eight or nine candidates" for the final selection at Government House, Wellington. He notes that his "known pacifist convictions" as well as appearing "rather immature" may have counted against him (49).

LG: I see myself as a Christian humanist with my values and thinking coming out of the Christian tradition—I don't deny I am a Christian—but labels are a bit of a nuisance really, though they are useful to distinguish.

The time in which we live is one of very fast transition to, I hope, one of global citizenship. Nationality must be seen as a very relative thing, for example, the debate whether we should allow land to be bought by overseas people. What does it matter, for we have to live globally?

MG: What about being a New Zealander?

LG: For me, being a New Zealander is now seen in only relative terms. I do take great pride in the All Blacks[a] and all that, but that is just a bit of fun and enjoyment and not to be taken too seriously.

Being a New Zealander—it's a fact in the sense of being born here and I feel at home. But it is more important to live a life that contributes to the unity of the whole world.

MG: How do you explain that shift in focus?

LG: It could be part of Christianity itself.

MG: Why do you think New Zealand has so responded to you?

LG: It puzzles me, to be quite honest. I think I have been able to articulate what a lot of people really feel but have been unable to put into words. Leaving aside the real fundamentalists, most people who are still going to church or have left the church they went to once, know they have valued the Christianity of the past but [also] know that [the] Christianity of the past doesn't fit the world they live in. ... They want to hold on to the value of the past but don't know how to do it, so they fall within the stance of being indifferent. They feel I can put into words what they are feeling. It was just an accident of history that the heresy trial took

---

a. The colloquial name for the New Zealand Rugby football team.

place—and coupled with my going to Victoria where, by a series of accidents, I developed a series of seminars which attracted a lot of people because my name was well known because of the heresy trial. This led to my writing a column for the *Auckland Star*,[a] which in turn led to my *Listener* column.[b]

MG: It's clear you found far greater theological freedom in academia than you did in the church.

LG: Yes—very much in the move to Victoria. When you come to think of it, it's a tragedy when a church that proclaims freedom actually imprisons people.

MG: Is there any freedom in the church now, do you think, really?

LG: No. It's an interesting point isn't it? Why does the church imprison when it should be freeing? That's the great message of Paul—freedom, freedom from the Law—and the church is now imprisoned by doctrine. Christians don't believe in Christ anymore, they believe in Christian doctrine—as if that is what will save them! They have to have the right belief. It's a very big confusion that faith is identified now as having certain beliefs.

MG: So doctrine is secondary for you?

LG: Yes, it has become more and more secondary. John Henderson used to call his course dogmatics because he was a Barthian; when Barth was first becoming known, John Dickie

---

a. A daily evening newspaper published in Auckland, 1970–91. Under the heading "Religion Today" Geering wrote a weekly 600–900 word column for them, 1971–83; this then became a monthly column, 1983–Jan 1986 and then a monthly weekend column, Sept 1986–Dec 1988. This, as much as his trial and other works, helped make him a public figure in New Zealand.

b. Geering wrote a column, "Horizons," for the *New Zealand Listener*, 1987–88. A public intellectual since the heresy trial, Geering undertook—and continues to undertake—a variety of media appearances: articles, reviews, interviews, public, across print, radio, and television as well as on-going public talks.

warned us against him; Dickie would never see theology as dogmatic.

MG: Looking back over your lifetime, who would you say are your major influences?

LG: Well, as I write in my new little book from Polebridge,[12] I have five mentors. There's Schleiermacher, who I came to via John Dickie; Feuerbach, who I came to via teaching at Victoria; Teilhard de Chardin, who was a great influence from the 1960s onwards (I read the *Phenomenon of Man* over one weekend about 1962 and that was a great influence); John Robinson with *Honest to God*; and Jung.

MG: What was it about Schleiermacher?

LG: Schleiermacher changed theology from the study of revealed doctrines to the study of revealed experience. I came to him via John Dickie and his influence that the theological process is the way in which Christians think through their experiences and relate them to all other knowledge. While John Dickie looks pretty traditional today, the seeds of growth are there.

MG: Of the five, who is the most important?

LG: The one who comes closest to my point of view is Feuerbach, for he really appreciated the importance of Christianity and what Christianity was. His book is really a tour de force—but you have to allow for the fact that it is almost two hundred years old, but I am interested that Don Cupitt never refers to Feuerbach.

Feuerbach made sense. In the second-year course in religion, "Religion and Change," I always used to enjoy the point when we came to Feuerbach.

MG: It is interesting that it is Feuerbach who is most important, because from your books it could seem that the most important were Nietzsche or Jung.

LG: Well, not so much Nietzsche because I find his thoughts are all over the place, so he is more a stimulator, while Feuerbach had a completeness.

MG: Can I ask why you went for Jung over Freud?

LG: The problem for me with Freud is that he is very anti-religious, whereas Jung saw religion as a way of overcoming—but there are aspects of Jung to leave behind, for example, Jung's collective unconscious is a type of mysticism that doesn't gel with me at all.

MG: Have you noticed how Hegel has made a comeback over the past ten to fifteen years?

LG: I think Hegel is important, and I have come to have quite a respect for him, even though I have come to see him through Feuerbach's eyes. It was Feuerbach who turned him upside down, not Marx.

MG: Would it be fair to say that your influences position you against mainstream orthodox thought in the New Zealand Church?

LG: I feel they are the continuum of the influence of the mainstream. I feel the Presbyterian Church today is living in the past.

MG: Do you think there is a future for the church?

LG: Not as it was in the past—and it has been fragmenting more and more since the Reformation. Christianity is becoming dissipated in organized form.

MG: So what is the future from your perspective?

LG: I see the modern secular world, particularly after the Enlightenment, as the logical expression of Christianity.

MG: So in this secular world that is the expression of Christianity, where and how is theology now done?

LG: It's a reinterpretation of the Incarnation, so out of the doctrine of the Incarnation: God took human flesh. Feuerbach says this: the problem with God is that we send him back to heaven again. Yet in the Incarnation, the Divine, ... the Otherworldly, has enfleshed itself in the human condition, and today we see the human species displaying many of the characteristics of omnipresence and omnipotence—both in science and technology.

MG: So what does this mean for theology? Is traditional theology at an end?

LG: It depends on how one interprets the word "God." I interpret it as a symbolic word that captures up the unity of the universe and has an associated ethic—the study of these ideas is properly called theology.

MG: So given this, where do you draw theology from? What are the resources to do theology from? Are you still doing theology?

LG: Yes, I am still doing theology. There's the Bible of course, which I don't read a lot these days, as it has become so much a part of me. So really it is trying to understand the world in the light of all modern knowledge, attempting to see purpose and unity.

MG: So central to your theology is the notion of purpose and unity?

LG: Yes indeed, that's right.

MG: I increasingly get the sense that too often it's only conservatives who want to talk about "God" or use "God"—and so there are always issues where you have to say you don't mean what they do.

LG: That's right, there's always a problem of being misunderstood when you don't believe in God in the traditional way.

MG: So is there a better word than "God" to use?

LG: I'd like to think that there was, but I can't find one—the important thing about monotheism is not the *theism* but the *mono*.

MG: So the notion of the singular is central?

LG: Yes, the way it is all held together—we get it in the universe—in the word "uni"—everything is held together.

MG: Would you describe yourself as a radical?

LG: I do—if you interpret radical as getting to the root of the matter, but not if it is used as a pejorative term, that is, as irrational.

MG: So would this sense of radial, of the radix, the root, arise out of your original focus and work in the Old Testament?

LG: I suppose it did start in that sense. By the time I was involved in Old Testament studies it was already taken for granted that it was a human set of scriptures to be understood in a human context: that of the Middle East. This understanding, then, led me into my interest in the History of Religion School that sees Christianity as a historical phenomenon.

I don't mind the term radical and I know John Robertson called himself a radical. Do you know I met John Robertson when he came to New Zealand, and he treated me as a fellow heretic! And, Jim Veitch got Robertson to write for my *festschrift*.[13]

MG: So given this, what do you say is "the root of the matter"?

LG: It has to do with historical origins and sort of what is fundamentally true—but I think truth is a difficult term these days. I don't believe in an absolute truth these days. I did for a time … For me truth is a quality.

MG: So you are seen as a theological radical; does this also translate over into you being a political and or social radical also?

LG: I am, on the social spectrum, on the left and always on the left; as for radical, well for me I see radical in the form of radix—

of getting to the root of the matter and not just in being or being seen as a renegade.

MG: And in the 1960s?

LG: First of all, Robinson's *Honest to God* (in 1963) and the student turmoil from California all had an impact. The student turmoil had the effect of shaking up the structure of authority in the university. But certainly theologically I think the radical view was fairly widespread. I found Gregor Smith very radical stuff.

MG: Do you have any hope for theology at the moment?

LG: Not altogether. When one uses traditional terms, it is very hard to get away from what they stood for. For me the word "God" is the most important word in the English language but it changes. Its use and meaning changes. Gordon Kauffman was the most help here: he helped me see "God" as the word at the centre of what means the most. Because of the human mind's tendency to unify experiences, "God" is the word used to link experiences. So in this sense there is a future for theology, but in the meantime theology itself is not a term to be used much. For most people it stands for something that has become redundant.

MG: Would you call yourself a postmodernist?

LG: I don't like labels too much. I had moved to Don Cupitt's position before he had. It was not until *Taking Leave of God* that I became interested in Cupitt. When I first met him, I felt he was a bit conservative and I was surprised that he had read my work. So I was surprised that in his book *The Sea of Faith* he ended with Nietzsche, as I had already done so in *Faith's New Age*, and also that he called Nietzsche "a prophet of the New Age" as I had done. Actually, Peter Munz had read that book for me, chapter by chapter, and he congratulated me on making Nietzsche the last Nietzschean.

MG: Who in your opinion comes after Nietzsche?

LG: When I was doing *Faith's New Age* I had the impression that the scholarly world had dismissed Hegel's work on the philosophy of religion. Yet Hegel saw … the biblical myth as playing an important role before Strauss, and he then interpreted the story of Adam and the Garden of Eden as not a fall but a rise to reality—to see reality as it truly is.

Movements seem to come in waves. There was the liberal movement in liberal theology which went from 1890 to World War II. Henry Major* was part of this particular period, but it faded. Very few of the old liberals became radical.

MG: But you would be one of those who did so?

LG: Yes, I would say what I do could be termed "radical theology."

MG: So given you are a twentieth-century liberal who transitioned into a radical, would you be happy to also be describes as the last modernist?

LG: Yes, I would. When I ended my teaching I thought, "I have at last reached the point where I don't have to defend anything. I am now free to think."

MG: How do you see the future of Christianity? Is it as a type of what could be called New Age Christianity?

LG: As I see it, the future of Christianity is a secular world which continues to promote its highest human values. It won't be called "Christian." It could well be called a "human" world. This is the consequence of a primary Christian doctrine: the Incarnation. The future is one in which the highest values—which we call "God"—become incarnated in the human race. As one looks back now, from Paul onwards we lost the sense of earthliness that sits at the heart of the Incarnation and became so heavenly minded that we saw earth and earthly behaviour as holding us back. But from the Renaissance onwards this heavenly move has been reversed. The focus of Christianity and our world has become this-worldly, which is what I mean by secular.

MG: In your essay on "Idolatry in the Church,"[14] you reference three future types of membership for the church as outlined by Kirsopp Lake in 1925.[a] Thinking of you, I wondered if you have moved from the Institutionalists to the Experimentalists?

LG: I actually think I had the seeds of the Experimentalist at the beginning. This is mainly because, having no church background, I did absorb up to a point what I was being taught, but I was not wholly convinced by theology. I was always out on the fringes of theology. You could really regard John Dickie as an Experimentalist, for he was of that tradition going right back to Schleiermacher. If you see how Schleiermacher came to his thought, Schleiermacher was really the beginning of Experimentalism in many ways.

MG: In 1990, you warned the Church that it was in danger of becoming a sect rather than a Church.[15] How do you see the mainstream churches now? Are they sects?

LG: The churches have become sects, and there is always this tendency in Christianity, which goes back to the East-West break in the church of 1054. This was a break into geographical areas whereby they were competing only at a distance. Sectarianism was emphasized in the Reformation and the churches are sects in today's world, including the Catholic Church.

MG: Why do you think there has been a revival of evangelical and Pentecostal Christianity?

---

a. Geering (*Reimagining God*, 155) presents Lake's three types as:
  1. The Fundamentalists who have strong convictions but are both spiritually arrogant and intellectually ignorant.
  2. The Experimentalists. Today these would be the radicals; they seek a faith relevant to the current cultural and intellectual climate.
  3. The Institutionalists are what we could term the mainstream broad-church. They saw themselves as liberals, were very critical of fundamentalists but were also very wary of the Experimentalists. They aimed for a middle way and affirmed watered-down traditional dogmas.

LG: They want to be modern in everyday things but want to have touch with some non-physical reality. Pentecostalism is a revival of religious enthusiasms—a second or third wave of what took place in the Methodist movement. It is a revival of feeling, a sense that academic theology is too rational for the inner spirit. We need to understand that people feel liberated inside by Pentecostalism, and that is the focus on feelings. These new churches, that's what feeds them: a sense of feeling and what's important is the fellowship, and I would support this.

I don't see any future for Pentecostalism myself. I see it as a bit of a fizzer. It may die out altogether but there will always be a seedbed for it.

MG: What are your thoughts on Islam?

LG: I feel that Islam is running behind the Western world by two hundred to three hundred years, and this has resulted in a love-hate relationship between the Muslim world and the West, as they are admirers of what has been done and of Western technology. The Islamic world also wants to preserve Islamic traditions, but in spite of itself the Islamic world is becoming more secular. It is difficult not to absorb secular ideas. Science is reliable knowledge that we have accumulated on a purely human and non-revelatory basis, and this undermines all knowledge accumulated on a revelatory basis.

MG: One of the major global changes of the past thirty years has been the rise of Islam as radical, political force. I would like to understand how you see this contemporary rise of what we may call radical Islam?

LG: Well, this is a very complex issue and one has to see what lies behind it. Remember Islam had a marvellous existence from the ninth to the twelfth century, where its society and knowledge and culture [were] far superior to Christendom. But this predominance disintegrated and was parcelled out in national forms, enabling the expansion of the West, from the sixteenth century onwards, to conquer Islam except for the Turkish Empire—and when the Turkish Empire fell at the end of the First World War, Islam was in disarray. I think the best Muslims look back to the past and would seek to reconstruct the Islamic world.

MG: So do you still have hope?

LG: Yes, I do. My hope is that which arises from looking back over one hundred years and seeing things that have improved: we are more aware of the needs of others; we are leaving racism behind; there is greater equality of the sexes and more acceptance of homosexuality. The real disaster is that the Islamic world is not doing this.

MG: Can I ask why even now you are writing new books and so, effectively, you have never retired?

LG: I never saw myself as a writer at all until I was fifty [years old], and even now I see myself as just a person who passes on what I have received—a teacher. So my books are a form of teaching. When I retired, lecturing became a continuous activity as John Murray* got me into doing lunch-hour lectures. I have been giving them for over twenty-five years now.

MG: How did you find the transition from university life to what could be called these post-retirement lectures?

LG: I never felt in the early stages that I was doing more than assembling knowledge and putting it in a form that people could understand. In fact, I never felt for a long time that I was breaking new ground.

MG: So when was it that you did feel you were doing so, that you were breaking new ground?

LG: It was with *Christianity without God*. The germ of the idea started off being a bit facetious. I was to give a lecture at a Sea of Faith Conference. It started as a lecture with an absurd title—Noel Cheer* put it in the web site—and it was drawn to the attention of Bob Funk* in the USA. Funk said to put it into a book and so I decided to try. In fact, I had an email from a theologian in South Africa saying it was the best Trinitarian sketch she had come across.

MG: So I must ask—are you a Trinitarian?

LG: I still am a Trinitarian—but a radical one. I am not thinking any more of final truth, rather of developing truth. The modern secular world reverses how the Trinity went off the rails.

MG: Can you be Christian without being Trinitarian?

LG: I don't know what it means to be Christian these days.

MG: Let me then ask a similar question in a different way. Would you describe yourself as a Christian Presbyterian or a Presbyterian Christian?

LG: I am Presbyterian by belonging to that organization. I am shaped by the Christian tradition but "Christian" becomes more and more narrow in its claims and meanings. Today "Christian" tends to mean fundamentalist.

MG: Did you know Richard Dawkins claims to be a cultural Anglican?[16]

LG: Yes, I did. I was pretty critical of Dawkins' *The God Delusion*, but I have come to quite like the man. In that dialogue between Dawkins and the Archbishop of Canterbury[a] I felt the Archbishop was a bit pitiable, while I agreed with everything Dawkins said.

MG: So in a similar way, do you think we could describe you as a cultural Presbyterian or even a cultural Christian?

LG: Yes, you could.

---

a. In 2012, hosted by Oxford University, Dawkins took part in a televised debate with the Archbishop of Canterbury, Rowan Williams. Chapter 5: Lloyd Geering's Notebook

MG: So I get the sense that for you Christian seems an identity to be left behind. Therefore, if you can't use Christian, what would you use?

LG: Labels are a bit of a nuisance but provided that we use them in a very general way I could state that I am shaped by the Christian tradition and have tried all my life to explore it.

MG: So this is the identity you would claim?

LG: I am a human being basically trying to explore all factors that have enabled us to become human and all the potential of being human. In one way I am a humanist but that word is a bit narrow.

MG: But you do still partake in the Eucharist; why is that?

LG: Yes, I do. I see it more as the symbolism of a fellowship meal and as an expression of community. It goes right back to the beginning of things: in the original Semitic setting people were bound together by what they ate together. Unfortunately, what spoilt it all was Paul.

MG: Why do you think you have had the success you have enjoyed?

LG: I think I have a very clear, lucid approach. I don't like things being woolly, which means I keep revising and revising. My struggle is to make the wordy thinking of institutions clear. ... Theology came to have a very bad reputation, being regarded as a lot of words that don't say anything, so my response is to bring out what it does mean.

MG: What does it mean for you?

LG: The curious thing is—the further I go along this general direction—the great themes like Incarnation and so on are still there and become more meaningful to me. Like the Trinity. I am very keen on the doctrine of the Trinity—as a model it is useful to help understanding.

As for the future, I feel New Zealand has a unique role to play in the coming global culture. While we are the most isolated nation, there are some positive consequences. We are one of the most well-read populations and one of the most-travelled also. These two features have turned us into a kind of melting pot where ideas get spread about and fertilised. It is not accidental that New Zealand is a social leader.

MG: I get a very strong sense that movement, that progress, is very important to you and your thinking?

LG: Yes, well I feel there is still progress to be made going forward. Evolution has come to be a very important way of understanding the nature of change. Life is change, and it can change for the worst, but overall I am very interested in how we can participate in change for some better attainment.

MG: Do you think about death? What is your view of what happens when we die?

LG: I see death as a coming to an end. The only regret I have is that I won't see things that I would like to see happen—and I am still interested in the world and how it is progressing. One is sorry to have to get off the train, and while that's the only thing that concerns me, I feel very grateful that I have reached this stage. Ideas come to me very quickly these days— but there is lots of rewriting and rephrasing. I'm a bit puzzled that new ideas keep coming, but I seem able to keep putting things together and see them in a new light.

MG: Looking back, what has made the most difference?

LG: I think I've been a sort of public voice who has articulated what a lot of people have thought but not articulated.

MG: So who do you talk to and write for?

LG: The intelligent citizen. They tend to be people who have had a reasonable education and have done some thinking themselves and are open-minded, and I think it important myself to remain open-minded. I never considered resigning from the church or resigning from being a minister. I saw myself as continuing my original call, as I was grateful to the church and to Christianity because it provided a framework to orient myself and a framework for living. That is what Christianity gave to me. This is still part of my call.

5

Lloyd Geering's Notebook, 1965–1990

"Because of the controversy my reading speed trebled."

In answer to a question as to how his mind has changed over the years, Geering responded that it had enlarged from a rather narrow liberal, churchman mindset by virtue of reading. Much of this was also self-directed for, as he noted, "I haven't had the advantage of regular contacts along my lines to work it out."[a]

As part of my research for this book, Geering generously lent me the notebook in which he recorded all of his academic reading for the years 1965–90. A once-blue, now worn khaki small hardback, it is held together by rubber bands, the spine cracked from twenty-five years of annotation and use. The notes are often rudimentary, comprising various forms of author and title detail in what is primarily a very cramped script. In deciphering just who the author or just what the title was, I was continually grateful to be able to turn to online resources, including access to the University of Otago and Victoria University of Wellington library catalogues, as most of the books Geering read were also first accessed via his university libraries.

Books have always been expensive in New Zealand, the result of a combination of a small population and geographical isolation.

---

a. See chapter 4.

Consequently, many tertiary scholars made use of—and continue to use—institutional purchasing power to order books to read for teaching and research, especially in the days before the advent of on-line book purchasing. Furthermore, university library collections tended to reflect the particular teaching or research interests of the small number of academic staff in each discipline. Our tertiary library collections were, therefore, often highly eclectic and offered fascinating insights into the interests or otherwise of staff at a particular time. This also meant that when an academic started to read in an inter-disciplinary manner, or, as in Geering's case in Dunedin, embarked on a focus outside of their specialization, what they could access was pre-determined by the interests, and often the theological position of those who had oversight for that area at a given time in its history.

Perhaps the most fortunate event to happen to Geering was the chance to create the library collection for the new Religious Studies Department at Victoria University of Wellington. As the inaugural chair establishing the discipline at the university, Geering could primarily determine the collection in tandem with the courses taught and his research interests. It also, crucially, meant that the university finances were behind such an endeavour. Geering's fine legacy continues to be built on by those who followed, and in my opinion Victoria University holds the most impressive library collection for religious studies in the country. This is not to say that Geering has not assembled his own impressive personal library. Anyone fortunate enough to have visited him in his apartment in Herbert Gardens in Wellington will recall his book-lined study. Books were and are a central element of Geering's life. This is why a photograph of Geering standing in his study was the most appropriate cover image for *The Lloyd Geering Reader*.[1]

Looking back, that title now seems most apposite, for not only was it a collection of Geering's writings but it emphasized that first and foremost Geering was and is a reader. This is why his notebook is a fascinating and invaluable insight into his interests and influences: it demonstrates the way in which a liberal was radicalized by reading. For unlike theological radicals in other parts of the world, Geering was self-radicalized because he never had a community of fellow radical thinkers to draw upon for support. New Zealand was—and still is—a notably conservative theological country. It was and continues to be an anti-intellectual community,[2] and this makes Geering's transition and success all the more remarkable. Furthermore, both the theological community and the religious studies community are small. Theology was not taught in universities, only in small denominational seminaries. Religious studies was a very recent discipline. In both theology and religious studies, along with the humanities more generally at this time, the emphasis was always more on teaching than publications.

New Zealand is a long way geographically from the rest of the world, especially from the intellectual ferment of the northern hemisphere. This isolation meant New Zealand scholars, especially in Geering's time, did not have the same access to the conferences, seminars, and colleagues as radicals in the northern hemisphere. Books and journals had to be transported by boat from England and the United States. There was, therefore, at least a six-week transit lag-time as New Zealand caught up with what was happening in the Northern hemisphere. Study leave was a major and uncommon event, involving long distances and travel time with much correspondence to arrange it. New Zealand academics tended to either cram as much into such periods as they could, aware that it would be years before they could again be so stimulated, or treat it primarily as a form of unofficial holiday, a reward for long service, where tourism and family visits were often emphasized. The advent of long-distance air travel dramatically shortened the distance to the rest of the world. Before this happened, Geering's only extended experience of life outside New Zealand (outside the childhood years in Australia 1926–31) were his years teaching in Brisbane, which was where, in the late 1950s, he was opened to Bultmann and Tillich. This experience, however, occurred within the confines of a mainstream mid-century liberal but not radical theological environment. It is therefore not surprising that in the early 1960s, on his return to New Zealand, Geering could be described as an "old-fashioned Liberal."

From the late 1950s onward, not only did New Zealand academics manage to travel overseas, increasingly northern hemisphere academics also regularly travelled south, often on an Australasian tour. In particular, two such visits were very fruitful for Geering during this time of his notebook. The first was that of the Scottish theologian Ronald Gregor Smith. Having met in New Zealand,[a] Smith and Geering became friends, which also led to Geering's attendance at a three-day theological seminar in Germany with Smith while on study leave in 1964.[3] As is well known, in 1966 Geering's quotation from Smith's *Secular Christianity* about "the bones of Jesus" caused the outroar when published in an article on the Resurrection in *The Outlook* (2 April). How was this possible, given that *Secular Christianity* was not published in the United Kingdom until late January 1966? Geering noted in his autobiography that when invited in January (1966) to write for *The Outlook*, he "had just been reading" the newly published *Secular Christianity*.[4] However, it was not in the list of books Geering read for 1966, nor was it accessioned in the Knox Theological Library until 1973.[5] I discovered from Geering that he had been sent a proof copy by Smith, from which he quoted the controversial statement.[6] In his mind, in doing so he was not expressing espe-

---

a. In 1955 Gregor Smith, in his role as managing director and editor of SCM Press, toured New Zealand. As the *Knox Collegian* (1955) recorded in "Theological Hall Notes": "This year was notable in that at the end of the first term the Faculty of Theology presented its first series of open lectures. They were delivered by the Rev. Ronald Gregor-Smith, MA, Editor of the SCM Press. He spoke on the temporary deadlock in theological thought, and although everyone did not agree with Mr Smith, the large crowd of Professors, Ministers, laymen and students who heard him found him extremely stimulating" (p. 52). My thanks to Jane Bloore of the Presbyterian Archives, Dunedin for this information.

cially radical ideas or positions, for as he notes, Ronald Gregor Smith's *Secular Christianity* "never caused so much as a ripple in Scotland."[7] The difference, it seems, is that Geering highlighted a specific statement in isolation from *Secular Christianity* in his *Outlook* article. This, in combination with the title of the book and the fact that Geering was principal of the Theological Hall, was enough to inflame existing suspicions. While *Secular Theology* did not cause any controversy in Scotland when published, we need to remember that Geering was selectively quoting a small passage from a book unheard of in almost all of New Zealand at that time. Furthermore, while Gregor Smith would be known to some of the clergy, the book at that time was not available and had yet to be reviewed in overseas theological journals, which then had to make their way down to New Zealand by ship. The laity were therefore confronted with a wholly unfamiliar passage from an unfamiliar book written by an unfamiliar theologian.

Smith later wrote to Geering expressing his thanks, support, and encouragement.[a] He had read Geering's article and "the Moderator's round-robin" and noted, "In Scotland matters are quiescent, since in Scotland, as you may or may not know, there is no very articulate interest in modern lines in theology." He then talks of continuing the theme of *Secular Christianity*: "not indeed the resurrection as an isolated topic, which I think can be misleading, but rather an attempt to grapple with the whole matter of Christianity in its relation to its own past and to its further forms in a secular world."[8] In many ways this is as succinct a description as any of the task Geering then set out upon himself.

Ronald Gregor Smith's interests also proved to be influential on Geering's later reading and thought. As is evident from the notebook, Geering came to be a regular reader and re-reader of Martin Buber; Smith was the original English translator of Buber's *I and Thou* in 1937. Geering has confirmed that he first read Buber via

---

a. Gregor Smith also wrote a letter to *The Outlook* in 1967 in support of Geering.

Gregor Smith's translation, but noted that later, when teaching in Wellington, he used Walter Kaufman's translation (Scribner, 1970).[9] Similarly, Bonhoeffer is another shared interest, Gregor Smith having published Bonhoeffer's *Letters and Papers from Prison* when at SCM Press. He made subsequent use of Bonhoeffer in *Secular Christianity*, while Geering came to focus on Bonhoeffer in 1975 and 1976. When I asked why this was, Geering replied (in reference to Bonhoeffer's *Letters and Papers from Prison*): "My interest in Bonhoeffer stemmed from the fact that he more than others recognized that we had entered the new secular age in which, as he said, 'People can no longer be religious in the way they used to be.'"[10]

Geering's concentrated reading of Bonhoeffer occurred almost a decade after the conservative challenge to Geering and his branding as a radical. In *Wrestling with God* he recalls that on his return to New Zealand in the early 1960s, while he was part of a clerical reading group in Dunedin, he read Bonhoeffer's *Letters and Papers from Prison* amongst other texts. "Strangely, I was not greatly influenced by Bonhoeffer at the time," he said, "feeling he had received such wide attention because he was a modern martyr. It was only later that I came to realise what a creative thinker he was."[11]

In the 1960s it was rather Geering's colleague, the systematic theologian Frank Nichol, who was, at that time, the deep reader and supporter of Bonhoeffer. A Barthian in his student days at Knox in the late 1940s, Nichol was strongly influenced by reading Donald Baillie's *God was in Christ* (1948)[12] and consequently, when awarded the Begg Travelling scholarship, studied under Bailie at the University of St. Andrews. It was here that he befriended the later death-of-God theologian William Hamilton, who introduced Nichol to the works of Dietrich Bonhoeffer. The result is that Nichol's theology came to combine the influences of Barth, Baillie, and Bonhoeffer, and the latter made him of concern to the conservative factions, both lay and clerical, in the church of the 1960s. As Geering has noted, he stoutly defended Nichol when Geering's future accuser Blaikie (a staunch Barthian) had attacked Nichol during a theological school for ministers. In turn Nichol was a strong and committed defender of Geering during his own period of controversy. I note this because Geering has admitted that he had done very little theological reading at the time, and, as revealed in the notebook, his engagement with what could be termed radical theology was extremely limited for a number of years.

The other visitor who was to have a significant impact on Geering's reading and thought was the dissident German Catholic Theologian Hans Küng. Soon after he arrived to teach at Victoria University, Geering chaired a sold-out public lecture by Küng at short notice. Having just read (in late 1971)[13] Küng's *Infallible?*, Geering discovered via the lecture that "it was clear he and I shared a common concern about the future of Christianity in the modern world."[14] As the notebook records, Küng subsequently became one of the writers Geering read and re-read.

Five additional writers sit centrally in Geering's thought: Martin Buber, Pierre Teilhard de Chardin, Paul Tillich, Carl Jung, and John Maquarrie. They not only were included in the courses Geering came to teach in religious studies but also provided the basis for his evolving thought. In particular, Buber, Jung, and Teilhard also provided a focus for many of Geering's continuing education lectures and other talks in the wider community and around the country. Geering helped make these three in particular popular amongst a community of liberals that was struggling with an increasingly conservative church, as well as amongst the growing body of post-church liberals. These are the writers to whom Geering returned time and time again. They informed his teaching, his public talks and, increasingly, his writing. They are accompanied by an ongoing concentration on two topics: books on humanism (Christian and otherwise) and books on religion and science. The focus on humanism is an influence arising partly from Ronald Gregor Smith while the interest in religion and science is understandable given Geering's background as a mathematician.

It is my sense that those two themes in particular really helped Geering have such an impact in and upon New Zealand. For it is not that New Zealand really seeks intellectually or theologically to be secular, but we do have a strong modern and rational interest in humanism and especially in taking science as the underlying *raison d'etre* for life and thought (as a type of rational common sense and non-abstract ethos). If these interests can be expressed clearly—as Geering is most able to do so—then we engage positively, which also helps explain why Geering has moved from being a dissident 'heretic' to being a central, officially rewarded public intellectual. His concern is always that of "how to be modern" and his reading was and is concentrated in the main upon various answers and engagements with that question.

Here it is also important to note that Geering was and in many ways continues to be opposed to what he has described as the abstract nature of much theology. Furthermore, Geering has himself also observed that it was not until 1963, whereupon he had been ordained for twenty-one years, that he "was forced to undertake my first piece of theological research."[15] Tellingly, this research came about in relation to questions of theology and science, for Geering had been asked to participate in a series of public lectures on the impact of Darwin's *On the Origin of Species*. Consequently, we can understand Geering's reading history as outlined in his notebook. His radical turn is not that of a theologian, nor even that of a theologian influenced strongly by comparative religion as, say, the influence of Eliade and Wach on Altizer, but rather that of a scientific mind venturing from Old Testament studies in search of truth, proof, and clarity. Geering's secular vision is likewise not so much that of a secular culture as that of a secular scientific culture. The difference is important to note. Geering has never made any pretension of the fact that his is foremost a scientific mind and outlook rather than one centrally informed by the arts, culture, and literature. Hence his "radical turn" of 1966–67 was a result of finally grappling with theology more directly. Therefore while Geering was certainly aware of the rise of radical theology in the United States, his own radical turn is not driven by similar concerns. Nor did he undertake anything more than a cursory reading in the death-of-God theology of the 1960s and its aftermath. Rather his turn is firstly that of an Old Testament scholar, influenced by Bultmann, reading New Testament scholarship.[a] It is also part of a "catch-up" of current writing on the relationship between theology/religion and science.

Geering, it can be argued, was not and never was, a theologian in the sense of one who centrally engages with theological texts and ideas. Rather, and this is no criticism, he is a religious thinker approaching the question of religion and modernity from the perspective of a scientific mind. His is not a mind of philosophical conjecture and debate, nor one seeking to make sense of intense personal religious and theological experience. It is rather a curious, inquisitive, sharp mind of the convert reading to seek evidence for a position of rational understanding of being Christian in the modern world.

Consequently, Geering's search for an understanding of Christianity is the reason why he first turns to reading on Christian origins and the resurrection in particular. Geering's engagement does not proceed first from a position of disciplinary expertise or, it could be argued, central interest. Rather, having written a clear assessment of how a modern Christian might—and perhaps should—think in a type of public sermon in *The Outlook*, Geering has to change tack, from expressing a position a clergyman might in a sermon to that of a church intellectual. The reading is, therefore, first undertaken to ensure he is sure in his self-defence. As he observed regarding his keeping the notebook, "The reason it started is that 1966 was the year my reading speed suddenly accelerated as a result of the controversy over my article in the resurrection. It

---

a. As he observed when I sent him the typed up list of his reading, "I do not know how I got through so many but I know that my reading speed trebled after the kerfuffle over my article on the resurrection of Jesus. You will notice that I read everything on the resurrection that I could find."
Email: Geering to Grimshaw, 26 February 2016.

made me fear my ignorance may have let me down on the topic of the resurrection. ... I read everything on the resurrection I could find and have a whole shelfful [of books] now. Strangely, today it all seems old hat."[16]

Geering's reading in religious studies proved influential in transitioning his thinking from that of a liberal to that which may truly be called radical. He had always, from his days as a theological student, expressed a strong interest in comparative religion, but until he took up the chair at Victoria University most of that interest had occurred within the wider study of the Old Testament. As his notebook shows, from 1971 Geering undertook a radical and wide-ranging crash-course in reading about non-Christian religions and also on issues in religious studies theory and methodology more generally. He also went back, repeatedly, to Schleiermacher and Nietzsche. He read not only to teach but also to understand—the topics and religions themselves as well as, crucially, how religion in the modern world operated and what it meant to be modern, both secular and religious. Reading with the underlying mind of a scientist and convert, Geering properly and truly self-radicalized in the 1970s. The number of books he read is impressive. In total, he noted reading nearly two thousand books, a number of them, of course, more than once over the years. The sheer volume of this concentrated, disciplined reading led to Geering's self-radicalization. But the transformation also occurred out of the task of communicating the fruits of his reading to undergraduates and a wider public who were, at the very least, in a critical, questioning position to mainstream, institutional Christianity. What is interesting from the notebook is how the Old Testament professor became centrally focussed on questions of Christian origins and identity, continuing throughout the notebook and into the present day.

It can be conjectured that if Geering had never read the proofs of Gregor Smith's *Secular Christianity* before being asked to write his Easter article for *The Outlook* in 1966, not only would there never have been a trial for heresy but Geering would have remained "an old fashioned liberal." Certainly it can be vouchsafed that his reading never would have reached such volume or breadth.

In conclusion, it is also worth mentioning that the record of his reading began when Geering was forty-seven years old and continued until he reached the age of seventy-two. Of course his reading and writing have only continued since then.

Appendix 1

Geering's Reading, 1965–1990

The following is a transcription of the reading journal kept by Geering, 1965–90. It contains the names of authors and books he read, as he read them. The number next to the year is how many books are recorded as being read that year.

Note: As this is a transcription, no attempt has been made to provide bibliographic details as none are recorded. Author names have been kept as he recorded them.

1965 (25)
J.B. Segal: *Hebrew Passover from the Earliest times to AD 70*.
T. K. Cheyne: *Founders of Old Testament Criticism: Biographical, Descriptive and Critical Studies*.
Denis Baly: *The Geography of the Bible*.
Stewart Perowne: *The Life and Times of Herod the Great*.
W. Robertson Smith: *The Old Testament in the Jewish Church: A Course of Lectures on Biblical Criticism*.
John Gray: *The Canaanites*.
E.A. Edgehill: *The Evidential Value of Prophecy*.
R.W. McNeur: *Space, Time, God*.
C. Westermann: *Essays on Old Testament Hermeneutics*.
Em. Anati: *Palestine before the Hebrews*.
Abraham Heschel: *The Prophets*.
J.N. Schofield: *Introducing Old Testament Theology*.
J.A.T. Robinson: *The New Reformation*.
A.S. Kapelrud: *The Ras Sharma Discoveries and the Old Testament* (recorded as *The Ras Sharma Discoveries—Masada—1955–56*).
Nelson Glueck: *The River Jordan*.
Hester Chapman: *Lady Jane Grey*.

Nineham, (ed): *The Church's Use of the Bible: Past and Present.*
R.E. Clements: *God and Temple.*
Hester Chapman: *Mary II, Queen of England.*
J. Jeremias: *The Central Message of the New Testament.*
F.C. Grant: *How to Read the Bible.*
R.C. Dentan: *Preface to Old Testament Theology.*
A.R. Johnson: *The One and the Many in the Israelite Conception of God.*
A.B. Starrat: *The Real God.*
F.F. Bruce (ed): *Promise and Fulfilment.*

1966 (61)
K. Slack: *The British Churches Today.*
J. Henderson: *Ratana. The Man, The Church, The Movement.*
P. Tillich: *Ultimate Concern.*
J.M. Holt: *The Patriarchs of Israel.*
P. Tillich: *Christianity and the Encounter of World Religions.*
C.J. Gadd: *The Dynasty of Agade and the Gutian Invasion.*
F.H. Stubbings: *Secular Christianity.*
Isaac Levy: *The Synagogue.*
H.J. Schoeps: *The Jewish-Christian Argument.*
Werner Foerster: *Palestinian Judaism in New Testament Times.*
J.R. Porter: *Moses and Monarchy.*
C. von Weizsacker: *The Relevance of Science: Creation and Cosmogony.*
James Barr: *Old and New in Interpretation: A Study of the Two Testaments.*
David Jenkins: *A Guide to the Debate About God.*
E.O. James: *The Nature and Function of Priesthood.*
R. de Vaux: *Studies in Old Testament Sacrifice.*
J.B. Lightfoot et al.: *Excluded Books of the New Testament.*
B.F. Westcott: *The Gospel of the Resurrection.*
B.F. Westcott: *The Revelation of the Risen Lord.*
W. Milligan: *The Resurrection of Our Lord.*
James Denney: *Jesus and His Gospel. Christianity Justified in the Mind of Christ.*
K. Lake: *Historical Evidence for the Resurrection of Jesus Christ.*
P. Gardener-Smith: *The Narratives of the Resurrection.*
John Knox: *The Churches and the Reality of Christ.*
Hans Grass: *Ostergeschchen und Osterberichte.*
R. Marten-Achard: *From Death to Life: A Study of the Development of the Resurrection in the Old Testament.*

Appendix 1: Geering's Reading 137

Colin Williams: *Faith in a Secular Age.*
A. Richardson (ed): *Four Anchors from the Stern.*
L. Newbiggin: *Honest Religion for the Secular Man.*
R. Bultmann: *New Testament Theology*, vol. 1.
R. Bultmann: *New Testament Theology*, vol. 2.
D.E. Newnham et al: *Historicity and Chronology in the New Testament.*
F.C. Happold: *Religious Faith and Twentieth Century Man.*
L. Hodgson: *The Doctrine of the Trinity.*
N. Smart: *Philosophers and Religious Truth.*
P. Tillich: *The Courage to Be.*
Edgar Jones: *The Triumph of Job.*
Roy A. Stewart: *Rabbinic Theology: An Introductory Study.*
R.M. Grant: *The Interpretation of the Bible.*
R. Bultmann: *Kergyma and Myth.*
James McLeman: *Resurrection: Then and Now.*
W. Hordern: *Speaking of God.*
H. Berkhof: *Christ the Meaning of History.*
A. Harnack: *What Is Christianity?*
W.A. Whitehouse: *Christian Faith and the Scientific Attitude.*
C.F. Von Weizsacker: *The History of Nature.*
R.E. Clements: *Prophecy and Covenant.*
G. von Rad: *The Problem of the Hexateuch, and Other Essays.*
W. Kunneth: *The Theology of the Resurrection.*
John Dillenberger: *Protestant Thought and Natural Science.*
H.C. Yee & F.W. Young: *The Living World of the New Testament.*
John McIntyre: *The Shape of Christology.*
Morton Scott Enslin: *Christian Beginnings Parts I & II.*
Thomas W. Ogletree: *The 'Death of God' Controversy.*
John McIntyre: *The Christian Doctrine of History.*
H. Anderson: *Jesus and Christian Origins.*
Harvey Cox: *The Secular City.*
F. Gerald Downing: *Has Christianity a Revelation?*
James Barr: *Biblical Words for Time.*
G.W. Anderson: *The History and Religion of Israel.*
A.E. Taylor: *Does God Exist?*

1967 (82)
A. Richardson: *Christian Apologetics.*
N. Smart: *World Religions: A Dialogue.*
John Knox: *The Church and the Reality of Christ.*

Teilhard de Chardin: *The Phenomenology of Man.*
H. Montefiore: *Truth to Tell.*
C. Dawson: *Religion and Culture.*
A. Hanson (ed): *Vindications.*
Alan Isaacs: *The Survival of God in the Scientific Age.*
W. Wightman: *The Growth of Scientific Ideas.*
E. Lampe & D.M. McKinnon: *The Resurrection: A Dialogue Arising from Broadcasts.*
H.J. Kraus: *Worship in Israel.*
A. Richardson: *Religion in Contemporary Debate.*
R. Bultmann: *Jesus Christ and Mythology.*
D.E. Nineham: *A New Way of Looking at the Gospels.*
Joel Carmichael: *The Death of Jesus.*
D. Bonhoeffer: *The Cost of Discipleship.*
J. Haroutunian: *God With Us: A Theology of Transpersonal Life.*
S.P.C.K. (no. 3): *The Miracles and the Resurrection.*
John Macquarrie: *Principles of Christian Theology.*
A. van Leuven: *Christianity and World History.*
J. Weiss: *Earliest Christianity*, vol. 1.
G.F. Moore: *Judaism*, vol. 1.
James Martin: *Did Jesus Rise from the Dead?*
Daniel Callahan: *Honesty In The Church.*
Daniel Jenkins: *Beyond Religion: The Truth and Error in "Religionless Christianity".*
G.P. Fisher: *History of Christian Doctrine.*
G. von Rad: *Old Testament Theology*, vol. 2.
A. Alt: *Essays on Old Testament History and Religion.*
K. Kenyon: *Archaeology in the Holy Land.*
Gordon Childe: *What Happened in History.*
Robert Aron: *The God of the Beginnings.*
Stephen Neill: *The Interpretation of the New Testament 1861–1961.*
H. von Camperhousen: *The Virgin Birth in the Theology of the Ancient Church.*
Paul Tillich: *The Eternal Now.*
M. Unamuno: *The Tragic Sense of Life.*
G. Bornkamm: *Jesus of Nazareth.*
John Knox: *Myth and Truth.*
J.H. Plumb: *The Penguin Book of the Renaissance.*
J.A. Coleman: *Relativity for the Layman.*
W.H. Thorpe: *Science, Man and Morals.*

Appendix 1: Geering's Reading

Gabriel Vahanian: *Wait Without Idols.*
H.H. Farmer: *Towards Belief in God.*
N. Micklem: *A Religion for Agnostics.*
Paul Tillich: *The Shaking of the Foundations.*
T. Francis Glasson: *Greek Influence in Jewish Eschatology.*
Evode Beaucamp: *The Bible and the Universe: Israel and the Theology of History.*
R.P.C. Hanson (ed): *Difficulties for Christian Belief.*
James McLeman: *Jesus in Our Time.*
Mircea Eliade: *The Myth of the Eternal Return.*
Nels. F.S. Ferre: *The Living God of Nowhere and Nothing.*
T.J.J. Altizer & W. Hamilton: *Radical Theology and the Death of God.*
W.R. Matthews: *The Hope of Immortality.*
J.A.T. Robinson: *Jesus and His Coming.*
J.S. Habgood: *Religion and Science.*
R. Gregor Smith (ed): *World Come of Age.*
John Macquarrie: *God-Talk.*
J.M. Robinson, J.B. Cobb (ed): *The New Hermeneutic.*
J.J. Stamm, M.E. Andrew: *The Ten Commandments in Recent Research.*
Amos Wilder: *New Testament Faith for Today*
H.H. Rex: *Did Jesus Rise from the Dead?*
Harvey Cox: *God's Revelation and Man's Responsibility.*
Daniel Callahan (ed): *The Secular City Debate.*
H.J. Schultz: *Conversion to the World.*
David E. Jenkins: *The Glory of Man.*
John Knox: *The Humanity and Divinity of Christ.*
Jürgen Moltmann: *Theology of Hope.*
Dean Pearman: *Frontline Theology.*
Neville Clark: *Interpreting the Resurrection.*
Gerhard Ebeling: *God and Word.*
S.H. Hooke: *The Resurrection of Christ.*
H.D.A. Major: *A Resurrection of Relics: A Modern Churchman's Defence in a Recent Charge of Heresy.*
Erich Fromm: *You Shall Be As Gods.*
John McIntyre: *On the Love of God.*
Charles Davis: *God's Grace in History.*
J.G. Davies: *Dialogue with the World.*
J. Weiss: *Earliest Christianity*, vol. 2.
Samuel Butler: *The Fair Haven.*
J.A.T. Robinson: *Exploration into God.*

Arnold E. Loen: *Secularization: Science without God?*
John Bright: *The Authority of the Old Testament.*
Hoskyns & Davey: *The Riddle of the New Testament.*
Earl H. Brill: *Sex Is Dead and Other Post-mortems.*

1968 (115)
Ian G. Barbour: *Issues in Science and Religion.*
H.H. Rowley: *Worship in Ancient Israel: Its Forms and Meaning.*
James Mitchell (ed): *The God I Want.*
Gerhard Ebeling: *Word and Faith.*
Murray Newman: *The People of the Covenant.*
Peter Hamilton: *The Living God and the Modern World.*
F.C. Grant: *A Introduction to New Testament Thought.*
F.L. Boschke: *Creation Still Goes On.*
John H. Otwell: *A New Approach to the New Testament.*
J.A. Schep: *The Nature of the Resurrection Body.*
Norman Pittenger: *God in Process.*
Charles Davis: *A Question of Conscience.*
G. von Rad: *Deuteronomy.*
Walter Beyerlin: *Origins and History of the Oldest Sinaitic Traditions.*
W.F. Albright: *New Horizons in Biblical Research.*
Th. C. Vriezen: *The Religion of Ancient Israel.*
Kathleen Kenyon: *Amorites and Canaanites.*
Grahame Clark: *World Prehistory.*
Errol E. Harris: *The Foundations of Metaphysics in Science.*
John C. Trevor: *The Untold Story of Qumran.*
Eric Berne: *The Games People Play.*
Christopher Dawson: *Religion and the Rise of Western Culture.*
Christopher Dawson: *The Dynamics of World History.*
J. Lindblom: *Prophecy in Ancient Israel.*
G.H. Shriver: *American Religious Heretics: Formal and Informal Trials in American Protestantism.*
T.S. Kuhn: *The Structure of Scientific Revolutions.*
Sebastian Moore: *God Is a New Language.*
Otto Betz: *What Do We know about Jesus?*
Schubert Ogden: *The Reality of God.*
F.G. Healey (ed): *Prospect for Theology: Essays in Honour of H.H. Farmer.*
W.G. Williams: *Archaeology in Biblical Research.*
Herbert W. Richardson: *Theology For A New World.*

Appendix 1: Geering's Reading

John Knox: *The Death of Christ: The Cross in New Testament History and Faith.*
Rollo May: *Man's Search for Himself.*
B. Farrington: *Greek Science.*
H.H. Rowley: *From Moses to Qumran.*
C.G. Starr: *A History of the Ancient World.*
James Kavanaugh: *A Modern Priest Looks at His Outdated Church.*
H. Holmes Hartshorne: *The Faith to Doubt.*
Maurice Goguel: *Jesus and The Origins of Christianity*, vol. 1.
John B. Cobb: *A Christian Natural Theology.*
Paul Tillich: *On The Boundary.*
Michael Green: *Man Alive.*
C.F.D. Moule (ed): *The Significance of the Message of the Resurrection for Faith in Jesus Christ.*
K.H. Miskotte: *When the Gods Are Silent.*
Ian Ramsay: *Religious Language.*
Bernard Basset: *We Agnostics: On the Tightrope to Eternity.*
A. Flew & A. MacIntyre (ed): *New Essays in Philosophical Theology.*
Richard R. Niebuhr: *Resurrection and Historical Reason.*
Dietrich Bonhoeffer: *No Rusty Swords.*
Peter Munz: *Problems of Religious Knowledge.*
Hans von Balthasar: *Who Is a Christian?*
Charles Gore: *Belief in God.*
Paul Tillich: *Perspectives on 19th and 20th Century Protestant Theology.*
R.M. Grant: *The Formation of the New Testament.*
F. Schleiermacher: *The Christian Faith.*
H.R. McIntosh: *Types of Modern Theology.*
M. Goguel: *Jesus and The Origins of Christianity*, vol. 2.
Georges Roux: *Ancient Iraq.*
D.S. Russell: *The Method and the Message of Jewish Apocalyptic.*
Karl Barth: *A Shorter Commentary on Romans.*
A.N. Whitehead: *Science and the Modern World.*
A.N. Whitehead: *Religion in the Making.*
W. Eichrodt: *Man in the Old Testament.*
Samuel H. Miller: *Man the Believer.*
Carl E. Braaten: *History and Hermeneutics.*
Martin Noth: *The Old Testament World.*
Ludwig Feuerbach: *Lectures on the Essence of Religion.*
Christopher Dawson: *The Formation of Christendom.*
W. Stringfellow & A. Towne: *The Bishop Pike Affair.*

Ved Mehta: *The New Theologian.*
Bryan Wilson: *Religion in Secular Society.*
G.B. Shaw: *Shaw on Religion.*
Paul Tillich: *A History of Christian Thought.*
John Macquarrie: *God and Secularity.*
Peter L. Berger: *The Noise of Solemn Assemblies: Christian Commitment and the Religious Establishment in America.*
Paul Tillich: *Systematic Theology*, vol. 1.
Thomas McPherson: *The Philosophy of Religion.*
Paul Tillich: *Systematic Theology*, vol. 2.
Gabriel Vahanian: *The Death of God.*
Xavier Leon-Dufour: *The Gospels and the Jesus of History.*
Marcus Aurelius: *Meditations.*
Lucretius: *The Nature of the Universe.*
John J. Vincent: *Secular Christ.*
M.A. Beck: *A Short History of Israel.*
W.F. Albright: *History, Archaeology and Christian Humanism.*
E. M. Blaiklock: *Layman's Answer.*
Austin Farrer: *A Science of God?*
Joseph Fletcher: *Situation Ethics.*
E.F. Scott: *The Fourth Gospel.*
Harvey Cox (ed): *The Situation Ethics Debate.*
Christopher Dawson: *The Making of Europe.*
F. Gerald Downing: *A Man for Us and a God for Us.*
Stanley Frost: *Patriarchs and Prophets*
Henry Chadwick: *The Early Church.*
Martin Noth: *The Laws in the Pentateuch and Other Essays.*
Maurice Goguel: *The Birth of Christianity.*
A.M. Ramsey: *Sacred and Secular.*
Descartes: *Discourse on Method.*
S.P.C.K. (no. 6): *Historicity and Chronology in the New Testament.*
Yvonne Lubboch: *Return to Belief.*
H. Anderson (ed): *The New Testament in Historical and Contemporary Perspective.*
Leslie Dewart: *The Future of Belief.*
G. Rattray Taylor: *The Biological Time-bomb.*
W. Pannenberg: *Jesus—God and Man.*
William Hamilton: *The New Essence of Christianity.*
Johannes Munck: *Paul and the Salvation of Mankind.*
G.R. Cragg: *From Puritanism to the Age of Reason.*

Norman Pittenger: *God's Way with Men.*
M. Sullivan: *A Funny Thing Happened on the Way to St. Paul's.*
B.M.G. Reardon: *Religious Thought in the Nineteenth Century.*
Leslie Paul: *The Death and Resurrection of the Church.*
G. Ernest Wright: *Shechem: The Biography of a Biblical City.*
Bertrand Russell: *Autobiography*, vol. 1.
Bertrand Russell: *Autobiography*, vol. 2.

1969 (87)
John B. Cobb: *The Structure of Christian Existence.*
R. Gregor Smith: *The Free Man.*
F.C. Grant: *The Gospels.*
Julian Huxley: *Essays of a Humanist.*
Ronald Clements: *God's Chosen People.*
N. W. Porteous: *Living the Mystery.*
J.V. Langmead Casserley: *Toward a Theology of History.*
Lee Belford: *Introduction to Judaism.*
Bernard Basset: *Born for Friendship: The Spirit of Sir Thomas More.*
J. Bronowski: *Science and Human Values.*
Sabatino Moscati: *The Face of the Ancient Orient.*
Martin Thornton: *The Rock and the River.*
Christoph F. Barth: *Introduction to the Psalms.*
Paul Tillich: *Systematic Theology*, vol. 3.
H. von Camperhausen: *The Events of Easter and the Empty Tomb.*
Helmer Ringgren: *Israelite Religion.*
N.F.F. Furniss: *The Fundamentalist Controversy 1918–1931.*
P.R. Ackroyd: *Exile and Restoration.*
S. Toulmin & J. Goodfield: *The Fabric of the Heavens: The Development of Astronomy and Dynamics.*
Paul van Buren: *Theological Explorations.*
W. Russell Hindmarsh: *Science and Faith.*
Karl Marx: *The Communist Manifesto.*
O. Eissfeldt: *The Hebrew Kingdom.*
R.H. Lightfoot: *The Gospel Message of St. Mark.*
Roger L. Shinn: *Man: The New Humanism.*
W & L. Pelz: *God Is No More.*
Teilhard de Chardin: *Science and Christ.*
The Biblical Archaeological Reader 2.
T.W. Manson: *The Servant Messiah.*
Paul Hessert: *Christian Life.*

W.F. Adeney: *The Greek and the Eastern Churches.*
Ronald Clements: *Abraham and David.*
Eugene A. Nida: *Religion across Cultures: A Study in the Communication of the Christian Faith.*
Raymond E. Brown: *Jesus, God and Man.*
G.H. Boobyer: *St. Mark and the Transfiguration Story.*
F. Nielson: *The Ten Commandments: New Perspectives.*
N.K. Sandars: *The Epic of Gilgamesh.*
Martin Buber: *The Kingship of God.*
C.F.D. Moule: *The Phenomenon of the New Testament.*
Albert. H. Van den Heuvel: *The Humiliation of the Church.*
Ronald Gregor Smith: *The Free Man.*
Ronald Gregor Smith: *Secular Christianity.*
Peter L. Berger: *Invitation to Sociology.*
Stewart Lawton: *Truth That Compelled.*
Phillipe Wolff: *The Awakening of Europe.*
S. Toulmin & J. Goodfield: *The Discovery of Time.*
H. Ringgren: *Sacrifice in the Bible.*
Ian G. Barbour (ed): *Science and Religion.*
M. Goldsmith & A. MacKay (ed): *The Science of Science. Society in the Technological Age.*
R.S. Lee: *Freud and Christianity.*
H.J. Blackham: *Humanism.*
N.H. Snaith: *The Book of Job.*
Samuel Sandmel: *Old Testament Issues.*
Jaroslav Pelikan: *The Shape of Death.*
R.N. Whybray: *The Succession Narrative.*
Donald Hudson: *Ludwig Wittgenstein.*
J.M. Morrison: *Honesty & God.*
W.F. Albright: *Yahweh and the Gods of Canaan.*
C.F. Schaeffer: *The Cuneiform Texts of Ras Shamra-Ugarit.*
Robert C. Denton: *The Knowledge of God in Israel.*
F.R. Barry: *Secular and Supernatural.*
F.C. Happold: *The Journey Inwards: A Simple Introduction to the Practice of Contemplative Meditation by Normal People.*
J. Bronowski & Bruce Mazlish: *The Western Intellectual Tradition: From Leonardo to Hegel.*
R.H. Charles (ed): *The Book of Enoch.*
Hans-Joachim Schoeps: *Jewish Christianity.*
Ian Breward: *Authority and Freedom.*

Heinz Zahrnt: *The Question of God: Protestant Theology in the Twentieth Century.*
F. Hahn, W. Lohff, G. Bornkamm: *What Can We Know about Jesus?*
J.A.T. Robinson: *On Being the Church in the World.*
M. De la Bedoyere (ed): *The Future of Catholic Christianity.*
Bertrand Russell: *Autobiography*, vol. 3.
The Bible Speaks Again: A Guide from Holland.
H. Frankfort: *The Intellectual Adventure of Ancient Man: An Essay on Speculative Thought in the Ancient Near East.*
A.J. Ayer (ed): *The Humanist Outlook.*
D.G. Bloesch: *The Christian Witness in a Secular Age.*
C.H.C. MacGregor & A.C. Purdy: *Jew and Greek, Tutors unto Christ. The Jewish and Hellenistic Background of the New Testament.*
Neville Clark: *Interpreting the Resurrection.*
Willi Marxsen: *Introduction to the New Testament.*
R. Martin-Achard: *From Death to Life: A Study of the Doctrine of the Resurrection in the Old Testament.*
Samuel Sandmel: *The First Christian Century in Judaism and Christianity.*
R.H. Charles: *Eschatology.*
Stephen G. Mackie: *Patterns of Ministry.*
Hugh Montefiore: *The Question Mark.*
David L. Edwards: *The Last Things Now.*
J.A.T. Robinson: *In the End, God: A Study of the Christian Doctrine of the Last Things.*
Desmond Morris: *The Naked Ape.*
E. Kasemann: *Jesus Means Freedom.*

1970 (72)
Bertrand Russell: *A History of Western Philosophy.*
Ernst Benz: *Evolution and Christian Hope: Man's Concept of the Future from the*
Church Fathers to Teilhard de Chardin.
K. Stendahl (ed): *Immortality and Resurrection.*
C.V. Pilcher: *The Hereafter in Jewish and Christian Thought.*
John Knox: *Jesus, Lord and Christ.*
C.F. Evans: *Resurrection and the New Testament.*
John Hinton: *Dying.*
M.E. Dahl: *The Resurrection of the Body.*
James Orr: *The Resurrection of Jesus.*

G.W.H. Lampe & D.M. MacKinnon: *The Resurrection: A Dialogue.*
W. Nicholls: *Systematic & Philosophical Theology.*
J.N.D. Kelly: *Early Christian Doctrines.*
David Martin: *The Religious and the Secular.*
J.M. Robinson & J.B. Cobb (ed): *Theology as History.*
W.J. Sparrow Simpson: *The Resurrection and Modern Thought.*
James Mellart: *Earliest Civilizations of the Near East.*
M.E.L. Mallowan: *Early Mesopotamia and Iran.*
David E. Jenkins: *Living with Questions.*
J.I. Durham & R.J. Porter (ed): *Proclamation and Presence.*
David L. Edwards: *Religion and Change.*
Claus Westermann: *Das Alte Testament und Jesus Christus.*
Norman Hampson: *The Enlightenment.*
Basil Willey: *Religion Today.*
Peter L. Berger: *The Social Reality of Religion.*
S.H. Hooke (ed): *Myth and Ritual.*
S.I. Curtiss: *Primitive Semitic Religion Today.*
Alisdair Macintyre: *Marxism and Christianity.*
Edward Schillebeeckx: *The Concept of Truth and Theological Renewal.*
M. Staniforth: *Early Christian Writings.*
G.R. Dunstan: *The Sacred Ministry.*
F.W.R. Nichol: *Jesus Today.*
Edmund Leach: *Genesis as Myth.*
L.J.J. Nye: *Man the Fool.*
T.H. Gaster: *The Scriptures of the Dead Sea Sect.*
John Bowden: *Who Is a Christian?*
Martin E. Marty: *The Modern Schism.*
Dietrich Bonhoeffer: *The Way to Freedom.*
Donald MacKinnon: *Borderlands of Theology.*
Donald Evans: *Communist Faith and the Christian Faith.*
M. Holmes Hartshorne: *The Faith to Doubt.*
Homer: *Odyssey.*
John Bowden: *What about the Old Testament?*
A.O. Dyson: *Who Is Jesus Christ?*
J. Austin Baker: *The Foolishness of God.*
Augustine: *Confessions.*
James A. Coleman: *Relativity for the Layman.*
Ronald Gregor Smith: *The Doctrine of God.*
Robert Mullen: *The Mormons.*
Tertullian: *The Resurrection of the Body.*

Appendix 1: Geering's Reading

James L. Map: *Hosea.*
R.G. Collingwood: *An Autobiography.*
C.H. Dodd: *Interpretation of the Fourth Gospel.*
Norman Pittenger: *Christology Reconsidered.*
Thomas P. Collins: *The Risen Christ in the Fathers of the Church.*
Goodspeed & Grant: *A History of Early Christian Literature.*
Robert J. Blaikie: *Secular Christianity and the God Who Acts.*
Willi Marxsen: *The Resurrection of Jesus of Nazareth.*
John Allegro: *The Sacred Mushroom and the Cross.*
J.A. Wharton: *The Occasion of the Word of God. An Unguarded Essay on the Character of the Old Testament as the Memory of God's Story with Israel.*
J.A.T. Robinson: *But That I Can't Believe!*
S.P.C.K. (no. 13): *The Christian Hope.*
Arnold Toynbee etc: *Man's Concern with Death.*
R. Bultmann etc: *Life and Death.*
W. Hordern: *New Directions in Theology Today*, vol. 1.
R.G. Jones & A.J. Wesson: *Towards a Radical Church.*
G.E. Wright: *The Old Testament and Theology.*
T.W. Ogletree (ed): *Openings for Marxist-Christian Dialogue.*
J.D. Bernal: *Science in History*, vol. 1.
John Knox: *Limits of Unbelief.*
Claus Westermann: *The Old Testament and Jesus Christ.*
M.J. Savage: *Haddon of Glen Leith.*
J.D. Bernal: *Science in History*, vol. 2.
J.D. Bernal: *Science in History*, vol. 3.

1971 (83)
G.E. Wright: *The Old Testament and Theology.*
Juan Mascaro: *The Bhagavad Gita.*
John Hick: *The Philosophy of Religion.*
H.N Wieman: *Religious Inquiry.*
J.D. Bernal: *Science in History*, vol. 4.
Peter L. Berger: *The Sacred Canopy.*
John Gray: *Near Eastern Mythology.*
Roger Garaudy: *Marxism in the Twentieth Century.*
Norman Pittenger: *The Last Things in Process Perspective.*
C. Roth: *A Short History of the Jewish People.*
D.Z. Phillips: *Death and Immortality.*
R. Swinburne: *The Concept of Miracle.*

Mircea Eliade: *Myth and Reality.*
Vernon Pratt: *Religion and Secularization.*
Trevor Ling: *A History of Religion East and West.*
M. Peissel: *Mustang: A Lost Tibetan Kingdom.*
C. Dawson: *The Crisis of Western Education.*
K.M. Sen: *Hinduism.*
Ewing Stevens: *Sunday alive: a story of youth and the Church.*
W.P. Morrell: *The University of Otago.*
E.A. Burtt: *Man Seeks the Divine: Study of the History and Comparison of Religions.*
John A. Hutchison: *Paths of Faith.*
Ninian Smart: *Secular Education and the Logic of Religion.*
Ninian Smart: *The Philosophy of Religion.*
Alan W. Watts: *The Way of Zen.*
A.K. Coomaraswamy: *Buddha and the Gospel of Buddhism.*
E. Conze: *Buddhism, its Essence and Development.*
R.C. Zaehnev: *Concordant Discord.*
Sam Keen: *To a Dancing God.*
H. von Glasenapp: *Buddhism, a Non-theistic Religion.*
A.J. Bahm: *Philosophy of the Buddha.*
Eric Vogelin: *Order and History,* vol. 1. *Israel and Revelation.*
Paul Tillich: *What Is Religion?*
Matthew Arnold: *Literature and Dogma.*
J.C. Cooper: *The Roots of the Radical Theology.*
E.O. James: *Christianity and Other Religions.*
C. Humphreys: *Buddhism.*
John Blofeld: *The Wheel of Life.*
D.M. High (ed): *New Essays on Religious Language.*
D.K. Swearer: *Buddhism in Transition.*
Louis Jacobs: *We Have Reason to Believe.*
E.K. Nottingham: *Religion and Society.*
Joachim Wach: *The Comparative Study of Religions.*
F.J. Streng: *Understanding Religious Man.*
Bryan Wilson (ed): *Rationality.*
S. Radhakrishnan: *The Principal Upanishads.*
Juan Mascaro: *The Upanishads.*
S.C. Thakur: *Christian and Hindu Ethics.*
H.G. Sarwar: *Muhammad, the Holy Prophet.*
Ninian Smart: *The Religious Experience of Mankind.*
A.L. Basham: *The Wonder That Was India.*

Appendix 1: Geering's Reading   149

D.S. Sharma: *Hinduism through the Ages.*
H.J. Blackham: *Objections of Humanism.*
S. Radhakrishnan: *The Hindu View of Life.*
A.J. Arberry (trans): *The Doctrine of the Sufis.*
W.M. Watt (trans): *The Faith and Practice of Al-Ghazali.*
C. Dawson: *The Historic Reality of Christian Culture.*
R.A. Nicholson: *The Mystics of Islam.*
Joseph Blau: *Modern Varieties of Judaism.*
W.C. Smith: *The Meaning and End of Religion.*
Peter L. Berger: *A Rumour of Angels.*
Hans Küng: *Infallible? An Enquiry.*
A.J. Arberry: *Sufism, An Account of the Mystics of Islam.*
Tor Andrae: *Mohammed, the Man and His Faith.*
Arthur F. Wright: *Buddhism in Chinese History.*
Fazlur Rahman: *Islam.*
Harbans Singh: *Guru Nanak and the Origins of the Sikh Faith.*
R.F. Spencer: *Religion and Change in Contemporary Asia.*
John Blofeld: *Mahayana Buddhism in South East Asia.*
Richard H. Robinson: *The Buddhist Religion.*
James R. Ware (trans): *The Sayings of Confucius.*
M. Gandhi: *An Autobiography.*
Alistair Kee: *The Way of Transcendence.*
H.G. Creel: *Confucius and the Chinese Way.*
J.C.H. Wu (trans): *Tao Teh Ching.*
Howard Smith: *Chinese Religions.*
N.G. Munro: *Ainu, Creed and Cult.*
H. Byron Earhart: *Japanese Religion: Unity and Diversity.*
Thomas Fawcett: *The Symbolic Language of Religion.*
G.B. Offner: *Modern Japanese Religions.*
B.B. Ahmad: *Ahmadiyya Movement.*
W. Pannenberg: *What Is Man?*
Martin C. D'Arcy: *Humanism and Christianity.*

1972 (113)
Frederick Ferre: *Language, Logic and God.*
Allama M. Iqbal: *The Reconstruction of Religious Thought in Islam.*
Robert B. Ekuall: *Religious Observances in Tibet.*
John D. Gay: *The Geography of Religion in England.*
J.B. Chethimattan: *Patterns of Indian Thought.*
M. Ono: *Shinto: The Kami Way.*

J. Bowden: *A Reader in Contemporary Theology.*
K.W. Morgan (ed): *The Religion of the Hindus.*
C.H. Hamilton (ed): *Buddhism. A Religion of Infinite Compassion.*
Stuart Piggott: *Prehistoric India.*
R. Duff: *The Ramayana.*
W.E. Soothill: *The Lotus of the Wonderful Law.*
D.T. Suzuki: *The Training of the Zen Buddhist Monk.*
Jacob Needleman: *The New Religions.*
D.C. Holtom: *Modern Japan and Shinto Nationalism.*
D.T. Suzuki: *The Essence of Buddhism.*
John B. Magee: *Religion and Modern Man.*
Jan de Vries: *The Study of Religion.*
Mircea Eliade: *The Quest: History and Meaning in Religion.*
Ernst Cassirer: *Language and Myth.*
Langdon Gilkey: *Religion and the Scientific Future.*
H.D. Lewis & R.H. Slater: *The Study of Religions.*
Joseph Campbell (ed): *Myths, Dreams and Reality.*
M. Eliade & J.M. Kitagawa (ed): *The History of Religions: Essays in Methodology.*
F.P. Dunne (ed): *The World Religions Speak.*
John Morton: *Man, Science and God.*
E. Schweitzer: *Jesus.*
Masaharu Anesaki: *History of Japanese Religion.*
W. Norman Brown: *Man in the Universe.*
S. Radhakrishnan: *The Hindu View of Life.*
J.M. Kitagawa (ed): *History of Religions: Essays on the Problem of Understanding.*
Charles Davis: *Christ and the World Religions.*
M.P. Pandit: *The Upanishads.*
J. Hinnells (ed): *Comparative Religion in Education.*
C.H. Dodd: *The Founder of Christianity.*
Winston L. King: *Buddhism and Christianity.*
M. Isherwood: *Searching for Meaning.*
D.T. Suzuki: *Outlines of Mahayana Buddhism.*
Brevard S. Childs: *Biblical Theology in Crisis.*
J.M. Kitagawa: *Modern Trends in World Religions.*
G.W.H. Lampe: *The Phenomenon of Christian Belief.*
Louis Renou: *Religions of Ancient India.*
J.N. Farquhar: *Modern Religious Movements in India.*

Appendix 1: Geering's Reading

Gopal Singh: *The Religion of the Sikhs.*
Lawrence G. Thompson: *Chinese Religion: An Introduction.*
Will Herberg: *Judaism and Modern Man.*
Fred Hoyle: *The New Face of Science.*
Robert N. Bellah: *Beyond Belief.*
Manfred Weippert: *The Settlement of Israelite Tribes in Palestine.*
A.T. Welford: *Christianity. A Psychologist's Translation.*
Noah S. Branner: *Soka Gakkai.*
A.C. Bouquet: *Religious Experience: Its Nature, Types and Validity.*
Hans Küng: *Truthfulness, the Future of the Church.*
Hans Mol: *Christianity in Chains.*
Yu-Lan Fung: *A Short History of Chinese Philosophy.*
H.G. Creel: *Chinese Thought from Confucius to Mao Tse-Tung.*
J.M. Katagawa: *Religion in Japanese History.*
G.R. Urban (ed): *Can We Survive Our Future?*
Ichiro Hori: *Folk Religion in Japan.*
Dogen: *A Primer of Soto Zen.*
H. Neill McFarland: *The Rush Hour of the Gods.*
Ralph E. James: *The Concrete God.*
Altizer & Hamilton: *Radical Theology and the Death of God.*
J. Duchesne-Guillemin: *Zoroastriansim, Symbols and Values.*
F.G. Healy (ed): *Preface to Christian Studies.*
John Bowden: *Karl Barth.*
Jeffrey K. Hadden: *Religion in Radical Transition.*
H.A. Williams: *True Resurrection.*
Isidore Epstein: *Judaism.*
Jacob Neusner: *The Way of Torah.*
Nicolas Zernov: *Eastern Christendom.*
Johannes Weiss: *Jesus' Proclamation of the Kingdom of God.*
R.C. Zaehner: *The Dawn and Twilight of Zoroastrianism.*
Victor Frankl: *Man's Search for Meaning.*
Abraham Heschel: *Who Is Man?*
Jacob Neusner: *American Judaism.*
W.H. McLeod: *Guru Nanak and the Sikh Religion.*
R. Michaelsen: *The Study of Religion in American Universities.*
Thomas Luckmann: *The Invisible Religion.*
Robert D. Baird: *Category Formation and the History of Religions.*
R. Caporale (ed): *The Culture of Unbelief.*
K.W. Morgan (ed): *Islam. The Straight Path.*

Timothy Ware: *The Orthodox Church.*
P. Ramsey & J.F. Wilson (ed): *The Study of Religion in Colleges and Universities.*
Jan Milic Lochman: *Church in a Marxist Society.*
M. Chaning-Pearce: *Soren Kierkegaard: A Study.*
Abraham Cronbach: *Reform Movements in Judaism.*
Robert L. Wilken: *The Myth of Christian Beginnings.*
E.K. Nottingham: *Religion: A Sociological View.*
Robert Mullen: *The Mormons.*
E.E. Plowman: *The Jesus Movement.*
John Macquarrie: *Paths in Spirituality.*
David L. Edwards: *Religion and Change.*
M. Hayward (ed): *Religion and the Soviet State.*
Arnold Toynbee: *Change and Habit.*
A. Vidler (ed): *Objections to Christian Belief.*
Alvin Toffler: *Future Shock.*
T.R. Miles: *Religious Experience.*
E.J. Jurji: *Religious Pluralism and World Community.*
Paul van Buren: *The Edges of Language.*
J.B. Bury: *A History of Freedom of Thought.*
B.E. Meland: *The Secularization of Modern Cultures.*
A. Macintyre: *Secularization and Moral Change.*
D.L. Munby: *The Idea of a Secular Society.*
A.T. van Leeuwen: *Christianity in World History.*
W.C. Smith: *Islam in Modern History.*
L. Feuerbach: *The Essence of Christianity.*
S. Radhakrishnan: *Religion in a Changing World.*
A. Kloosterman: *Contemporary Catholicism.*
Patrick Masterson: *Atheism and Alienation.*
Wolfhart Pannenberg: *The Apostles Creed.*
K. Bliss: *The Future of Religion.*

1973 (122)
Martin E. Marty: *The Search for a Usable Future.*
Eric Lund (ed): *A History of European Ideas.*
Kenneth Morgan (ed): *The Path of the Buddha.*
Abraham Cronbach: *Judaism for Today.*
Jaroslav Pelikan: *The Christian Intellectual.*
Dean M. Kelley: *Why Conservative Churches Are Growing.*

Appendix 1: Geering's Reading

Georgia Harkness: *Women in Church and Society.*
F.C. Grant: *The Gospels: Their Origin and Growth.*
James Thrower: *A Short History of Western Atheism.*
Marty, Rosenberg and Greeley: *What Do We Believe? The Stance of Religion in America.*
Martin Noth: *A History of Pentateuchal Traditions.*
R.C. Zaehner: *Hinduism.*
Paul Younger: *Introduction to Indian Religious Thought.*
S.C. Leslie: *The Rift in Israel: Religious Authority and Secular Democracy.*
H.H. Price: *Essays in the Philosophy of Religion.*
G. Parrinder: *Upanishads, Gita and the Bible.*
H. Saddhatissa: *The Buddha's Way.*
J. Blenkinsoff: *Gibeon and Israel.*
E.M. Blaiklock (ed): *Why I am still a Christian.*
Helmut Hoffmann: *The Religion of Tibet.*
Shankara: *Crest—Jewel of Discrimination.*
H. Zimmer: *Philosophies of India.*
R.H. Fuller: *The Formation of the Resurrection Narratives.*
R.E. Whitson: *The Coming Convergence of World Religions.*
Julian Huxley: *Religion without Revelation.*
W.D. Dean: *Coming To: A Theology of Beauty.*
Edward L. Bode: *The First Easter Morning.*
Paul Tillich: *Christianity and the Encounter of the World Religions.*
A.F. Wright: *Buddhism in Chinese History.*
Martin Buber: *I and Thou.*
C.H. Dodd: *The Interpretation of the Fourth Gospel.*
Edward Caird: *Hegel.*
D.T. Suzuki: *Shir Buddhism.*
Ian G. Barbour: *Science and Religion.*
Marx & Engels: *On Religion.*
S. Freud: *The Future of an Illusion.*
G.J. Holyoake: *The Origin and Nature of Secularism.*
F. Nietzsche: *The Anti-Christ.*
Charles Boyall: *The Man for Others.*
G.W.F. Hegel: *Early Theological Writings.*
Ewing Stevens: *Jesus.*
John Hick: *Philosophy of Religion.*
Reimarus: *Fragments.*

David Martin: *A Sociology of English Religion.*
C.E.M Joad: *An Introduction to Modern Political Theory.*
A. Solzhenitsyn: *A Lenten Letter to Pimen, Patriarch of All Russia.*
J.C. Livingstone: *Modern Christian Thought.*
J.W. Parker (ed): *Essays and Reviews.*
E. Troeltsch: *The Absoluteness of Christianity.*
C.G. Jung: *Man and His Symbols.*
G. Murray: *The Five Stages of Greek Religion.*
M. Mead: *Twentieth Century Faith: Hope and Survival.*
George Widengren: *Mani and Manichaeism.*
Ormond Burton: *To Whom Shall We Go?*
George Tyrrell: *Christianity at the Cross-Roads.*
A. Harnack: *History of Dogma,* vol. 1.
W.C. Smith: *Islam in Modern History.*
H.A.R. Gibb: *Modern Trends in Islam.*
H.M. Ahmad: *Ahmadiyya Movement.*
Kenneth Cragg: *Counsels in Contemporary Islam.*
Jacob Neusner: *Judaism in the Secular Sage.*
W.H. van der Pol: *The End of Conventional Christianity.*
Roger Garaudy: *Marxism in the Twentieth Century.*
Will Herberg: *Protestant, Catholic, Jew.*
K.K. Aziz: *Ameer Ali: His life and work.*
Abd Assamii Misry: *Principles of Islam.*
J. Edgar Burns: *The Christian Buddhism of St John.*
Dag Hammarskjold: *Markings.*
M. Chaning-Pearce: *Soren Kierkegaard: A Study.*
Jacob Neusner: *American Judaism.*
W. Hamilton: *The New Essence of Christianity.*
P. van Buren: *The Secular Meaning of the Gospel.*
Joseph L. Blau: *Modern Varieties of Judaism.*
W. Berkowitz: *Ten Vital Jewish Issues.*
Simon Noveck: *Contemporary Jewish Thought.*
Hayyim Schauss: *Guide to Jewish Holy Days.*
J.A.T. Robinson: *The Human Face of God.*
Russell Aldwinckle: *Death in the Secular City.*
R.N. Bellah (ed): *Religion and Progress in Modern Asia.*
A.M. Greeley: *Religion in the Year 2000.*
M. Novak: *Belief and Unbelief.*
R.C. Zaehner: *Evolution in Religion: Study in Sri Aurobindo and Pierre Teilhard de Chardin.*

Appendix 1: Geering's Reading

Teilhard de Chardin: *Le Milieu Divin.*
N.M. Wildiers: *An Introduction to Teilhard de Chardin.*
Claude Cuenot: *Teilhard de Chardin.*
A.M. Greeley: *The Persistence of Religion.*
M. Novak: *Ascent of the Mountain, Flight of the Dove.*
Thubten Jigme Norbu: *Tibet. Its History, Religion and People.*
David Knowles: *Christian Monasticism.*
Paul Tillich: *The Future of Religions.*
Henri de Lubac: *Teilhard de Chardin: The Man and His Meaning.*
C.L. Manschreck: *Erosion of Authority.*
Don Cupitt: *Crisis of Moral Authority.*
H. Zimmer: *Myths and Symbols in Indian Art and Civilization.*
A. Hodes: *Martin Buber, an Intimate Portrait.*
Martin Buber: *Eclipse of God.*
Jacques Monod: *Chance and Necessity. An Essay on the Natural Philosophy of Modern Biology.*
W.H. Capps: *Ways of Understanding Religion.*
Vitezslav Gardavsky: *God Is Not Yet dead.*
T.I. Idinopulos: *The Erosion of Faith.*
Guy Swanson: *The Birth of the Gods.*
H. Gollwitzer: *The Christian Faith and the Marxist Criticism of Religion.*
Claude Cuenot: *Science and Faith in Teilhard de Chardin.*
Teilhard de Chardin: *The Phenomenon of Man.*
C.E. Raven: *Teilhard de Chardin: Scientist and Seer.*
Henri de Lubac: *The Eternal Feminine.*
Teilhard de Chardin: *Hymn of the Universe.*
A.A. Cohen: *Martin Buber.*
P.B. Medawar: *The Hope of Progress.*
T. Fawcett: *Hebrew Myth and Christian Gospels.*
L. Gilkey: *Naming the Whirlwind.*
Julian: *Revelations of Divine Light.*
T. Dobzhansky: *The Biology of Ultimate Concern.*
M. Buber: *I and Thou.*
M. Buber: *Daniel: Dialogues on Realization.*
E. Bentz: *Buddhism or Communism?*
M.L. Diamond: *Martin Buber: Jewish Existentialist.*
M. Buber: *Two Types of Faith.*
MacGregor and Morton: *The Structure of the Fourth Gospel.*
Paul Tillich: *My Search for Absolutes.*
Grete Schaeder: *The Hebrew Humanism of Martin Buber.*

1974 (88)
N. Anderson: *A Lawyer among the Theologians.*
Rissho-Kosei-Kai
G. Jackson: *People's Prison.*
A.M. Hunter: *According to John.*
H.J. Birx: *Pierre Teilhard de Chardin's Philosophy of Evolution.*
K. Barth: *The Humanity of God.*
P. Tillich: *The Courage to Be.*
Alan Watts: *The Temple of Konarak.*
Ninian Smart: *The Phenomenon of Religion.*
R. Otto: *The Idea of the Holy.*
R.M. Grant: *The Formation of the New Testament.*
B. Delfgaauw: *Evolution. The Theory of Teilhard de Chardin.*
Teilhard de Chardin: *The Future of Man.*
Teilhard de Chardin: *Man's Place in Nature.*
Teilhard de Chardin: *The Prayer of the Universe.*
R. Otto: *Religious Essays.*
Henri Bergson: *Creative Evolution.*
Teilhard de Chardin: *The Vision of the Past.*
Teilhard de Chardin: *The Phenomenon of Man.*
Raphael Patai: *Myth and Modern Man.*
N.M. Wilders: *An Introduction to Teilhard de Chardin.*
Michael Gough: *The Origins of Christian Art.*
Teilhard de Chardin: *Let Me Explain.*
Martin Buber: *Between Man and Man.*
Donald Wilber: *Persepolis.*
Gordon Kaufmann: *God the Problem.*
Martin Buber: *The Tales of Rabbi Nachman.*
Mircea Eliade: *Patterns in Comparative Religion.*
Helmer Ringgren: *Religions of the Ancient Near East.*
Martin Buber: *Hasidism and Modern Man.*
Teilhard de Chardin: *Human Energy.*
Martin Buber: *I and Thou.*
Martin Buber: *Paths in Utopia.*
Martin Buber: *Mamre.*
Geoffrey Parrinder: *The Indestructible Soul.*
Kenneth Morgan: *The Religion of the Hindus.*
M. Friedman: *Searching in the Syntax of Things.*
Sidney Spencer: *Mysticism in World Religions.*
Samuel Sandmel: *The Enjoyment of Scripture.*

Appendix 1: Geering's Reading

Paul Tillich: *Ultimate Concern.*
Paul Tillich: *The Courage to Be.*
A. Van Leeuwen: *Critique of Heaven.*
E. Lord & C. Bailey: *A Reader in Religious and Moral Education.*
Marcus Aurelius: *Meditations.*
Alastair Macleod: *Paul Tillich. An Essay on the Role of Ontology in his Philosophical Theology.*
D. Howard Smith: *Confucius.*
Christopher Evans: *Cults of Unreason.*
Paul Tillich: *The Courage to Be.*
F. Karl & L. Hamalian: *The Existential Imagination.*
A.D. Galloway: *Wolfhart Pannenberg.*
Sri Aurobindo: *The Human Cycle.*
J. Sanders: *The Fourth Gospel in the Early Church.*
Robert Tucker: *Philosophy and Myth in Karl Marx.*
William Nicholls: *Systematic and Philosophical Theology.*
Alan Watts: *The Joyous Cosmology.*
Ninian Smart: *The Science of Religion and the Sociology of Knowledge.*
D.H. von Daalen: *The Real Resurrection.*
Bernard Delfgaauw: *The Young Marx.*
David Hume: *On Religion.*
Samuel Sandmel: *The First Christian Century in Judaism and Christianity.*
D.T. Suzuki: *An Introduction to Zen Buddhism.*
F.F. Bruce: *Jesus and Christian Origins outside the New Testament.*
D.T. Suzuki: *The Zen Doctrine of No Mind.*
Marten Redeker: *Schleiermacher: Life and Thought.*
F.R.J. Verhoeven: *Islam.*
F.C. Happold: *Mysticism.*
W.M. Watt: *Muhammed at Mecca.*
F. Vallot (ed): *Human Rights.*
F. Nietzsche: *Twilight of the Idols.*
Trevor Ling: *The Buddha.*
C. Cameron (ed): *Who is Guru Mahraj Ji?*
F. Schleiermacher: *On Religion.*
J.S. Trimingham: *The Sufi Orders in Islam.*
Robert H. King: *The Meaning of God.*
Harvey Cox: *The Seduction of the Spirit.*
Hannah Tillich: *From Time to Time.*
Maurice Wiles: *The Remaking of Christian Doctrine.*

John Hick: *God and the Universe of Faiths.*
A.S. Tritton: *Muslim Theology.*
Green & Hooper: *C.S. Lewis: An Biography.*
R.C. Zaehner: *Our Savage God.*
W.L. King: *Introduction to Religion.*
Meister Eckhart.
George Grey: *Polynesian Mythology.*
C. Batson et al: *Commitment without Ideology.*
Karl Rahner: *The Shape of the Church to Come.*
William James: *The Varieties of Religious Experience.*
A. von Harnack: *History of Dogma*, vol. 2.

1975 (122)
Rollo May: *Paulus.*
C.L. Manschreck: *A History of Christianity in the World.*
V.B. Ficker: *The Revolution in Religion.*
Juan Mascaro: *The Bhagavad Gita.*
G.S. Kirk: *Myth. Its Meaning and Function.*
C.F. Potter: *The Lost Years of Jesus Revealed.*
Claus Westermann: *Creation.*
Karl Jaspers: *Philosophy of Existence.*
Werner Manheim: *Martin Buber.*
Leslie Dewart: *The Foundations of Belief.*
St John of the Cross: *The Dark Night of the Soul.*
M & H.R.F. Keating: *Understanding Teilhard de Chardin.*
Don Cupitt: *Christ and the Hiddenness of God.*
R.C. Zaehner: *Hindu and Muslim Mysticism.*
H. Hubert & Mauss: *Sacrifice. Its Nature and Function.*
S.N. Dasgupta: *Hindu Mysticism.*
Browning, Alioto & Farber (ed): *1971 Symposium: Teilhard de Chardin. In Quest of the Perfection of Man.*
E.O. James: *Origins of Sacrifice.*
W.R. Smith: *The Religion of the Semites.*
E. Trocme: *Jesus and his Contemporaries.*
Morton Smith: *The Secular Gospel.*
R. Money-Kryle: *The Meaning of Sacrifice.*
R. Otto: *The Idea of the Holy.*
H.W. Turner: *Commentary on The Idea of the Holy.*
Malachi Martin: *The Encounter: Religions in Crisis.*
Aubrey Menen: *The New Mystics.*

Appendix 1: Geering's Reading

S.G.F. Brandon: *Man and His Destiny in the Great Religions.*
Eldson Best: *The Maori.*
Mircea Eliade: *The Sacred and the Profane.*
Peter De Rosa: *Jesus Who Became Christ.*
A.M. Hunter: *The Gospel According to John.*
M. Buber: *Two Types of Faith.*
A. van Gennep: *The Rites of Passage.*
E.J. Tinsley: *Paul Tillich.*
N.C. Chaudhuri: *Scholar Extraordinaire: The Life of Professor the Rt. Hon. Friedrich Max Muller.*
Geza Vermes: *Jesus the Jew.*
Ian Ramsey: *Christian Empiricism.*
John Macquarrie: *Existentialism.*
Stephen Sykes: *Friedrich Schleiermacher.*
Martin Buber: *I and Thou.*
W.W. Fletcher: *Modern Man looks at Evolution.*
J. Bowden (ed): *A Reader in Contemporary Theology.*
Alan Richardson: *Creeds in the Making.*
Ernst Cassirer: *The Philosophy of the Enlightenment.*
Trevor Beeson: *Discretion and Valour.*
Trevor Beeson: *The Church of England in Crisis.*
Henry J. Koren: *Marx and the Authentic Man.*
Paul Tillich: *The Courage to Be.*
John Macquarrie: *Thinking about God.*
G.E.H. Abraham: *Nietzsche.*
R. Speaight: *Teilhard de Chardin: A Biography.*
David Robey: *Structuralism.*
Gerald O'Collins: *The Easter Jesus.*
Henri Frankfort: *Ancient Egyptian Religion.*
Raymond Brown: *The Virginal Conception and the Bodily Resurrection of Jesus.*
John S. Dunne: *The Way of All the Earth.*
J. Moltmann: *The Crucified God.*
W.L. King: *Introduction to Religion.*
Teilhard de Chardin: *The Phenomenon of Man.*
Alastair Kee (ed): *A Reader in Political Theology.*
T.S. Szasz: *The Second Sin.*
R.C. Monk et al: *Exploring Religious Meaning.*
University of Pennsylvania bicentennial conference: *Religion and the Modern World.*

D. Stafford-Clark: *Five Questions in Search of an Answer.*
Michael Hill: *The Religious Order.*
Philip Toynbee: *Towards the Holy Spirit.*
Azriel Eisenberg: *The Synagogue through the Ages.*
A. McIntyre & P. Ricouer: *The Religious Significance of Atheism.*
Nigel Nicholson: *Portrait of a Marriage.*
Bertrand Russell: *Why I Am Not a Christian.*
W.H. van der Pol: *The End of Conventional Christianity.*
Os Guiness: *The Dust of Death.*
Peter Gay: *The Rise of Modern Paganism.*
James Barr: *The Bible in the Modern World.*
Ernst Bloch: *Man on His Own.*
David Hume: *Dialogues Concerning Natural Religion.*
Arnold Toynbee: *Christianity Among the World Religions.*
Malachi Martin: *Jesus Now.*
W. T. de Bary: *Sources of Indian Tradition*, vol. 2.
H.J. Richards: *The Miracles of Jesus.*
H.J. Richards: *The First Christmas.*
J.A. Schneiderfranken: *The Wisdom of St. John.*
John S. Dunne: *A Search for God in Time and Memory.*
Richard Rubenstein: *After Auschwitz.*
James McLeman: *The Birth of the Christian Faith.*
Religious Education in Secondary Schools.
John Macquarrie: *The Faith of the People of God.*
Una Kroll: *TM: A signpost for the World.*
Thomas Flynn: *The Charismatic Renewal and the Irish Experience.*
R. Johnson et al: *Critical issues in Modern Religion.*
D.T. Suzuki: *What is Zen?*
John S. Dunne: *The City of the Gods.*
J. Moltmann: *Man.*
John V. Taylor: *Enough is Enough.*
W. Harenberg: *Der Speigel on the New Testament.*
W.D. Zimmerman (ed): *I Knew Dietrich Bonhoeffer.*
William Kuhns: *In Pursuit of Dietrich Bonhoeffer.*
E. Troeltsch: *Christian Thought.*
K. Lake: *The Religion of Yesterday and Tomorrow.*
H.K. McArthur (ed): *In Search of the Historical Jesus.*
C.F. Mooney: *The Making of Man.*
Miguel de Unamuno: *The Agony of Christianity.*
Dietrich Bonhoeffer: *Letters and Papers from Prison.*

Appendix 1: Geering's Reading

Dietrich Bonhoeffer: *The Cost of Discipleship.*
Charles Combaluzier: *God Tomorrow.*
Dietrich Bonhoeffer: *Sanctorum Communio.*
T.F. Torrance: *Space, Time and Incarnation.*
I. Breward: *Grace and Truth.*
Richard Church: *The Voyage Home.*
A. Manchenko: *My Testimony.*
H.N. Glatzer: *The Dimensions of Job.*
Ugo Bianchi: *The History of Religions.*
John Macquarrie: *Christian Unity and Christian Diversity.*
Malcolm Muggeridge: *Jesus.*
Dietrich Bonhoeffer: *Christology.*
E.E. Evans-Pritchard: *Theories of Primitive Religion.*
R.A. Nicholson: *The Mysteries of Islam.*
Dietrich Bonhoeffer: *Ethics.*
Eric J. Sharpe: *Comparative Religion. A History.*
Andre Dumas: *Dietrich Bonhoeffer: Theologian of Reality.*
Pierre Montet: *Lives of the Pharaohs.*
Quentin Bell: *Bloomsbury.*

1976 (96)
W.T. Stace: *Religion and the Modern Mind.*
David Edwards: *Jesus for Modern Man.*
Francis Schaeffer: *The God Who Is There.*
Michael Perry: *The Resurrection of Man.*
Peter Baelz: *The Forgotten Dream: Experience, Hope and God.*
Anthony Duncan: *The Fourth Dimension.*
R. Preston (ed): *Theology and Change.*
K. Lake: *Immortality and the Modern Mind.*
C.H. Moore: *Ancient Beliefs in the Immortality of the Soul.*
R. Dermott (ed): *The Essential Aurobindo.*
R.J. Lifton: *Revolutionary Immortality: Mao Tse Tung and the Chinese Cultural Revolution.*
N. Smart (ed): *New Movements in Religious Education.*
A.M. Hanson: *Job.*
Robert Gordis: *The Book of God and Man: A Study of Job.*
Paul Sanders (ed): *Twentieth Century Interpretations of the Book of Job.*
E. Bethge: *Bonhoeffer: Exile and Martyr.*
Dietrich Bonhoeffer: *Act and Being.*
Keith Sinclair: *A History of New Zealand.*

E. Lester Smith: *Intelligence Came First.*
Dietrich Bonhoeffer: *No Rusty Swords.*
Theodore Roszak: *Where the Wasteland Ends.*
Dietrich Bonhoeffer: *The Way to Freedom.*
Heinrich Ott: *Reality and Faith.*
Dietrich Bonhoeffer: *True Patriotism.*
Dietrich Bonhoeffer: *Life Together.*
T.W. Ogletree (ed): *Openings for Marxist-Christian Dialogue.*
Mark Giffard: *Twentieth Century Men of Prayer.*
Martin E. Marty: *The Place of Bonhoeffer.*
E. Bethge: *Dietrich Bonhoeffer.*
E.H. Robinson: *Dietrich Bonhoeffer.*
J.H. Houlden: *Ethics and the New Testament.*
Ruben A. Alves: *A Theology of Human Hope.*
T. Penelhum: *Survival and Disembodied Existence.*
Peter Hebblethwaite: *The Runaway Church.*
F.H. Hock (ed): *Death and Eastern Thought.*
John A. Phillips: *The Form of Christ in the World.*
R. Gregor Smith (ed): *World Come of Age.*
Teilhard de Chardin: *Le Milieu Divin.*
R. Speaight: *Teilhard de Chardin: A Biography.*
K. Rahner: *On Heresy.*
J. Wach: *The Comparative Study of Religions.*
D. Chrystal: *Linguistics.*
T.H.L. Parker: *John Calvin.*
Eberhard Jungel: *Death: The Riddle and the Mystery.*
E. Troeltsch: *Protestantism and Progress.*
F. Gogarten: *Demythologizing and History.*
F.M. Young: *Sacrifice and the Death of Christ.*
Heinrich Ott: *God.*
Ninian Smart: *Philosophers and Religious Truth.*
Teilhard de Chardin: *The Future of Man.*
Martin Buber: *I and Thou.*
D.J. Moore: *Martin Buber: Professor of Religious Secularization.*
M.H. Harper: *Gurus, Swamis and Avatars.*
Jean Holm: *Teaching Religion in School.*
Helder Camara: *Race Against Time.*
Michael D. Ryan: *The Contemporary Explosion of Theology.*
Alan Watts: *In My Own Way.*
L. Feuerbach: *Principles of the Philosophy of the Future.*

Appendix 1: Geering's Reading

L. Feuerbach: *The Essence of Christianity.*
F. Engels: *Ludwig Feuerbach and the End of Classical German Philosophy.*
Hector Hawton: *The Humanist Revolution.*
J.B. Wilson: *Death by Decision.*
F. Nietzsche: *Thus Spake Zarathustra.*
Kenneth Slack: *Nairobi Narrative: the story of the Fifth Assembly of the World Council of Churches.*
John Charles Cooper: *The New Mentality.*
E.T. Long (ed): *Secularization and History.*
Keith Miller: *A Second Touch.*
The Common Catechism.
Martin Hengel: *The Son of God.*
Martin E. Marty: *Varieties of Unbelief.*
Max Muller: *Natural Religion.*
Jacob Neusner: *Between Time and Eternity.*
R. Rubenstein: *My Brother Paul.*
M. Bernstein: *Nuns.*
Maurice Wiles: *Working Papers in Doctrine.*
Paul Johnson: *A History of Christianity.*
Donald E. McInnes: *Religious Policy and Practice in Communist China.*
S. Kierkegaard: *Fear and Trembling.*
Martin E. Marty: *The Modern Schism.*
Paul Pruyser: *Between Belief and Unbelief.*
Aziz Atiya: *A History of Eastern Christianity.*
C.R. Hensman: *Sun Yat-Sen.*
R.A. Johnson: *Critical Issues in Modern Religion.*
E. Berkovits: *Major Themes in Modern Philosophies of Judaism.*
John Rogerson: *The Supernatural in the Old Testament.*
David E. Jenkins: *The Contradiction of Christianity.*
Marcus Braybrooke: *Faith in Fellowship.*
Donovan Joyce: *The Jesus Scroll.*
Ronald Blythe: *Akenfield: Portrait of an English Village.*
Philip A. Verhalen: *Faith in a Secularized World.*
Edgar Snow: *China's Long Revolution.*
Hans Schwarz: *The Search for God: Christianity, Atheism, Secularism, World Religions.*
Norman Young: *Creator, Creation and Faith.*
Johannes Hirschberger: *A Short History of Western Philosophy.*

Joseph B. Tyson: *A Study of Early Christianity.*
Leo Baeck: *The Essence of Judaism.*

1977 (97)
Peter Selby: *Look for the Living.*
Owen Chadwick: *The Victorian Church, Part II.*
J.V.L. Casserley: *The Retreat from Christianity.*
E. Troeltsch: *Christian Thought.*
S. Crites: *In the Twilight of Christendom.*
Daniel Jenkins: *The British: Their Identity and Their Religion.*
W.S. Smith: *The London Heretics 1870–1914.*
Anthony Symondson (ed): *The Victorian Crisis of Faith.*
Owen Chadwick: *The Secularization of the European Mind in the Nineteenth Century.*
David Martin: *A Sociology of English Religion.*
Eugene Kamenka: *The Philosophy of Ludwig Feuerbach.*
Ludwig Feuerbach: *Lectures of the Essence of Religion.*
Roland Stromberg: *Religious Liberalism in Eighteenth Century England.*
R.J.Z. Werblowsky: *Beyond Tradition and Modernity.*
Bernard M. Meland: *The Realities of Faith.*
Leslie Paul: *A Church by Daylight.*
David Martin: *Tracts against the Times.*
Owen Chadwick: *The Victorian Church, Part I.*
Karl Jaspers: *Man in the Modern Age.*
W. Humphrey Ward: *A Writer's Recollections.*
John P. Clayton: *Ernst Troeltsch and the Future of Theology.*
Moses Mendelssohn: *Jerusalem: and Other Jewish Writings.*
Karl Jaspers: *The Origin and Goal of History.*
Ernst Haeckel: *The Riddle of the Universe.*
William F. Lynch: *Christ and Prometheus. A New Image of the Secular.*
Arnold Toynbee: *A Study of History*, vol. 13.
Max Weber: *The Sociology of Religion.*
E. Gellner: *Thought and Change.*
Robert J. Miller (ed): *Religious Ferment in Asia.*
A.S. Farrar: *A Critical History of Free Thought in Reference to the Christian Religion.*
Hans Küng: *On Being a Christian.*
Philip H. Ashby: *The Conflict of Religions.*
S.R. Hopper: *The Crisis of Faith.*
E. Renan: *The Life of Jesus.*

Appendix 1: Geering's Reading

R.J. Campbell: *The New Theology.*
K.B. MacFarlane: *The Origins of Religious Dissent in England.*
P. O. Kristeller: *Renaissance Thought: The Classic, Scholastic and Humanist Strains.*
Jacob Buckhardt: *The Civilization of the Renaissance in Italy.*
Arnold Toynbee: *A Historian's Approach to Religion.*
Pieter Geyl et al: *The Pattern of the Past.*
Nicholas Berdyaev: *The Meaning of History.*
F.C. Copelston: *History of Philosophy*, vol. 6.
Horton Harris: *David Friedrich Strauss and his Theology.*
David Strauss: *The Old Faith and the New.*
P.A. Sorokin: *The Crisis of Our Age.*
Erich Kahler: *The Meaning of History.*
Herbert Butterfield: *Man on His Past.*
Bryan Wilson: *Contemporary Transformations of Religion.*
Trevor Ling: *Buddha, Marx and God.*
John MacMurray: *The Structure of Religious Experience.*
W.L. King: *A Thousand Lives Away. Buddhism in Contemporary Burma.*
W. Chan: *Religious Trends in Modern China.*
Stephen Neil: *Christian Faith and Other Faiths.*
Robert C. Lester: *Theravada Buddhism in South East Asia.*
Bede Griffiths: *Return to the Centre.*
Klaus Klostermann: *Hindu and Christian in Vrindaban.*
John Hick (ed): *The Myth of God Incarnate.*
Karl Rahner: *Christian at the Crossroads.*
Ian Sellers: *Nineteenth Century Nonconformity.*
David Elkind: *A Sympathetic Understanding of the Child.*
Nancy Mitford: *Voltaire in Love.*
Arnold Toynbee: *Surviving the Future.*
Eric Sharpe: *Faith Meets Faith.*
David Strauss: *The Life of Jesus Critically Examined.*
Paul Hazard: *The Crisis of the European Mind.*
Albert Schweitzer: *The Decay and Restoration of Civilization.*
Arnold Toynbee: *Mankind and Mother Earth.*
Paul Tillich: *The Dynamics of Faith.*
J. Ortega y Gasset: *Man and Crisis.*
B.R. Scharf: *The Sociological Study of Religion.*
Ronald Grimsby: *Rousseau and the Religious Quest.*
Norman Hampson: *The Enlightenment.*

Paul-Henri Michel: *The Cosmology of Giordano Bruno.*
John Caird: *Spinoza.*
J. Moltmann: *The Crucified God.*
Erasmus: *The Praise of Folly.*
Descartes: *Discourse on Method.*
Jan de Vries: *The Study of History.*
John Hibberd: *Kafka in Context.*
Rollo May: *The Courage to Be.*
W. & M. Pauck: *Paul Tillich: His Life & Thought*, vol. 1.
James O'Higgins: *Anthony Collins: The Man & His Work.*
Franz Kafka: *America.*
H. Faber: *Psychology of Religion.*
Paul Tillich: *The Continuation of the History of Religion in Schelling's Positive Philosophy.*
G. Hegel: *Philosophy of Religion*, vol. 1.
R. Kroner (ed): *Hegel's Early Theological Writings.*
G. Hegel: *Philosophy of Religion*, vol. 3.
W. Kaufmann (ed): *Hegel: Texts & Commentary.*
John Bowker: *The Sense of God.*
Jurgen Moltmann: *The Experiment of Hope.*
Karl Jaspers: *Nietzsche and Christianity.*
R.W. Harris: *Reason & Nature in Eighteenth Century Thought.*
Karl Lowith: *From Hegel to Nietzsche.*
L. Feuerbach: *Principles of the Philosophy of the Future.*
M. Rubel: *Marx without Myth.*
Roger Garaudy: *Karl Marx.*

1978 (56)
Peter Gay: *Age of Enlightenment.*
Virgil Topazio: *D'Holback's Moral Philosophy.*
A. Comte: *The Essential Comte.*
Hans Küng: *That the World May Believe.*
Emile Durkheim: *The Elementary Forms of the Religious Life.*
H. Misiak & V.S. Sexton: *History of Psychology.*
S. Freud: *The Future of an Illusion.*
Erich Fromm: *Psychoanalysis and Religion.*
C.G. Jung: *Psychology and Religion.*
C.G. Jung: *Psychological Reflections.*
Edward Stevens: *The Religion Game, American Style.*
T.W. Jennings Jr: *Introduction to Theology.*

Appendix 1: Geering's Reading

Karl Jaspers: *Nietzsche and Christianity*.
Brian Hebblethwaithe: *Evil, Suffering & Religion*.
B.M.G. Reardon: *Hegel's Philosophy of Religion*.
Lux Mundi.
E. Troeltsch: *The Absoluteness of Christianity*.
H. Kraemer: *Religion and the Christian Faith*.
A.C. Bouquet: *The Christian Faith and Non-Christian Religions*.
Maurice Wiles: *What is Theology?*
Martin Buber: *I and Thou*.
Michael Ramsey: *Holy Spirit*.
John Bowker: *Problems of Suffering in Religions of the World*.
Erich von Daniken: *Visions*.
G. Vermes: *The Dead Sea Scrolls*.
Frederick Sontag: *Sun Myung Moon*.
Dale Vree: *On Synthesizing Marxism and Christianity*.
Church of England: *Christian Believing*.
Paul Tillich: *The Courage to Be*.
W.E. Hocking: *Living Religions and a World Faith*.
Hans Küng: *On Being a Christian*.
M. Lukas: *Teilhard*.
Teilhard de Chardin: *The Future of Man*.
H.K. Schelling: *The New Consciousness in Science and Religion*.
Theodore Roszak: *Unfinished Animal*.
Alexandre Koyre: *From the Closed World to an Infinite Universe*.
John Hick: *Evil and the God of Love*.
Peter Kelley: *Searching for Truth*.
M. Buber: *Images of Good and Evil*.
V. Kuroyodov: *Church and Religion in the USSR*.
Susan Budd: *Varieties of Unbelief*.
L. Wiley (ed): *Cosmogony*.
Paul Carus (ed): *Kant's Prolegomena*.
John Macquarrie: *The Humility of God*.
Paul Tillich: *Systematic Theology*, vol. 2.
Alex Vidler: *Scenes from the Clerical Life*.
J. Moltmann: *The Open Church*.
Maurice Gee: *Plumb*.
V. Frankl: *Man's Search for Meaning*.
F. Nietzsche: *Beyond Good and Evil*.
Peter Berger: *Invitation to Pilgrimage*.
Peter Berger: *The Social Reality of Religion*.

Michael Hill: *A Sociology of Religion.*
Carlos Christo: *Letters from a Prisoner of Conscience.*
F. Nietzsche: *The Gay Science.*
F. Nietzsche: *Thus Spake Zarathustra.*

1979 (85)
Jan Myrdal: *Report from a Chinese Village.*
W. Rosenberg: *The Coming Depression.*
R.J. Hollingdale: *Nietzsche: The Man and his Philosophy.*
David Ogilvie: *Blood, Brains and Beer.*
F. Nietzsche: *Ecce Homo.*
V. Frankl: *The Unconscious God.*
Alan Watts: *The Wisdom of Insecurity.*
Morton T. Kelsey: *Myth, History & Faith.*
M. Eliade: *The Myth of the Eternal Return.*
Jacques Ellul: *The Betrayal of the West.*
R. Bultmann: *Jesus and the Word.*
M. Buber: *Eclipse of God.*
M. Eliade: *Myth and Reality.*
R. Bultmann: *Existence and Faith.*
R.E. Clements: *A Century of Old Testament Study.*
S.H. Nasr: *Ideals and Realities in Islam.*
I.G. Marquand: *New Life Movement.*
David Edwards: *A Reason to Hope.*
D.W.D. Shaw: *The Dissuaders.*
Peter Munz: *The Shapes of Time.*
Martin Buber: *I and Thou.*
M. Eliade: *Myths, Dreams and Mysteries.*
Teilhard de Chardin: *Christianity and Evolution.*
Martin Redeker: *Schleiermacher: Life and Thought.*
Ninian Smart: *The Science of Religion and the Sociology of Knowledge.*
Teilhard de Chardin: *The Phenomenon of Man.*
John Macquarrie: *An Existentialist Theology.*
Jacques Monod: *Chance and Necessity.*
F. Schleiermacher: *On Religion.*
E. Schillebeeckx: *Jesus.*
Hans Küng: *That the World May Believe.*
John Macquarrie: *Christian Hope.*
Ulrich Wilckens: *Resurrection.*
Heinrich Ott: *God.*

Appendix 1: Geering's Reading

Alan Watts: *The Book on the Taboo against Knowing Who You Are.*
R.K. St Cartmail: *The Love Ethic.*
L.G. Thompson: *Chinese Religion: An Introduction.*
S. Ono: *Shinto. The Kami Way.*
Paul Tillich: *The Courage to Be.*
C. F. Mooney (ed): *The Presence and Absence of God.*
Ernst Bloch: *Man on His Own.*
James P. Mackey: *Jesus. The Man and the Myth.*
Ben Meyer: *The Aims of Jesus.*
Richard Purtill: *Thinking about Religion.*
Stefan Zweig: *Erasmus.*
Stepan Zweig: *The Right to Heresy.*
Yoshinori Hyuga: *Awakening to the Truth through Buddhism.*
Peter Donovan: *Interpreting Religious Experience.*
Arthur Osborne: *The Incredible Sai Baba.*
Robert L. Wilken: *The Myth of Christian Beginnings.*
Peter Slater: *The Dynamics of Religion.*
Karl Rahner: *The Spirit of the Church.*
Billy Graham: *The Holy Spirit.*
H.J. Blackham: *Six Existential Thinkers.*
Gordon Leff: *Medieval Thought. St. Augustine to Ockham.*
Stephen Sykes: *Friedrich Schleiermacher.*
James Richmond: *Ritschl, a Reappraisal.*
Albert Ritschl: *Justification and Reconciliation.*
Adolf Harnack: *What is Christianity?*
Pope John Paul II: Encyclical *Redemptor Hominos.*
John Dillenberger: *Protestant Christianity.*
Claude Geffre: *A New Age in Theology.*
Martin Buber: *Meetings.*
G.E. Pugh: *The Biological Origins of Human Values.*
Ronald Eyre: *On the Long Search.*
Hans Ruedi Weber: *The Cross.*
Rupert Davies: *The Church in Our Times.*
Martin Buber: *The Eclipse of God.*
Nicholas Lash: *Doing Theology on Dover Beach.*
C.S. Lewis: *The Dark Tower and Other Stories.*
J.M. Clark (ed): *Meister Eckhart.*
C.S. Lewis: *The Pilgrim's Regress.*
O. Cullmann: *The Johannine Circle.*
J. Miranda: *Being and the Messiah.*

Gerhard Speigler: *The Eternal Covenant.*
Peter Stuhlmacher: *Historical Criticism and Theological Interpretation of Scripture.*
Don Cupitt: *The Debate about Christ.*
Bruce Reid: *The Dynamics of Religion.*
Edward Norman: *Christianity and World Order.*
Michael Goulder: *Incarnation and Myth: The Debate Continued.*
R. Bultmann: *Jesus and the Word.*
H. Ridderbos: *Bultmann.*
G.H. Jansen: *Militant Islam.*
Noman Perrin: *The Promise of Bultmann.*
Peter Berger: *The Heretical Imperative.*

1980 (62)
Lionel Blue, *A Backdoor to Heaven.*
Morris Ashcraft, *Rudolf Bultmann.*
A.C. Moore, *Rudolf Bultmann and his approach to theology.*
W.C. Smith, *Faith and Belief.*
Hedrieck Smith: *The Russians.*
Don Cupitt: *The Nature of Man.*
John Macquarrie: *God-Talk.*
T.J. Altizer: *The Descent into Hell.*
Hans Küng: *His Work and His Way.*
H.W. Bartsch: *Kerygma and Myth*, vol. 1.
R. Bultmann: *Existence and Faith.*
B.S. Childs: *Introduction to the Old Testament as Scripture.*
Norman Pittenger: *The Lure of Divine Love.*
George Steiner: *Heidegger.*
Martin Kahler: *The So-called Historical Jesus and the Historical Biblical Christ.*
F. Schleiermacher: *The Life of Jesus.*
John Macquarrie: *God-Talk.*
Schubert Ogden: *Christ without Myth.*
Rudolf Bultmann: *Jesus Christ and Mythology.*
Charles Kegley: *The Theology of Paul Tillich.*
W.C. Smith: *Belief and History.*
G. von Rad: *The Form-Critical Problem of the Hexateuch.*
M. Chaning-Pearce: *Soren Kierkegaard: A Study.*
Raymond Brown: *After Bultmann, What?*
Paul Tillich: *Systematic Theology*, vol. 1.

Martin Noth: *A History of Pentateuchal Tradition*.
Ronald Eyre: *Ronald Eyre on The Long Search*.
P. Donovan: *Beliefs and Practices in New Zealand*.
Benedick Ogden et al: *Myths in the Old Testament*.
Rosemary Radford Ruether: *Mary. The Feminine Face of the Church*.
C.C. Adams: *Islam and Modernism in Egypt*.
M. Iqbal: *The Reconstruction of Religious Thought in Islam*.
Ninian Smart: *The Phenomenon of Christianity*.
Albert Hourani: *Arabic Thought in the Liberal Age*.
John Hick: *God Has Many Names*.
Gerd Theisen: *On Having a Critical Faith*.
Paul Tillich: *Systematic Theology*, vol. 2.
J.A. Soggin: *Introduction to the Old Testament*.
Antonio Perez-Esclarin: *Atheism and Liberation*.
Alistair Kee: *A Reader in Political Theology*.
Harper & Veitch (ed): *The Heritage of Christian Thought*.
G.W. Anderson: *Tradition and Interpretation*.
Colless & Donovan: *Religion in New Zealand Society*.
Raymond Brown: *The Community of the Beloved Disciple*.
David Tracy: *Blessed Rage for Order*.
Patrick Burke: *The Fragile Universe*.
Paul Tillich: *Systematic Theology*, vol. 3.
R Aubert: *The Church in a Secularized Society*.
Harry M. Johnson (ed): *Religious Change and Controversy*.
Martin E. Marty: *A Nation of Believers*.
W.A. Johnson: *On Religion*.
H.L. Fries: *Schleiermacher's Soliloquies*.
R.R. Niebuhr: *Schleiermacher on Christ and Religion*.
W.B. Selbie: *Schleiermacher. A Critical and Historical Study*.
George Cross: *The Theology of Schleiermacher*.
James D. Boulger: *Coleridge as a Religious Thinker*.
David L. Mueller: *An Introduction to the Theology of Albert Ritschl*.
Alfred A. Garvie: *The Ritschlian Theology*.
William Herman: *Faith and Morals*.
Adolf Harnack: *Christianity and History*.

1981 (49)
M. Buber: *Meetings*.
M. Buber: *Daniel*.
Alan D. Gilbert: *The Making of Post-Christian Britain*.

D.L. Carmody: *Women and World Religions.*
Leonard Swidler: *Biblical Affirmations of Woman.*
M. Buber: *I and Thou.*
S. Kierkegaard: *Fear and Trembling.*
W. Manheim: *Martin Buber.*
K.A. Popper & John Eccles: *The Self and Its Brain.*
Karl Marx: *Selected Writings in Sociology.*
George Rupp: *Beyond Existentialism and Zen.*
S. Kierkegaard: *The Concept of Dread.*
P. Tillich: *The Courage to Be.*
E.H. Cousins (ed): *Process Theology.*
Alvin Toffler: *The Third Wave.*
Nikki Keddie: *An Islamic Response to Imperialism.*
S. Kierkegaard: *Philosophical Fragments.*
A.N. Whitehead: *Science and the Modern World.*
R.A. Johnson: *Critical Issues in Modern Religion.*
Don Cupitt: *Jesus and the Gospel of God.*
Carl Jung: *Man and His Symbols.*
John Cobb: *Process Theology: An Introductory Exposition.*
C.G. Jung: *Psychology and Religion.*
A.C. Webster. *A Study of New Zealand Clergy.*
E.A. Bennet: *C.G. Jung.*
R. Sohl & A. Carr: *The Gospel According to Zen.*
W.A. Johnson: *The Search for Transcendence.*
L. Van der Post: *Jung and the Story of Our Time.*
E.A. Bennet: *C.G. Jung.*
Encyclical: *Dives in Misericordia.*
B.M.G. Reardon: *Religious Thought in the Victorian Age.*
Mecca, the Muslim Pilgrimage. [note: only information given]
Colin Brown: *Forty Years On.*
Robert Nowell: *A Passion for Truth.*
Hans Küng: *Does God Exist?*
H.J. Richards: *Death and After: What Will Really Happen?*
Basant Kumar Lal: *Contemporary Indian Philosophy.*
Donald E. Miller: *The Case for Liberal Theology.*
K. S. Latourette: *History of the Expansion of Christianity*, vol. 1.
Rudolf Augstein: *Jesus Son of Man.*
Paul Tillich: *The Religious Situation.*
Charles B. Ketcham: *A Theology of Encounter.*
James L. Crensaw: *Gerhard von Rad.*

Muhammad Iqbal: *The Secrets of the Self.*
Muhammad Iqbal: *Javid-Nama.*
A. Schimmel: *Gabriel's Wing.*
P. Tillich: *Dynamics of Faith.*
Dorothee Solle: *Choosing Life.*
Charles S. McCoy: *When Gods Change.*

1982 (90)
Michael Peissel: *Mustang: A Lost Tibetan Kingdom.*
W.H. Forbes: *Fall of the Peacock Throne.*
K.S. Latourette: *A History of the Expansion of Christianity*, vol. 2.
Young Oon Kim: *Unification Theology.*
John Hick (ed): *Christianity and Other Religions.*
Jo Spark: *The Religious Structures of a Secular Society.* [VUW MA Thesis]
Kevin Sharpe: *Building a Ladder with Science and Theology.*
Paul Tillich: *My Search for Absolutes.*
Paul Tillich: *The World Situation.*
Paul Tillich: *What Is Religion?*
Paul Tillich: *Theology of Culture.*
Gustaf Aulen: *Jesus in Contemporary Historical Research.*
Rosemary Radford Ruether: *Religion and Sexism.*
Dennis C. Duling: *Jesus Christ through History.*
Paul Tillich: *Christianity and the Encounter with World Religions.*
W. Cantwell Smith: *Towards a World Theology.*
James M. Robinson: *A New Quest for the Historical Jesus.*
H.J. Richards: *The First Easter: What Really Happened.*
Calvin S. Hall & V.J. Nordby: *A Primer of Jungian Psychology.*
Victor White: *God and the Unconscious.*
Martin Buber: *I and Thou.*
Carl Jung: *Man and His Symbols.*
Jolande Jacobi: *The Psychology of C.G. Jung.*
Antonio Moreno: *Jung, Gods and Modern Man.*
C.G. Jung: *Four Archetypes.*
Vincent Browne: *Jung, Man and Myth.*
C.A. Meier: *Jung's Analytical Psychology and Religion.*
H.D.A. Major: *The Gospel of Freedom.*
Walter Kaufmann: *Existentialism, Religion and Death.*
S. Daniel Breslauer: *The Chrysalis of Religion.*
Carol P. Christ (ed): *Womanspirit Rising.*

David Stacey (ed): *Is Christianity Credible?*
Paul Tillich: *The Dynamics of Faith.*
Rosemary Ruether: *New Woman, New Earth.*
Phillipe Aires: *The Hour of Our Death.*
Tom Driver: *Christ in a Changing World.*
Phillipe Aries: *Western Attitudes towards Death.*
Martin Kahler: *The So-called Historical Jesus and the Historic Biblical Christ.*
J.K. Elliot: *Questioning Christian Origins.*
Judith M. Brown: *Men and Gods in a Changing World.*
F.O. Bennett: *The Road from Saddle Hill.*
Leo Baeck: *The Essence of Judaism.*
Saul L. Goodman: *The Faith of Secular Jews.*
Claus Westermann: *The Structure of the Book of Job.*
Robert Stout: *Evolution and Theism (1881).*
George Higenbotham: *Science and Religion (1883).*
Thomas Bracken: *Pulpit Pictures.*
Robert Stout: *What is Freethought?*
E. Whitehouse: *Freethought.*
Abd-al-Rahman Azzam: *Eternal Message of Muhammad.*
Walter Kaufman: *The Future of the Humanities.*
Alisdair I.C. Heron: *A Century of Protestant Theology.*
Tefilio Cabestrero: *Faith. Conversations with Contemporary Theologians.*
Antonio Perez-Esclarin: *Atheism and Liberation.*
William Henderson: *Christianity and Modern Thought (1861).*
Alistair Kee (ed): *The Scope of Political Theology.*
Paul Tillich: *Morality and Beyond.*
A.F. Chalmers: *What is this thing called science?*
John Losee: *A Historical Introduction to Philosophy of Science.*
Antonio Moreno: *Jung, Gods and Modern Man.*
Walter Wink: *Transforming Bible Study.*
John Hick (ed): *The Myth of God Incarnate.*
R.A. Johnson (ed): *Critical Issues in Modern Religion.*
Letty M. Russell: *The Future of Partnership.*
Letty M. Russell (ed): *The Liberating Word.*
Martin H. Cressey: *The Church in Dialogue.*
James Bentley: *Between Marx and Christ.*
Charles S. Boyall: *A Living Force.*

Frederick Hiebel: *Treasures of Biblical Research and the Conscience of the Times.*
Geza Vermes: *Jesus the Jew.*
Naomi Goldenberg: *Changing of the Gods.*
Letty M. Russell: *Human Liberation in a Feminist Perspective—a theology.*
Dorothy Solle: *Christ the Representative.*
Mary Daly: *Beyond God the Father.*
Leonardo Boff: *Jesus Christ Liberator.*
Joan C. Englesman: *The Feminine Dimension of the Divine.*
Milan Machovec: *A Marxist Looks at Jesus.*
Friedrich Schleiermacher: *On Religion.*
Don Cuppitt: *The World to Come.*
Patrick Leigh Fermor: *A Time of Gifts.*
John H.S. Kent: *The End of the Line.*
Keith F. Nickle: *The Synoptic Gospels.*
G.A.F. Knight: *Theology in Pictures.*
T.E. Pollard: *Fullness of Humanity. Christ's Humanity and Ours.*
Maurice Andrew: *The Old Testament and New Zealand Theology.*
Alastair Kee: *Constantine versus Christ.*
Joachim Kohl: *The Misery of Christianity.*
Evelyn Waugh: *Brideshead Revisited.*
Ninian Smart: *Beyond Ideology.*

1983 (32)
Michael Talbot: *Mysticism and the New Physics.*
Ayn Rand: *For the New Intellectual.*
Reimarus: *Fragments.*
James W. Fowler: *Stages of Faith.*
David G. Bromley & A.D. Sharpe: *'Moonies' in America, Cult, Church and Crusade.*
John Macquarrie: *In Search of Humanity.*
Albert Schweitzer: *The Quest of the Historical Jesus.*
David G. Bromley & A.D. Sharpe: *'Moonies' in America, Cult, Church and Crusade.*
Carol Ochs: *Behind the Sex of God.*
Chogyom Trungpa: *Cutting Through Spiritual Materialism.*
Tenzin Gyatso: *The Buddhism of Tibet and the Key to the Middle Way.*
H. Richard Niebuhr: *Radical monotheism and Western Culture.*

A.E. Harvey: *Jesus and the Constraints of History.*
R.A. Johnson: *Cultural issues in Modern Religion.*
Carol P. Christ: *Diving Deep and Surfacing.*
Michael Goldberg: *Theology and Narrative.*
Martin Kahler: *The So-called Historical Jesus and the Historic Biblical Christ.*
James M. Robinson: *A New Quest of the Historical Jesus.*
J.K. Elliot: *Questioning Christian Origins.*
James Atkinson: *Martin Luther and the Birth of Protestantism.*
W. Cantwell Smith: *Towards a World Theology.*
Paul Tillich: *On the Boundary.*
Leander E. Keck: *A Future for the Historical Jesus.*
Gordon Kaufmann: *The Theological Imagination.*
Wallace B. Clift: *Jung and Christianity.*
Naomi Goldberg: *The Changing of the Gods.*
Gerhard Ritter: *Luther. His Life and Work.*
Jim Wallis: *The Call to Conversion.*
Alan Race: *Christians and Religious Pluralism.*
Dorothy Solle: *Of War and Love.*
George Orwell: *Nineteen Eighty Four.*
Michael Goulder and John Hick: *Why Believe in God?*

1984 (68)
C.G. Jung: *Memories, Dreams, Reflections.*
John G. Gager: *Kingdom and Community.*
Rosemary Radford Ruether: *To Change the World.*
George Knight: *I Am: this is my name.*
C.G. Jung: *The Undiscovered Self.*
C.G. Jung: *The Integration of the Personality.*
Geza Vermes: *Jesus and the World of Judaism.*
J.M. Coetzee: *Waiting for the Barbarians.*
John Morton: *Redeeming Creation.*
C.G. Jung: *Answer to Job.*
Hazel E. Barnes: *The University as the New Church.*
William Johnston: *The Mirror Mind.*
John Mortimer: *Clinging to the Wreckage.*
Rosemary Radford Ruether: *Sexism and God-Talk.*
Karl Jaspers: *The Idea of the University.*
Harold K. Schelling: *The New Consciousness in Science and Religion.*
Ray Galvin: *A Nuclear-Free New Zealand Now.*

Appendix 1: Geering's Reading

Kevin Sharpe (ed): *Religion and Nature.*
John Bowden: *Karl Barth, Theologian.*
Joseph Klausen: *Jesus of Nazareth.*
Ian Wilson: *Jesus, the Evidence.*
Keith Ward: *Holding Fast to God.*
Julian Jaynes: *The Origin of Consciousness in the Breakdown of the Bicameral Mind.*
Karl Kautsky: *Foundations of Christianity.*
Edward Schillebeecx: *Interim Report.*
G.W.H. Lampe: *God as Spirit.*
Elizabeth and Jurgen Moltmann: *Humanity in God.*
Elizabeth Kubler-Ross: *Death and the Final Stage of Growth.*
Gerald H. Anderson (ed): *Christ's Lordship and Religious Pluralism.*
Mortimer J. Adler: *How to think about God.*
W.H. van de Pol: *The End of Conventional Christianity.*
James Irwin: *An Introduction to Maori Religion.*
Evelyn Reed: *Sexism and Science.*
Elizabeth Cody Stanton & Susan B. Anthony: *Correspondence, Writings, Speeches.*
Martin Buber: *I and Thou.*
Carol Ochs: *Beyond the Sex of God.*
Samuel Hill & D. Owen: *The New Religious Political Right in America.*
Evelyn Reed: *Women's Evolution.*
Jim Garrison: *The Darkness of God: Theology after Hiroshima.*
Jan Sobrino: *Christology at the Crossroads.*
Hans Küng: *Eternal Life.*
Gordon Kaufman: *The Theological Imagination.*
Gordon Kaufman: *God the Problem.*
Gordon Kaufman: *An Essay on Theological Method.*
John O'Grady: *Models of Jesus.*
Phyllis Trible: *Texts of Terror.*
Rosemary Ruether: *Faith and Fratricide.*
Bob Consedine: *New Zealand (1984) Ltd.*
Tom Driver: *Christ and a Changing World.*
Gordon Kaufman: *The Theological Imagination.*
Rustum Roy: *Experimenting with Truth.*
Stewart R. Sutherland: *Faith and Ambiguity.*
Charlotte Klein: *Anti-Judaism in Christian Theology.*
Jim Garrison: *The Darkness of God: Theology After Hiroshima.*
John Macqaurrie: *In Search of Deity.*

Norton T. Kelsey: *Christo-Psychology.*
Christopher Bryant: *Jung and the Christian.*
Judith M. Brown: *Men and Gods in a Changing World.*
A. Roy Eckardt: *Elder and Younger Brothers.*
Michael Harrington: *The Politics at God's Funeral.*
Renny Westra: *The Faith of a Radical.*
J. Veitch: *New Light on the New Testament.*
A.R. Peacocke (ed): *The Sciences and Theology in the Twentieth Century.*
Eric J. Sharpe: *Understanding Religion.*
Jonathan Schell: *The Fate of the Earth.*
Joseph McCabe: *The Testament of Christian Civilization.*
Leslie Paul: *Alternatives to Christian Belief.*
Wilford W. Spradlin & Patricia Porterfield: *The Search for Certainty.*

1985 (97)
Don Cupitt: *The Sea of Faith.*
Umberto Eco: *The Name of the Rose.*
W. Wrede: *The Messianic Secret.*
Derek Brewer: *Chaucer in his Time.*
Graham Greene: *Monsignor Quixote.*
Paul Theroux: *The Kingdom by the Sea.*
Burns H. Weston (ed): *Towards Nuclear Disarmament and Global Security.*
R.H. Tawney: *Religion and the Rise of Capitalism.*
James P. Carse: *Death and Existence.*
Harvey Cox: *Just as I am.*
William Strawson: *Teachers and the New Theology.*
David Thomson: *Woodbrook.*
William Cooper: *Scenes from Later Life.*
Russell Aldwinkle: *Death in the Secular City.*
B.A. Gerrish: *A Prince of the Church.*
James M. Wall (ed): *Theologians in Transition.*
David Strauss: *The Christ and Faith and the Jesus of History.*
Russell Aldwinkle: *Jesus—A Saviour or the Saviour?*
Stephen Neill: *Crisis of Belief.*
Horst Kruger: *A Crack in the Wall.*
Kirsopp Lake: *Immortality and the Modern Mind.*
James P. Mackey: *The Christian Experience of God as Trinity.*
Anthony Trollope: *The Warden.*

Elaine Pagels: *The Gnostic Gospels.*
Gerald Priestland: *Priestland's Progress.*
T.J. Altizer et al: *Deconstruction and Theology.*
Basil Willey: *Samuel Taylor Coleridge.*
R. Richard Niebuhr: *Christ and Culture.*
John Prickett (ed): *Death.*
Jacob Neusner: *Judaism in the beginning of Christianity.*
Arnold Toynbee et al: *Life After Death.*
John P. Dowley: *C.G. Jung and Paul Tillich: The Psyche as Sacrament.*
Calvin S. Hall & V.J. Nordley: *A Primer of Jungian Psychology.*
Peter Homans: *Jung in Context.*
John Hick: *Death and Eternal Life.*
John G. Gager: *The Origins of Anti-Semitism.*
Michael Binyon: *Life in Russia.*
Paul Van Buren: *Discerning the Way.*
John J. McNeill: *The Church and the Homosexual.*
Paul Davies: *God and the New Physics.*
S.P.C.K. (theological collection 13): *The Christian Hope.*
Albert Schweitzer: *The Psychiatric Study of Jesus.*
John Riches: *Jesus and the Transformation of Judaism.*
James Coriden: *Sexism and Church Law.*
Pinchas Lapide: *The Resurrection of Jesus.*
Norman Pittenger: *Time for Consent.*
James B. Nelson: *Embodiment.*
Hans Schwarz: *Beyond the Gates of Death.*
Helmut Thielicke: *Living with Death.*
Geddes MacGregor: *Reincarnation in Christianity.*
Paul Badham: *Christian Beliefs about Life after Death.*
Norbert Weiner: *God and Golem.*
Paul F. Knitter: *No Other Name?*
John Hick & Brian Hebblethwaite (ed): *Christianity and Other Religions.*
Robin H.S. Boyd: *India and the Latin Captivity of the Church.*
John Hick: *God and the Universe of Faiths.*
Peter Randall: *Not without Honour. Tributes to Beyers Naude.*
Elizabeth S. Fiorenza: *In Memory of Her.*
Don Cupitt: *Only Human.*
Gerd Thiesen: *Biblical Faith. An Evolutionary Approach.*
John Naisbitt: *Megatrends.*
Pamela McCorduck: *Machines who think.*

Stewart R. Sutherland: *God, Jesus and Belief.*
Alec Smith: *Now I Call Him Brother.*
Jeffrey Frates & William Moldrup: *Computers and Life.*
Sherry Turkle: *the Second Self: Computers and the Human Spirit.*
Hugh Trowell: *The Unfinished Debate on Euthanasia.*
Geoff Simons: *Are Computers Alive?*
F.H. George: *Cybernetics.*
Norbert Weiner: *Cybernetics.*
Barrie Sherman: *The New Revolution.*
Jeremy Rifkin: *Algeny.*
Bryan Wilson: *Religious Sects.*
Ludwig Feuerbach: *Thoughts on Death and Immortality.*
M. Sarfatti Larson: *The Rise of Professionalism.*
Bryan Magee: *Popper.*
Robert Dingwall & Philip Lewis: *The Sociology of Professions.*
Charles Allan: *A Mountain in Tibet.*
Digby Anderson (ed): *The Kindness that Kills.*
Alan H. Goldman: *The Moral Foundations of Professional Ethics.*
Albert Nolan: *Jesus before Christianity.*
Darrell Reeck: *Ethics for the Professions.*
Edmund Pellegrino: *Humanism and the Physician.*
Ivan Illich: *Limits to Medicine.*
C.G. Jung: *Memories, Dreams, Reflections.*
Owen T. Jenkin: *Thorns in my Crown.*
Leonardo Boff: *Church, Charism and Power.*
Louis B. Savaray et al: *Dreams and Spiritual Growth.*
Nancy Harrison: *Winnie Mandela.*
Gerald O'Collins: *Interpreting Jesus.*
John Welch: *Spiritual Pilgrims.*
Christian Montenat: *How to Read the World. Creation in Evolution.*
John Durant: *Darwinism and Divinity.*
Liliane Frey-Robin: *From Freud to Jung.*
Generals for Peace & Disarmament: *Arms Race to Armageddon.*
Fred Hoyle: *The Intelligent Universe.*
Brian Mackrell: *Halley's Comet over New Zealand.*

1986 (73)
Anne Scott-James: *Sissinghurst.*
Colm Connellan: *Why Does Evil Exist?*
John Sandford: *Evil. The Shadow Side of Reality.*

Richard W. Knopf: *Evil and Evolution. A Theodicy.*
Bernard Levin: *Enthusiasms.*
Samuel Sandmel: *Anti-Semitism in the New Testament.*
Virginia Glendinning: *Vita.*
David Edwards: *Christian England*, vol. 3.
Philip Curtis: *A Hawk among the Sparrows.*
Carl Kerenyi et al: *Evil.*
Howard Didsbury (ed): *Creating a Global Agenda.*
H.L. Philp: *Jung and the Problem of Evil.*
Eileen Barker: *The Making of a Moonie.*
James D.G. Dunn: *The Evidence for Jesus.*
Pinchas Lapide: *The Resurrection of Jesus.*
John Gribbin: *The Search for Schrodinger's Cat: Quantum Physics and Reality.*
Derek Stanesby: *Science, Reason and Religion.*
Hans Mol: *The Faith of Australians.*
Josephine Grierson: *The Hell of It. Early Days in the New Zealand Party.*
Freya Stark: *Prelude to Travel.*
John Hick: *Problems of Religious Pluralism.*
G.R. Evans: *Augustine on Evil.*
James H. Schaub (ed): *Engineering Professionalism and Ethics.*
Graham Green: *The Human Factor.*
Stephen H. Unger: *Controlling Technology.*
W. Barnes Tatum: *In Search of Jesus.*
Ruth Page: *Ambiguity and the Presence of God.*
Russell Stannard: *Science and the Renewal of Belief.*
Anthony Kenney: *The Logic of Deterrence.*
T.M. Schoof: *A Survey of Catholic Theology.*
Alvin Toffler: *Previews and Premises.*
Peter Ackroyd: *T.S. Eliot.*
Ken Wilber: *A Sociable God.*
Peter Singer: *Animal Liberation.*
Bernard Campbell: *Human Ecology.*
John Passmore: *Man's Responsibility for Nature.*
Witold Rybczynski: *Taming the Tiger.*
Barbara C. Sproul: *Primal Myths. Creating the World.*
Heinz Zahrnt: *The Question of God.*
Alastair Kee: *The Way of Transcendence.*
Don Cupitt: *Taking Leave of God.*

Paul Davies: *God and the New Physics.*
Mary Midgely: *Evolution as a Religion.*
Richard Jones: *How Goes Christian Marriage.*
John Gribben: *Timewarps.*
Peter Berger: *Sociology: A Biographical Approach.*
Rustum Roy: *Experimenting with Truth.*
Ivan Illich: *Deschooling Society.*
Paulo Freire: *Education for Critical Consciousness.*
Paulo Freire: *Pedagogy of the Oppressed.*
Robin Barrow: *The Philosophy of Schooling.*
George Bryant: *The Church on Trial.*
George Bryant: *Is Life Not Sacred Anymore?*
Ernest Crane: *I Can Do No Other.*
Louis B. Baer: *Let the Patient Decide.*
Robert F. Weir: *Ethical Issues in Death and Dying.*
Peter Medawar: *The Limits of Science.*
Fred Hoyle: *The New Face of Science.*
A.F. Chalmers: *What is this thing called science?*
Frei Betto: *Fidel and Religion.*
Edward J. Hughes: *Wilfred Cantwell Smith. A Theology for the World.*
Bernard Levin: *Hannibal's Footstep.*
John Pawlikowski: *Christ in the Light of Jewish-Christian Dialogue.*
Barbara Ward: *The Home of Man.*
Edwin Eames & Judith Goode: *Anthropology of the City.*
John Mortimer: *Paradise Postponed.*
Harvey Cox: *Religion in the Secular City.*
John Macquarrie: *The Concept of Peace.*
P.J. Shaw: *Geering: The Southern Reaction 1965–7.*
Paul Clifford: *Interpreting Human Experience.*
Roger Haight: *An Alternative Vision. An Interpretation of Liberation Theology.*
Leonard Woolf: *Sowing: An Autobiography of the Years 1880–1904.*
Leonard Woolf: *Beginning Again: An Autobiography of the Years 1911–1918.*

1987 (76)

Keith Ward: *The Living God.*
Leonard Wolf: *Downhill All The Way: An Autobiography of the Years 1919–1939.*
P.D. James: *A Taste of Death.*

Appendix 1: Geering's Reading

Leonard Woolf: *The Journey Not The Arrival Matters: An Autobiography of the Years 1939–1969.*
James Lees-Milne: *Another Self.*
David Hollenbach: *Nuclear Ethics. A Christian Moral Argument.*
Sidney A. Burrell (ed): *The Role of Religion in Modern European History.*
Alan Paton: *Towards the Mountain.*
Paul Collins: *Mixed Blessings.*
C.G. Jung: *Modern Man in Search of a Soul.*
C.G. Jung: *Psychological Types.*
C.G. Jung: *The Integration of the Personality.*
Jolan Jacobi: *The Psychology of C.G. Jung.*
Alistair Kee: *Domination or Liberation.*
Gerald Priestland: *Something Understood. An Autobiography.*
Trevor Shaw: *E.M. Blaiklock. A Christian Scholar.*
E.M. Blaiklock: *Kathleen. A Record of Sorrow.*
Robert McAfee Brown: *Gustavo Gutierrez.*
John L. Kater: *Christians on the Right.*
Keith Ward: *The Turn of the Tide.*
L. Van der Post: *Jung and the Story of Our Time.*
Gustavo Gutierrez: *A Theology of Liberation.*
Adrian Hastings: *In Filial Disobedience.*
Paul Oestreicher: *The Double Cross.*
Jack Sommerville: *Jack in the Pulpit.*
Leonardo Boff: *Church, Charism and Power.*
J.L. Adams et al: *The Thought of Paul Tillich.*
Joland Jacobi: *The Psychology of C.G. Jung.*
Sherwin T. Wine: *Judaism beyond God.*
Rinny Westra: *Signs of the World to Come.*
Phillipe Wolff: *The Awakening of Europe.*
Hugh Trevor-Roper: *The Rise of Christian Europe.*
Gordon Kaufmann: *Theology for a Nuclear Age.*
J. Bronowski & Bruce Mazlish: *The Western Intellectual Tradition.*
O.L. Zangwill: *An Introduction to Modern Psychology.*
Samuel S. Hill: *The New Religious Political Right in America.*
W.G. de Burgh: *The Legacy of the Ancient World.*
Iain Browning: *Jerash and the Decapolis.*
James A. Beckford: *New Religious Movements and Rapid Social Change.*
William Barrett: *Death of the Soul.*

Paul Hazard: *The Crisis of the European Mind 1680–1715.*
Adam Ford: *Universe: God, Man and Science.*
Don Cupitt: *Life Lines.*
Iris Murdoch: *The Nice and the Good.*
S.G. Shanker (ed): *Philosophy in Britain Today.*
Bruce Lincoln: *Myth, Cosmos and Society.*
Iris Murdoch: *The Good Apprentice.*
Don Cupitt: *The Sea of Faith.*
Morton T. Kelsey: *Myth, History and Faith.*
T.J. Tapp: *Humanism. Its History and Nature.*
Donald Offwood: *Reincarnation and Christianity.*
Sylvia Cranston & Carey Williams: *Reincarnation: A New Horizon in Science, Religion and Society.*
Christian Faith and Practice in the Society of Friends.
Morton T. Kelsey: *Myth, History & Faith.*
Don Cupitt: *The Sea of Faith.*
The Catholic Presbyterian: Essays in honor of Frank Nichol.
John Searle: *Minds, Brains and Science.*
John Eccles & Daniel Robertson: *The Wonder of Being Human: Our Brain and Our Mind.*
John D. Lawry: *Guide to the History of Psychology.*
John Eccles: *The Brain and the Unity of Conscious Experience.*
Karl Popper & John Eccles: *The Self and Its Brain.*
John Eccles: *The Human Mystery*, vol. 1.
John Eccles: *The Human Mystery*, vol. 2.
John Eccles & Daniel Robertson: *The Wonder of Being Human: Our Brain and Our Mind.*
Joseph Campbell (ed): *Myths, Dreams and Religion.*
Lee W. Gibbs & T.W. Stevenson: *Myth and the Crisis of Historical Consciousness.*
Thomas Keneally: *Three Cheers for the Paraclete.*
Tiziano Terzani: *Behind the Forbidden Door.*
Janet Malcolm: *In the Freud Archives.*
Harvey Falk: *Jesus the Pharisee.*
George Steiner: *Nostalgia for the Absolute.*
Olivia Manning: *The Levant Trilogy.*
James Wellard: *Desert Pilgrimage.*
A History of Islam [note: no other details]
Willis B. Glover: *Biblical Origins of Modern Secular Society.*
Lord Longford: *Francis of Assisi.*

1988 (93)
Gerd Theissen: *The Shadow of the Galilean.*
David Bivin: *Understanding the Difficult Words of Jesus.*
J.R. Staude: *The Adult Development of C.G. Jung.*
John Robinson: *Where Three Ways Meet.*
Don Cupitt: *The Long-Legged Fly.*
James D.G. Dunn & James P. Mackey: *New Testament Theology in Dialogue.*
Barbara Hannah: *Jung: His Life and Work.*
Alfred Loisy: *The Birth of the Christian Religion.*
Gerald O'Collins: *Jesus Risen.*
Gavin Young: *Slow Boats to China.*
Vernon Wilkinson: *A God for the 21st Century.*
Kenneth Wapnick: *The Meaning of Forgiveness.*
Madeleine P. Cosman: *Medieval Holidays and Festivals.*
Ann Belford Ulanov: *The Feminine in Jungian Psychology and Christian Theology.*
Wallace B. Cliff: *Jung and Christianity.*
Jean & Wallace Cliff: *Symbols of Transformation in Dreams.*
David Knowles: *Christian Mysticism.*
John Selby Spong: *Into the Whirlwind.*
Gordon Leary: *The Search. A Faith for the New Age.*
John Meyendorff: *Byzantine Theology.*
Hans Lietzmann: *The Beginnings of Christianity.*
Willy Rordorf: *Sunday.*
Mary Jean Irion: *From the Ashes of Christianity.*
James Hitchcock: *What Is Secular Humanism?*
Alan Watts: *Beyond Theology.*
Viktor E. Frankl: *The Doctor and the Soul.*
Jacob Neusner: *Death and the Birth of Judaism.*
Alan Bullock: *The Humanistic Tradition in the West.*
George Gallup: *The American Catholic People.*
Gordon Thomas: *The Trial.*
John P. Dourley: *C.G. Jung and Paul Tillich.*
Basil Willey: *Samuel Taylor Coleridge.*
Paul Erdman: *What's Next?*
Stewart Perowne: *The Life and Times of Herod the Great.*
Stewart Perowne: *The Later Herods.*
Gordon Kaufmann: *Theology for a Nuclear Age.*
A.J. Ayer (ed): *The Humanist Outlook.*

Ludwig Feuerbach: *Thoughts on Death and Immortality.*
Paul Kurtz (ed): *The Humanist Alternative.*
Corliss Lamont: *The Philosophy of Humanism.*
Paul Kurtz (ed): *Sidney Hook. Philosopher of Democracy and Humanism.*
Grace Halsell: *Prophecy and Politics.*
K. Eric Drexler: *Engines of Creation.*
Konrad Lorenz: *The Waning of Humaneness.*
Tony Moss (ed): *In Search of Christianity.*
Monica Furlong (ed): *Feminine in the Church.*
T. Dobzhanzky & E. Boesiger: *Human Culture.*
Richard E. Leakey: *The Making of Mankind.*
Bernt Engelmann: *In Hitler's Germany.*
Ron Elisha: *Two.*
Rene Dubios: *Beats or Angel?*
Ernst Becker: *The Birth and Death of Meaning.*
Dietrich Ritschl: *The Logic of Theology.*
Sallie McFague: *Models of God.*
John de Gruchy (ed): *The Kairos Document.*
John Bowden: *Jesus. The Unanswered Questions.*
Paul Kurtz: *The Transcendental Temptation.*
Karl Popper: *The Open Society*, vol. 1.
Karl Popper: *The Open Society*, vol. 2.
Karen Armstrong: *The First Christian.*
Trevor Pateman: *What is Philosophy?*
Eric James: *A Life of Bishop John A.T. Robinson.*
Bernard Levin [note: no other details]
Ninian Smart: *Religion and the Western Mind.*
Brian Hebblethwaithe: *The Ocean of Truth.*
Matthew Fox: *Manifesto for a Global Civilization.*
Wayne Proudfoot: *Religious Experience.*
Anne Freemantle: *The Age of Belief.*
Victoria Glendinning: *Rebecca West.*
William Henderson: *Christianity and Modern Thought (1861).*
John Gammell: *The Pre-Christian Jesus (1903).*
Hugh Juror Brown: *Atheism Philosophically Refuted (1887).*
Samuel Butler: *The Evidence of the Resurrection of Jesus Christ.*
Clement Partridge: *Theological and Metaphysical Essays* (1869).
Henry Smythies: *Education of Man (1873).*

James P. Mackey: *Modern Theology.*
Gordon Kaufmann: *An Essay on Theological Method.*
Richard Layard: *How to Beat Unemployment.*
Emil Brunner: *Justice and the Social Order.*
J. Maxwell Miller: *Introducing the Holy Land.*
Alberic Stacpoole (ed): *Vatican II Revisited.*
Matthew Fox: *Western Spirituality.*
Hans Küng: *Why I am Still a Christian.*
Scott Cowdell: *Atheist Priest? Don Cupitt and Christianity.*
Don Cupitt: *The New Christian Ethics.*
Stephen Hawking: *A Brief History of Time.*
James A. Sanders: *From Sacred Story to Sacred Text.*
Konrad Lorenz: *The Waning of Humaneness.*
Ira M. Lapidus: *A History of Islamic Societies.*
Sally McFague: *Models of God.*
Karen Armstrong: *The Gospel According to Woman.*
Susanne Heine: *Women and Early Christianity.*

1989 (6)
Don Cupitt: *Crisis of Moral Authority.*
H.E. Peters: *Red Jenny. A Life with Karl Marx.*
Werner Blumenberg: *Karl Marx.*
David McLellan: *Karl Marx.*
David McLellan: *Karl Marx. Interviews and Recollections.*
Don Cupitt: *The Radicals and the Church.*

1990 (25)
Peter de Rosa: *Vicars of Christ.*
Rupert Sheldrake: *A New Science of Life.*
Fritjof Capra: *The Turning Point.*
Robin Gill: *Beyond Decline.*
William Lunny: *The Sociology of the Resurrection.*
Quakers: *Bridging the Invisible into the Heights.*
Peter C. Hodgson: *Revisioning the Church.*
W.B. Selbie: *Schleiermacher.*
A.E. Taylor: *Does God Exist?*
John Hick: *An Interpretation of Religion.*
Edward Lohse: *The New Testament Environment.*
Don Cupitt: *The Radicals and the Church.*

Alan M.G. Stephenson: *The Rise and Decline of English Modernism.*
Ulrich Simon: *Sitting in Judgment 1913–1963.*
Dorothy Solle: *Suffering.*
Peter Eaton (ed): *The Trial of Faith.*
John Macquarrie: *Existentialism.*
Richard D. Chessick: *A Brief Introduction to the Genius of Nietzsche.*
Claudia Orange: *The Treaty of Waitangi.*
Jurgen Moltmann: *Creating a Just Future.*
David L. Edwards: *The Futures of Christianity.*
John Macquarrie: *Existentialism.*
Frederick Sontag: *A Kierkegaard Handbook.*
Presbyterianism in Aotearoa.
H.J. Blackham: *Six Existentialist Thinkers.*

Appendix 2

Biographical Sketches

Allan, Rev. Dr John (1897–1979). After serving in World War I, he studied philosophy at Victoria University College, Wellington, then theology at New College Edinburgh, where he gained his DD. He returned to parish work in New Zealand, then appointed Professor of New Testament Studies, Knox Theological Hall, 1938–62 as well as serving as principal of the Theological Hall, 1947–62; Moderator of the General Assembly, 1955.

Altizer, Thomas J. J. (1927–). American radical theologian who was part of the "death-of-God" theology of the 1960s. Altizer is one of the most important theological thinkers of the twentieth century and continues to be a prolific writer of distinctive radical theology. For a comprehensive engagement with Altizer's more recent thought, see Grimshaw (ed), *This Silence Must Now Speak*. Geering read Altizer and Hamilton's *Radical Theology and the Death of God* in 1967, and in 1966 had read Thomas W. Ogletree: *The 'Death of God' Controversy*. But there is little evidence of American radical theology in his thought during the 1960s.

Arnold, Rollo (1926–98), Professor of Education at Victoria University of Wellington, Historian of New Zealand settler life. A central figure in the Association of Presbyterian Laymen.

Bates, Rev. Dr James (1903–81), MA in Philosophy, Otago University, Theological Hall, 1929–30; acting head of Philosophy, Otago University, 1933; studied for a PhD on "Calvin's Doctrine of the Church" under Brunner at Zurich, 1934–35. The thesis was not awarded on a technicality as, due to insufficient funds, Bates was unable to return to Zurich to defend it. Bates was a very important figure in introducing the then-new and radical neo-orthodox theology into New Zealand. This, with his support for ecumenism, saw him treated with suspicion by evangelicals. A parish minister (except time as Warden of Arana Hall, Dunedin, 1952–58), in 1948 when he was appointed convenor of the Doctrine Committee of the General Assembly (which included Geering) he wrote *A Manual of Doctrine* (Presbyterian Bookroom: Christchurch, 1950), the first such book for the New Zealand Presbyterian Church. Moderator of the General Assembly 1965, he was awarded an honorary LLD by Otago University, 1969.

Baxter, Archibald (1881–1970), Christian socialist, pacifist, and conscientious objector in World War I. Not accepted as a conscientious objector because he was not a Christadelphian, Seventh-day Adventist, or Quaker, Baxter was arrested in 1917, tried for court martial and sentenced to imprisonment. In 1918, on the orders of the Minister of Defence Sir James Allen, Baxter and thirteen others were sent to the Western Front in France where he was sentenced to field punishment no. 1. *We Will Not Cease*, his account of his experiences, was published in 1939.

Baxter, James Keir (1926–72), leading New Zealand poet, critic and playwright. A prolific and highly talented poet from a young age amidst itinerant life, work, and study, he converted to Anglicanism in 1948 and then to Catholicism in 1958. Baxter became a public figure on the strength of his writing and activism and in 1969 he established a religious commune on the Whanganui River, seeking to draw on Maori spiritual values to revitalize New Zealand Pakeha (European) urban society. See bookcouncil.org.nz/writers/baxterjk.html.

Bell, Robert (1876–1963), Scottish-born mathematician; Professor of Pure and Applied Mathematics, University of Otago, 1920–48.

Blaikie, Rev. Robert (1923–75). Born to missionaries in Kenya, educated and ordained in Scotland, parish minister in New Zealand, 1959–75. Member of the Doctrine Committee of the Presbyterian Church. A Barthian, Blaikie had attacked what he saw as the excessively liberal theology of Knox Theological Hall and from 1966 he became one of the two main accusers of Geering. Not wanting to be associated with fundamentalism or the Westminster Confession, Blaikie charged Geering with "gravely disturbing the peace and unity of the church by making statements which appear contrary to the church's teachings" (*Wrestling with God*, 170). Blaikie was clear that it was understood "I have not brought, and I do not intend to try, to prove specific changes of doctrinal error or 'heresy' against Principal Geering. All I claim in this area—and it surely needs no proof—is that to many he appears to have denied Christian doctrines which we believe to be 'fundamental doctrines of the Reformed Christian Faith,' or which are 'of the substance of the Faith.' Nor, I think, is it necessary for me to try to prove that the consequences of the principal's statements have been sufficiently deep, disturbing and divisive to require the serious consideration of the Assembly." See Presbyterian Church of New Zealand, *A Trial for Heresy*, 55. Blaikie's *Charges brought to the General Assembly* are on pp. 20–26. For *Blaikie's Address to the General Assembly*, see 55–70. In Blaikie's *Final Reply to the General Assembly* it is clear he situates Geering within his wider focus of concern, which is the rise of "Secular Christianity," 105.

Breward, Rev. Dr Ian (1934–), Student at Theological Hall, 1958–60, then PhD study at Manchester University. Professor of Church History, Knox Theological Hall, 1965–82; Professor of Church History, Ormond College University of Melbourne, Australia, 1982–99; archivist of Synod of Victoria and Tasmania, 2000–2013. Moderator of the General Assembly of Presbyterian Church of New Zealand, 1975. While Breward came from the evangelical wing of New Zealand Presbyterianism, he was wide-ranging in his support for ecumenism, women's ordination, homosexual law reform, and, while theologically conservative, supported Geering's acquittal in the heresy trial.

Cheer, Noel (1941–), newsletter editor and life member of Sea of Faith Network (NZ).

Cobb, John (1925–), American process philosopher and theologian and environmental thinker. Co-founder (with David Ray Griffin, 1939–), in 1973, and a director of the Centre for Process Studies, as part of Claremont School of Theology in Claremont, California.

Cupitt, Don (1934–), English philosopher, radical theologian and Anglican priest. In 2008 he stopped being a communicant member of the church. See doncupitt.com/don-cupitt. Geering read Cupitt's *Christ and the Hiddenness of God* (1971) in 1975 and, in *Wrestling with God* (215–16), notes he and his wife Elaine were in England on study leave in 1980 when the impact of Cupitt's *Taking Leave of God* broke, and so he contacted and met with Cupitt at Cambridge. This was the beginning of a friendship that continues to this day.

Dickie, Rev. Dr John (1875–1942; DD Aberdeen 1919), born in Scotland, educated at Edinburgh University and Jena University, Germany. Appointed by General Assembly of Presbyterian Church of

New Zealand as Professor of Systematic Theology, Ethics, Apologetics & New Testament Exegesis. Professor of Systematic Theology, Theological Hall Dunedin, in 1910. He also taught New Testament studies, 1910–19, and later also church history. Dickie was appointed First Principal of the Theological Hall, 1928, and Moderator of the General Assembly, 1934. Dickie was author of *The Organism of Christian Truth* (1934) that combined German and Scottish scholarship and traditions. He also gave the Gunning lectures in Edinburgh in 1936, later published as *Fifty Years of British Theology*. Dickie's virulent patriotism turned him against Germany during the First World War and made him a noted opponent of Helmut Rex's appointment in 1939, as well as an opponent to those pacifist students in the Theological Hall.

Dixon, Rev. Ian (1912–2006), student at Knox Theological Hall, 1935–37, parish minister then Chaplain, 2nd NZ Expeditionary Force, serving in New Zealand, Italy, then in Japan with the Allied occupation forces. Army service, 1945–47. Dixon was in Hiroshima in the first draft of the occupation forces, an experience that deeply affected his life and his ministry. Following parish work, Dixon was Professor of Pastoral Theology, Theological Hall Knox College, Dunedin, 1970–77. In retirement, he was a strong supporter of homosexual law reform and homosexuals in the church, coming out in his eighties after the death of his wife.

Elley, Reverend R. D. (1925–2012), studied at Knox Theological Hall, 1950–52; also undertook a ThM at Princeton, 1954–55. At this time, Minister at Khandallah Parish in Wellington, then lecturer at Bible College in Auckland, followed by missionary work in Malaysia.

Falloon, Rev. George (1911–88), Knox Theological Hall, 1938–40. In 1938 Falloon was New Zealand SCM Representative to the Madras conference. Geering took over Falloon's Kurow parish when Falloon went to war, 1942–46, as Chaplain to the NZ Thirty-fifth Battalion in the Pacific. Always a noted parish Minister and Churchman, Falloon was Moderator of the General Assembly in 1970.

Ferguson, Rev. Dr Graeme (1935–), student at Theological Hall, 1958–60, then PhD study at Westminster College, Cambridge. Parish Ministry at Kent Terrace, Wellington, New Zealand, 1965–75; then principal, United Theological College Sydney, 1975–89; then minster St David's, Auckland, 1989–2000.

Fraser, Rev. Dr Ian (1907–96). Student at Theological Hall, 1928–30; then three years post-graduate study at New College and University of Edinburgh; at Bonn University under Karl Barth and then at Union Theological Seminary under John Baillie. On return to New Zealand, co-edited *New Zealand Journal of Theology*, and served in a number of parishes and on numerous Assembly committees. A leading churchman, he was a strong advocate for women elders and ministers and for nuclear disarmament. Moderator of the General Assembly, 1968. Interestingly, in his entry in The Register of New Zealand Presbyterian Ministers, Deaconess & Missionaries, 1840–2015, it is stated: "After reading *Tomorrow's God* he feared he did not have Lloyd Geering's courage to ask the hard questions." (archives.presbyterian.org.nz/Page161.htm).

Funk, Robert (1926–2005), founder of the Jesus Seminar and the Westar Institute. Geering met Funk in 1998 when Funk visited New Zealand on a speaking tour organized by Jim Veitch.

Gosling, Rev. Colin Leslie (1913–98), student at Theological Hall, 1940–42; parish ministry 1943–68. Trained also as a journalist, he served as press officer for his presbyteries and for the General Assembly. In a signal as to how the mood of the church was already shifting in favour of the conservatives, following the death of Peter Smith, Gosling was appointed Editor of *The Outlook*, 1968–78 [thanks to Cassandra Farrin for pointing this out to me]. Gosling was chair of the Westminster Fellowship and first editor of the *Evangelical Presbyterian*.

Henderson, Rev. John (1897–1982). PhD (Edinburgh); Professor of Systematic Theology and Church History, Knox Theological Hall, 1943–62. Henderson was strongly influenced by a year of study in Germany in 1930 where he worked under Karl Heim and Gerhard Kittel at Tübingen and Karl Barth at Bonn. Appointed to Knox when a parish minister in Scotland, he seems to have continued that ethos. The official history of the Theological Hall notes, "he published little and made no major contributions to the theological debates of the forties and fifties. He was a parish minister in a chair, and opinion is divided about the contribution he made to the New Zealand church" (Breward, *Grace and Truth*, 60).

Hughes, George (1918–94), philosopher, logician, and Anglican priest. Born in Ireland to English parents, educated in Scotland (University of Glasgow), and a year at Cambridge where he was taught by Wittgenstein. After teaching in Welsh universities he was appointed to the first chair in Philosophy at Victoria University of Wellington in 1951. He held this position until retirement in 1984.

Kaufman, Gordon D. (1925–2011), Mennonite clergyman, liberal theologian and Professor at Harvard Divinity School, 1963–2009.

Laughton CMG, Very Reverend John (1891–1965), Orkney born, relocated to New Zealand with his family in 1908. Educated Otago University, from 1918 Laughton spent his ministry amongst Maori as part of the Presbyterian Maori Mission, learning the language and named "Hoani" as a mark of respect. In addition to his clerical duties, Laughton established schools, trained clergy, and also founded the Te Waka Karaitiana Press and in 1936 was appointed Superintendent of the Presbyterian Maori Missions. As well as being Moderator of the Presbyterian General Assembly 1942–43, from 1956–62 he was inaugural Moderator of the Maori Synod.

Lietzmann, Hans (1875–1942), German Lutheran Church Historian and theologian, best known for his four-volume history of the early church.

Major, Henry (1871–1961), Anglican clergyman and theologian. Born in England, his family moved to New Zealand in 1878. Major studied geology at Auckland university followed by theology at St John's College. Ordained a clergyman in 1896, he served in parishes until 1903 when he returned to England to study at Exeter College, Oxford. Eventually gaining his DD in 1924, from 1906 Major taught at Ripon Clergy college, and was principal 1929–48. Founder and editor (1911–54) of the *Modern Churchman*, he was a liberal churchman and supporter of theological modernism.

McCahon, Colin (1919–87), leading New Zealand artist whose work included landscape, figuration, abstraction, and use of painted text, many of which were drawn from biblical verses. The question of McCahon's personal beliefs, given the religious themes and imagery of many of his works, has been much discussed, McCahon being notably obtuse on this point. See: mccahon.co.nz.

Moore, Rev. Dr Albert (1926–2003), a student at the Theological Hall, 1949–51, he then earned his PhD in New Testament Studies at University of Manchester, 1954, followed by further study at University of Göttingen under Käsemann, Jeremias, and Gogarten. He then returned to New Zealand to parish ministry at Tapanui, 1955–64. Moore then undertook further study at Chicago in history of religions, 1964–65; taught at University of Southern Indiana, Bloomington, 1965–66; then returned again to New Zealand to found and teach phenomenology of religion at Otago University in 1967. Moore spent the rest of his academic career at Otago University, retiring in 1992. A world authority on religious iconography, he was also a noted jazz enthusiast.

Munz, Peter (1921–2006), historian and philosopher, born in Chemnitz, Germany, as a German-Jewish refugee he emigrated to New Zealand from Florence in 1940. At Canterbury University College, Christchurch, he completed his MA under Karl Popper, then in 1945 began a PhD at Cambridge University. Here he was a member of Wittgenstein's seminar, making him one of two students who studied under Karl Popper and Ludwig Wittgenstein. In 1949, he was appointed lecturer in History at Victoria University of Wellington, where he became Professor of History and a noted intellectual in medieval history, religious thought in modernity, and latterly the evolution of knowledge.

Murray, The Very Rev. John (1929–2017), parish minister, activist, founder of the New Zealand Hymnbooks trust, Moderator of the General Assembly of the Presbyterian Church of Aotearoa, New Zealand, 1990. While Minister at St Andrew's on the Terrace Wellington (1975–93), founded the St Andrew's Music Trust and the St Andrew's Trust for Religion and Society.

Nichol, Rev. Dr Frank (1925–2008). Student at Theological Hall, 1947–49; then PhD study at University of St Andrews, Scotland under Donald Baillie, where a fellow student and friend was William Hamilton, the noted radical theologian. Returned to parish ministry in New Zealand; then appointed Director of Theological Studies at Theological Hall of the Presbyterian Church of Western Australia, Perth March, 1955 (Appointed principal, 1958); Professor of Systematic Theology and Christian Ethics, Theological Hall Dunedin, 1963–85; principal of Theological Hall Dunedin, 23 Feb 1972–1985 (retired due to ill health). Primarily a Barthian, in the 1960s he was strongly influenced by Bonhoeffer—he was introduced to Bonhoeffer's theology by Hamilton, with whom he read and discussed *Letters & Papers from Prison*—and throughout was a public supporter of Geering.

Nordmeyer, Rev. Sir Arnold (1901–89). Student at Knox Theological Hall 1923–25, then parish minister, Kurow, North Otago, 1925–35. Kurow was both a rural parish and site of a hydro scheme during the depression. Nordmeyer, in tandem with the local doctor and headmaster, devised a scheme to alleviate the medical needs of the workers and their families. It became the basis of the national security scheme introduced by the first Labour Government. Nordmeyer resigned from the ministry in 1935 and, representing the Labour Party, was elected member for Oamaru, 1935–49, and then member for Brooklyn (1951 by-election), and finally Island Bay, 1954–69. He was Minister of Health, 1941–47, and became a noted Minister of Finance, 1957–60, entering popular notoriety with his 1960 "Black Budget" that imposed large tax increases on, notably, alcohol and tobacco. His "Black Budget" is considered to have been a significant reason for the defeat of the Labour government in 1960.

Pollard, Rev. Dr Evan (1921–2006), Australian born and educated, member of 647 Squadron RAF Bomber Command World War II; ordained 1949; PhD St Andrews, Scotland, 1954–56. Parish Ministry in Australia, 1949–62; also teacher of New Testament Studies at University of Sydney, 1959–63. Appointed Professor of New Testament Studies, Knox Theological Hall, 1963–82 (retirement due to ill health).

Prior, Arthur (1914–69), logician (founder of tense logic) and philosopher. Prior was, for a period, a student at Knox Theological hall (1935–Aug 1936), then completed his MA in Philosophy. His studies were followed by a time as an itinerant religious journalist and book reviewer in Britain, 1938–40. Returning to New Zealand, he undertook a number of odd-jobs, then served in the Royal New Zealand Air Force, 1943–45. A committed Barthian in the 1930s and early 1940s and also deeply interested in the Scottish reformers, he increasingly moved from theology into logic and philosophy, teaching at Canterbury University college (1946–58), Manchester University (1959–66), and finally Balliol College, Oxford (1966–69). See priorstudies.org.

Prior, Mary (1923–2012), daughter of Rev. Frank Wilkinson (1891–1965), born in Chinese Village Mission; went to school with Nancy Geering in Timaru. Involved in the SCM, she met and married Arthur Prior in 1943. In later life, a noted women's historian.

Read, Rev. Stanley (1905–77), a Solicitor for seven years before a student at Knox Theological Hall 1935–37; parish ministry then Army Chaplain, 1941–44 in Middle East and Italy followed by appointment as Commissioner of the NZ Patriotic Fund Board in London with the rank of Major. He returned to parish ministry 1946–71; Clerk of General Assembly, 1956–74; Moderator of General Assembly 1966.

Rex, Rev. Helmut (1913–67), born in Germany as Helmut Rebhien (changed to Rex in 1946), studied at Berlin university under Hans

Leitzmann and member of Confessing Church in 1934; came to New Zealand as pastor and refugee via London. His wife, Renate, had a Jewish mother, and their marriage application had been refused in Germany. Ordained in Presbyterian Church of New Zealand, 1939. Appointed Lecturer, 1939–53, then Professor of Church History, 1954–64, Knox Theological Hall. His own book on the resurrection, *Did Jesus Rise from the Dead?*, appeared posthumously, but as the preface by his wife, Renate, makes clear, "The book is not an 'answer to Professor Geering'; he had written most of it when the articles appeared" (p. 7). Rex was a significant influence on Geering, as expressed in his memories of Rex in Moore & Andrew, *A Book of Helmut Rex*, 13–16.

Richardson, Alan (1905–75), English Anglican theologian and priest; Professor of Christian theology, University of Nottingham, 1953–64; Dean of York, 1964–75.

Ryburn, Rev. Hubert (1897–1988). A son of the manse, his mathematics study at Otago University was interrupted by war service, 1917–19. He graduated with an MA from Otago University in 1921. An Otago representative in hockey, Ryburn was a Rhodes scholar, completing a BA at Oxford followed by a BD at Union Seminary, New York. Returned to New Zealand for parish ministry, 1926–41; then Master, Knox College Dunedin, 1941–64; Chancellor Otago University, 1955–70.

Somerville, Rev. John (Jack) (1910–99), ONZ, CMG, MC, MA, DD (Hon St. Andrews); LLD. (Hon Otago); student at Theological Hall, 1935–37; then Westminster College, Cambridge, 1937–38; parish minister at Tapanui; then Army Chaplain in Italy, 1942–46, where he was awarded the Military Cross for bravery. Minister, St. Andrews on the Terrace, Wellington, 1947–64; Master of Knox College, Dunedin, 1964–78; Moderator of the General Assembly, 1960–61; Pro-Chancellor of Otago University, 1970–76; Chancellor of Otago University, 1977–82. In many ways the last of the old-fashioned churchmen, Somerville was deeply involved in Presbyterian, Otago, University and community affairs and committees. He was awarded the highest exclusive honour of the Order of New Zealand. See his autobiography, *Jack in the Pulpit*.

Steele, Rev. James (1905–49). Theological Hall, 1927–29. Suffering TB of the eye and spine in 1929, he spent three years convalescing. His friend Jim Bates started the *New Zealand Journal of Theology* to give him something to do in his recovery. On recovery, he was ordained into North Otago parish of Duntroon where he stayed until his death. Steele was a noted scholar and in New Zealand had an unequalled knowledge of Calvin. After the *Journal*, he led a number of Synod refresher courses, often with a Calvinist focus.

Stevely, Rev. Alan (1886–1950), born and educated in Glasgow, Scotland. Following ordination in 1911, travelled to Australia and served in parishes in Victoria, 1912–30. Called to First Church, Dunedin, 1930, and served there until death. Stevely was Moderator of Presbyterian Synod of Otago & Southland, 1948, lecturer at Deaconess College Dunedin, Grand Master of the Masonic Lodge and Chaplain in the Royal New Zealand Navy amongst many offices and roles while minister. He was noted as a very effective preacher and pastor.

Sturm, Jacqueline (1927–2009), born in Opunake, Taranaki, New Zealand, poet and short story writer. In 1946, she enrolled at Otago University (where she was the only Maori woman on campus) to study medicine but decided to refocus on anthropology, which also required a shift to Canterbury University in late 1947. In 1949, she was the first Maori woman to complete an undergraduate degree (BA) at Canterbury University, followed by an MA in Philosophy at Victoria University of Wellington. She was also the first Maori woman writer to be published in English. Jacqui Sturm had met James K. Baxter in Dunedin and he followed her north to Christchurch where they married in 1948; they separated in 1969 when Baxter left to found the Jerusalem Commune on the Whanganui river.

Thornton, Jim (1928–), Philosopher of Religion. Taught philosophy of Religion at University of Canterbury 1963–88, then also in Religious Studies, University of Canterbury, 1966–88. In retirement he continued to tutor philosophy until 2000.

Turner, Rev. Dr Harold (1911–2002), student at Knox Theological Hall, 1936–38. In 1938 he combined attendance at a Moral Rearmament meeting in Switzerland with a term's study under John Baillie at New College, Edinburgh. He was University Chaplain, Otago University, 1942–47; founder of the university bookshop; and founder and first warden of university student residences Stuart House, Arana Hall, and Carrington Hall, 1941–51. Turner emigrated to Britain in 1954 and commenced an academic career, first in Old Testament Studies in Sierra Leone (1955–62); then in Religious Studies in University of Eastern Nigeria (1963–66), and University of Leicester (1966–70);

in World Religions at Emory University (1970–72), and Religious Studies at University of Aberdeen (1973–76). A noted scholar in African Indigenous Churches and also in New Religious Movements, Turner was also Founding Director, Centre for New Religious Movements, Selly Oak College, Birmingham. He returned to New Zealand in 1989 and founded Deep Sight Trust for "deep mission to deep culture" in 1990.

Veitch, Rev. Dr James (1940–). Veitch studied under Geering at Knox Theological Hall, 1963–65; completed a PhD at University of Birmingham (UK) and later a ThD from Australian College of Divinity. Variously a missionary and academic (Indonesia and Singapore), ongoing parish minister (New Zealand), and colleague of Geering in Religious Studies, Victoria University of Wellington 1978–2004. From 2005–11, he moved into security studies at Victoria University focussing on terrorism, intelligence studies, and transnational crime and then defence and security studies at Massey University, Wellington campus, 2011–13. Also a radical biblical scholar, Veitch is a fellow of the Westar Institute and the Jesus Seminar; he also holds the Westar Institute's David Friedrich Strauss medal (1999).

Waddell, Rev. Dr Rutherford (1852–1932), Northern Irish Presbyterian, arrived in New Zealand 1877 and after time as minister at Lincoln and Prebbleton, was minister of St Andrews Dunedin, 1879–1919. A noted social reformer, Waddell famously drew attention to sweated labour in Dunedin factories in a sermon in 1888. This led to a commission of inquiry and the eventual passing of the Arbitration Acts. He also helped establish kindergartens, was a member of the Prison Reform Association, and was the founder and first editor of *The Outlook*.

Winton, Rev. Frank (1911–77), student at theological hall, 1934–36; Parish minister and pioneer of Industrial chaplaincy in New Zealand—which included working in freezing works (abattoir and meat processing plants that froze meat for export) and on the wharves when a parish minister.

Yule, Rev. George (Morris) (1915–2012), student at Theological Hall, 1939–41; parish ministry 1942–95; helped found the Westminster Fellowship in 1950. At the time referenced, he was minister at St Stephens, Auckland.

Notes

Preface

1. Dyer, *Out of Sheer Rage: In the Shadow of D. H. Lawrence* (London: Little, Brown, 1997).
2. Dyer, *Out of Sheer Rage*, 2.
3. Dyer, *Out of Sheer Rage*, 4.
4. Hitchens, *Why Orwell Matters*, 39.

Introduction

1. Hobsbawm, *The Age of Extremes*.
2. Jenson, "Karl Barth," 2, 4.
3. Berger, *The Desecularization of the World*.
4. See Geering, *Wrestling with God*, 131.
5. Moore, "'A Western Heritage, an Asian Destiny,'" 10.
6. Moore, "'A Western Heritage, an Asian Destiny,'" 10.
7. See Geering, *Wrestling with God*, 164–65.
8. Geering, *Wrestling with God*, 170–71. For a copy of the transcript as presented to the General Assembly, see Presbyterian Church of New Zealand, *A Trial for Heresy*, 43–54.
9. Geering to Grimshaw, 5 August 2011.
10. "To Rollo Arnold from Austen Ward of 56 Waterhouse St Nelson 10 May 1967," MS Papers 2258 Folder 10 Letter D1, National Archives, Wellington.
11. "Robert Wardlaw of APL to Rollo Arnold 12 May 1967," MS Papers 2258 Folder 1 Letter 12, National Archives, Wellington. [Note: Letter 14 from Wardlaw to Arnold, 18 May 1967, thanks Arnold for the delivery of the recording and transcript on 15 May 1967.]
12. GA/82 Assembly Clerk S. C. Read papers, Doctrinal Debate 1967-Lloyd Geering (Folder 2 of 5) 97/74/17 AO 16/5. Presbyterian Archives, Dunedin. From a copy of letter from Austen Ward to Wardlaw Nelson, 21 May 1967. Wardlaw passed the copy to Read. Ward agreed to have this done.
13. See "Go into All the World," for a transcription of the points made in the second address that caused the concern.
14. "Go into All the World," {15}.
15. "Moore to Rex Tapanui 3.2.63." NZ 640 AC Moore Correspondence: Moore to Rex 1951–1967 2007/120/24 DC 17/3. Presbyterian Archives, Dunedin.
16. Jan Cormack, email message to Grimshaw, 29 August 2016.
17. Ron Cormack, email message to Grimshaw, 26 August 2016.

18. Geering, "Is a New Reformation Possible?" (Originally appeared in *The Outlook*, Sept 1965.)
19. "Letter to Mrs Arnold from R Bruce Fowler 48 Homewood Avenue Karori (23 November 1967)," MS Papers 2258 Folder 23. NZ Association of Presbyterian Laymen (Hereafter: APL papers), Alexander Turnbull Library, Wellington.
20. MS PAPERS 2258 FOLDER 23. APL papers, Alexander Turnbull Library, Wellington.
21. Geering in conversation with Grimshaw, 23 February 2017.
22. Geering, *Wrestling with God*, 143.
23. Peter Smith to Lloyd Geering, 15 June 1966, marked "confidential." Geering private correspondence files, 1966. Permission granted to reproduce.
24. Geering, *Wrestling with God*, 158.
25. "Nichol to Read 2.5.67," GA/82 Assembly Clerk S. C. Read papers, Doctrinal Debate 1966–67 (Folder 1 of 5) 97/74/17 AO 16/5. Presbyterian Archives, Dunedin.
26. 3/164 Pollard, T. E. (Prof) Correspondence: Geering Controversy 1966–70. 394/58/1 DC2/4. Pollard to Bow (H.O. Bowman-Balmoral church, Auckland) 2 Jan 1968. Presbyterian Archives, Dunedin.
27. GA/82 Assembly Clerk S. C. Read papers, Doctrinal Debate 1966–67 (Folder 1 of 5) 97/74/17 AO 16/5. Presbyterian Archives, Dunedin.
28. GA/82 Assembly Clerk S. C. Read papers, Doctrinal Debate 1967—Lloyd Geering (Folder 2 of 5) 97/74/17 AO 16/5. Stan Read to Blaikie, 6 June 1967, "confidential." Presbyterian Archives, Dunedin.
29. 3/72 Nichol, Frank W. F. (Dr) Correspondence—Geering Controversy 1967 396/27/1 DC 3/2. Ferguson to Nichol 9 Oct 67. Presbyterian Archives, Dunedin.
30. 3/72 Nichol, Frank W. F. (Dr) Correspondence—Geering Controversy 1967 396/27/1 DC 3/2. E: Letter of Ross Miller (Castor Bay) to Ferguson—and copy to Nichol, 12 Oct 1967. Presbyterian Archives, Dunedin.
31. Geering in conversation with Grimshaw, 23 February 2017.
32. Geering, *Wrestling with God*, 170.
33. Geering, *Wrestling with God*, 169–70.
34. 3/72 Nichol, Frank W. F. (Dr) Correspondence—Geering Controversy 1967 396/27/1 DC 3/2. E: Letter of Ross Miller (Castor Bay) to Ferguson—and copy to Nichol, 12 Oct 1967. Presbyterian Archives, Dunedin.
35. Geering, *Wrestling with God*, 173.
36. Nichol, "Theology—Into the Open?"
37. Harvey, "Reflections on the Teaching of Religion in America," 17.
38. Harvey, "Reflections on the Teaching of Religion in America," 21.
39. Harvey, "Reflections on the Teaching of Religion in America," 28.

40. Harvey, "Reflections on the Teaching of Religion in America," 28.
41. Harvey, "Reflections on the Teaching of Religion in America," 29.
42. Loos, "Ornament and Crime."
43. Brasch, "Notes," 5–6.
44. See Grimshaw, "Land and Literature."
45. See *Landfall* 77, vol. 20. no. 1 (March 1966), which was focused on religion in New Zealand with articles by W. H. Oliver, W. Merlin Davies, Lloyd Geering, P. J. Downey, John Harre, Frank Nichol, and Dennis McEldowney. This was the first *Landfall* issue to focus on religion and occurred during the first debate of the two-fold "Geering controversy." There was not another issue focussing on religion until *Landfall* 215, "Waiting for Godzone" (May 2008), edited by Paul Morris, Mike Grimshaw, and Harry Ricketts.
46. Geering, *Faith's New Age*, 25.
47. Geering, *Faith's New Age*, 18.
48. Geering, *Faith's New Age*, 319.
49. Geering, *Faith's New Age*, 22.
50. Geering, *The World of Relation*, 10, 43.
51. Geering, *On Becoming Human*, 24.
52. Geering, *On Becoming Human*, 37.
53. Geering, *On Becoming Human*, 144.
54. Geering, *On Becoming Human*, 144.
55. Geering, "Reshaping the Christian Culture Which Shaped Us."

Chapter 1: Early Life
1. Geering, *Wrestling with God*, 16.
2. See Geering, *Wrestling with God*, 40.
3. Geering, "The Faith to Doubt," in *Reimagining God*, 31.

Chapter 2: Parish Life
1. See *Wrestling with God*, 127.
2. Bultmann, "New Testament and Mythology."

Chapter 3: The Trial
1. See *Wrestling with God*, 142, where Geering recounts standing up to Blaikie in defence of Nichol.
2. Geering, *What Is Our Gospel?* Produced by the Faith and Order Commission of the National Council of Churches to engage with theological issues for the ecumenical movement. Geering not only edited the collection of seven studies, he also wrote Study 1 ("Why Ask the Question?"), Study 4 ("What Difference Can Science Make?"), Study 5 ("How Can Other Religions Compare?"), and Study 7 ("What then IS Our Gospel?"). The other studies have no authors named, being attributed to unnamed study groups.

Chapter 4: Public Theologian

1. See *The Fourth R* 38,5 (2015). These are articles Geering wrote for *The Outlook* 1966–67.

2. Geering, "Theology before and after Bishop Robinson's *Honest to God*," 10.

3. Bellah, "Religious Evolution."

4. Geering, *Christian Faith at the Crossroads*.

5. Geering, *Wrestling with God*, 147.

6. *Colin McCahon and Christianity*. A seminar in conjunction with the exhibition Colin McCahon in Gates and Journeys, Theatrette, National Art Gallery and Museum, Wellington, 17 June 1989. The speakers included Albert Moore; Francis Pound; Stuart McKenzie; Haare Williams; Lloyd Geering and Elizabeth Isichei.

7. The date of this is uncertain, but in email discussion with Geering it seems it was probably 1992, as there were subsequent talks on McCahon in Hamilton and Wanganui in 1993. Since then, Geering reports he has lectured on McCahon in at least a dozen places.

8. Geering, *Such Is Life*. Somewhere between 1980 and 1982, McCahon created two paintings: *I applied my mind* and *Is there anything of which one can say this is new?*, drawing on Ecclesiastes. See mccahon.co.nz/cm001660 and mccahon.co.nz/cm001300. There is also McCahon's last, unfinished painting drawing on Ecclesiastes, *I considered all the acts of oppression*, dating from 1981, that was discovered in his studio after his death. See mccahon.co.nz/cm000169.

9. See, for example, Cobb, *Toward a Mutual Transformation of Christianity and Buddhism*.

10. See Geering, *Wrestling with God*, 58. The original reference is "Comparative Religion is an admirable recipe for making people comparatively religious." See Knox, *The Hidden Stream*, 105. The misquote seems to at least be drawn from Ninian Smart, who uses it in his essay "Religious Studies and the Comparative Perspective" (republished in Smart, *Ninian Smart on World Religions*, 226).

11. See Batchelor, *Buddhism without Beliefs* and *Confession of a Buddhist Atheist*. Stephen Batchelor (1953–), Buddhist teacher and writer; Buddhist monk, 1974–85. See stephenbatchelor.org/index.php/en/.

12. Geering, *Reimagining God*.

13. Veitch, *Faith in an Age of Turmoil*. While Robinson died in 1983, he had expressed keenness to be part of a *festschrift* for Geering. Robinson's essay is "Religion in the Third Wave: The Difference in Being a Christian Tomorrow."

14. The essay is chapter 10 in Lloyd Geering, *Reimagining God*.

15. Geering, "The Theological Challenge to the Church."

16. Dawkins made this claim in 2013 (see spectator.co.uk/2013/09/interview-richard-dawkins-on-what-hed-miss-if-christianity-vanished/); and in 2014 claimed he was a secular Christian (see telegraph.co.uk/culture/hay-festival/10853648/Richard-Dawkins-I-am-a-secular-Christian).

Chapter 5: Lloyd Geering's Notebook

1. Morris and Grimshaw, *The Lloyd Geering Reader.*
2. See Simmons, *Speaking Truth to Power*. It includes an interview with Geering (pp.128–39).
3. See Geering, *Wrestling with God.*
4. See *Wrestling with God*, 143.
5. My thanks to Jane Bloore of the Presbyterian Archives, Dunedin for this information.
6. Email: Geering to Grimshaw, 6 January 2017.
7. See *Wrestling with God*, 144.
8. Ronald Gregor Smith to Lloyd Geering, 18 July 1966. [source: Geering's correspondence, Geering's private collection, 1966, Folio 3].
9. Email: Geering to Grimshaw, 26 January 2017. Geering further mentioned he met Kaufman at a 'Moonies' conference, one of three Geering attended, observing also, "I met a lot of Nobel Prize winners there."
10. Email: Geering to Grimshaw, 6 January 2017.
11. See *Wrestling with God*, 129.
12. So far the only comprehensive engagement with Nichol is Richard Shaw, "Invitation To Relate. The Theology of Frank Nichol," BA Honours Long Essay, University of Canterbury, 1993.
13. In the reading for 1971, Küng's *Infallible* is book 62 read for the year (out of a total of 83 books). It is recoded as being read between Peter Berger's *A Rumour of Angels?* and A.J. Arberry's *Sufism, An Account of the Mystics of Islam.*
14. See *Wrestling with God*, 203.
15. See *Wrestling with God*, 131.
16. Email: Geering to Grimshaw, 6 January 2017.

Bibliography

Batchelor, Stephen. *Buddhism without Beliefs*. New York: Riverhead, 1998.

———. *Confession of a Buddhist Atheist*. New York: Spiegel & Grau, 2010.

Bellah, Robert. "Religious Evolution." *American Sociological Review* 29,3 (June 1964) 358–74.

Berger, Peter, ed. *The Desecularization of the World: Resurgent Religion and World Politics*. Grand Rapids, MI: W. B. Eerdmans Pub. Co., 1999.

Berry, Christine. *The New Zealand Student Christian Movement, 1896–1996*. Christchurch: Student Christian Movement of Aotearoa, 1996.

Brasch, Charles. "Notes." *Landfall* 1,1 (March 1947) 3–8.

Breward, Ian. *Grace and Truth*. Dunedin: Theological Education committee, Presbyterian Church of New Zealand, 1975.

Bultmann, Rudolf. "New Testament and Mythology: The Problem of Demythologizing the New Testament Message." In *The New Testament & Mythology and Other Basic Writings*. Ed and trans. Schubert M. Ogden. Minneapolis, MN: Augsburg Fortress Publishers, 1984.

Cobb, John. *Toward a Mutual Transformation of Christianity and Buddhism: Beyond Dialogue*. Philadelphia: Fortress Press, 1982.

Falloon, Mary, Lillian Falloon, and Richard Falloon. *The Day Thou Gavest, Lord. An Account of the Life of George David Falloon, OBE, MC, BA, 1911–1988*. Christchurch, 1991.

Geering, Lloyd. *Christian Faith at the Crossroads*. Santa Rosa, CA: Polebridge Press, 2001.

———. *Every Moment Must Be Lived: The Story of Elaine*. Wellington: Lake Dunstan Press, 2004.

———. *Faith's New Age*. London: Collins, 1980.

———. *From the Big Bang to God*. Salem, OR: Polebridge Press, 2013.

———. "Go into All the World." Presbyterian Summer Conference, Gore 1962–63. 1 January 1963. Transcription by the author, 2016.

_____. "Is a New Reformation Possible?" Pp. 81–88 in *The Lloyd Geering Reader*. Eds. Paul Morris and Mike Grimshaw. Wellington: Victoria University Press, 2007.

_____. *On Becoming Human*. Wellington: St Andrews Trust, 1988.

_____. *Reimagining God: The Faith Journey of a Modern Heretic*. Salem, Oregon: Polebridge Press, 2014.

_____. "Reshaping the Christian Culture Which Shaped Us." Sea of Faith Network (NZ) Conference, Auckland, 21 September 2001. sof.wellington.net.nz/lgkey2001.htm.

_____. *Such Is Life. A Close Encounter with Ecclesiastes*. Wellington: Steele Roberts, 2010.

_____. "The Theological Challenge to the Church." An Address to the Presbyterian General Assembly, 1990. Pp 56–60 in *The Lloyd Geering Reader*. Eds. Paul Morris and Mike Grimshaw. Wellington: Victoria University Press, 2007.

_____. "Theology Before and After Bishop Robinson's *Honest to God*." *Sea of Faith Network (NZ) Newsletter* 108 (October 2013) 9–10.

_____. *Tomorrow's God*. Santa Rosa, CA: Polebridge Press, 2000.

_____, ed. *What Is Our Gospel? Studies Preparatory to the Faith and Order Conference, Massey College, February, 1964*. The Presbyterian Bookroom for The National Council of Churches in New Zealand, 1963.

_____. *The World of Relation: An Introduction to Martin Buber's I and Thou*. Wellington: Victoria University Press, 1983.

_____. *Wrestling with God*. Wellington: Bridget Williams Books, 2006.

Grimshaw, Mike. "Land and Literature: The 'Spiritual Resources' of Charles Brasch." *Relegere: Studies in Religion and Reception* 6,1 (2016) 61–71. relegere.org/relegere/article/view/705/796.

_____, ed. *This Silence Must Now Speak. Letters of Thomas J.J. Altizer 1995–2015*. New York: Palgrave Macmillan, 2016.

Harvey, Van A. "Reflections on the Teaching of Religion in America." *Journal of the American Academy of Religion* 38,1 (March 1970) 17.

Hobsbawm, Eric. *The Age of Extremes: The Short Twentieth Century, 1914–1991*. London: Michael Joseph/New York: Vintage, 1994.

Hoverd, William. "No Longer a Christian Country? Religious Demographic Change in New Zealand 1966–2006." *New Zealand Sociology* 23,1 (2008) 41–65.

Jenson, Robert W. "Karl Barth." Pp. 23–49 in *The Modern Theologians*. Vol. 1. Ed. David. F. Ford. Oxford: Basil Blackwell, 1989.

Knox, Ronald. *The Hidden Stream*. London: Burns Oates, 1952.
Kaufman, Gordon D. *An Essay on Theological Method*. Scholars Press, 1975.
_____. *God the Problem*. Harvard University Press, 1972.
_____. *The Theological Imagination*. Westminster Press, 1981.
_____. *Theology for a Nuclear Age*. Westminster Press, 1985.
Loos, Adolf. "Ornament and Crime" (1908). Pp. 226–31 in *Adolf Loos. Pioneer of Modern Architecture*. L. Munz and G. Kunster. London: Thames & Hudson, 1966.
McKinlay, John. "Hall Notes." *Knox Collegian* (1966) 71.
Moore, Albert and M. Andrew, eds. *A Book of Helmut Rex*. Dunedin: University of Otago, 1980.
Moore, Albert C. "'A Western Heritage, an Asian Destiny': Recent Theological Work in New Zealand." *Bulletin of Department of Theology, World Presbyterian Alliance* 5,2 (1964–65).
Morris, Paul and Mike Grimshaw, eds. *The Lloyd Geering Reader*. Wellington: Victoria University Press, 2007.
Morris, P., H. Ricketts, and M. Grimshaw, eds. *Spirit in a Strange Land. A Selection of New Zealand Spiritual Verse*. Auckland: Godwit, 2002.
Newton, John. *The Double Rainbow: James K. Baxter, Ngati Hau and the Jerusalem Commune*. Wellington: Victoria University Press, 2009.
Nichol, Frank. "Theology—Into the Open?" *Comment* 42 (November 1970) 19–21.
O'Brien, Gregory. "Somebody Say Something. Colin McCahon's Storm Warning, Wellington, 1999, A Scrapbook." Pp. 239–58 in *After Bathing at Baxter's. Essays and Notebooks*. Wellington: Victoria University Press, 2002.
Presbyterian Church of New Zealand. *A Trial for Heresy. Charges against Principal Geering*. Christchurch: Presbyterian Bookroom, 1968.
Rex, Helmut. *Did Jesus Rise from the Dead?* Auckland: Blackwood & Janet Paul Ltd, 1967.
Richardson, Alan. *The Bible in the Age of Science*. SCM Press, 1961.
Robinson, T. H. *A Short Comparative History of Religions*. London: Duckworth, 1951.
Simmons, Laurence, ed. *Speaking Truth to Power: Public Intellectuals Rethink New Zealand*. Auckland: Auckland University Press, 2007.

Simpson, Peter. "Candles in a Dark Room: James K. Baxter and Colin McCahon." *Journal of New Zealand Literature* 13 (1995) 157–88.

Smart, Ninian. *Ninian Smart on World Religions: Traditions and the Challenges of Modernity: Vol. 1, Religious Experience and Philosophical Analysis.* Ed. John J Shepherd. Ashgate Publishing, 2009.

_____. "Religious Studies and the Comparative Perspective." *The Forum* 2,1 (Spring 1986) 5–13.

Smith, Ronald Gregor. *Secular Christianity.* London: Collins, 1966.

Somerville, John S. *Jack in the Pulpit.* Dunedin: John McIndoe Press, 1987.

Veitch, James, ed. *Faith in an Age of Turmoil: Essays in Honour of Lloyd Geering.* London: Oriental University Press, 1990.

Lloyd Geering (1918 –) is a international scholar of religion and a noted radical religious thinker. In 1967, while Principal of Knox Theological Hall, Dunedin, New Zealand, Geering was put on trial by the Presbyterian Church of New Zealand for what was labelled heresy. A year earlier Geering had come to national attention when, in an Easter article, he questioned the bodily resurrection of Jesus. Controversy ensued and intensified when he questioned the immortality of the soul. Geering was acquitted and in 1971 took up the foundation Chair in Religious Studies at Victoria University of Wellington. He became a prolific author, religious commentator, and a popular public speaker on issues of religious thought and modern belief. A member of the Sea of Faith and of the Westar Institute which awarded him its David F. Strauss medal, Lloyd Geering's status and influence as scholar of religion and public intellectual was recognized with a knighthood, as well as with the New Zealand Order of Merit in 2001 and New Zealand's highest honour, membership in The Order of New Zealand in 2007.

About the Author

Mike Grimshaw (Ph.D. University of Otago) is a sociologist at University of Canterbury, New Zealand, who has studied and written on Lloyd Geering for almost thirty years. Grimshaw works at the intersections of radical theology, continental thought, and cultural and social theory. An author and editor of books and articles on radical theology, he is also a founder and series co-editor of *Radical Theologies* (Palgrave Macmillan) and co-founder and co-editor of the journal *Continental Thought & Theory*.